CONTENTS

Introduction   vii

Contributors   xi

ONE   Get in Formation   1

Featuring: Patrisse Khan-Cullors, Christopher Rashad Green, Tarana Burke, Bianca Xunise, Kareem "Tef Poe" Jackson

TWO   The Struggle Is Real   29

Featuring: Constance Malcolm, Asali Solomon, Quinn Gee, John Jennings, Marlon Peterson, Shane McCrae

THREE   Laugh to Keep from Crying   55

Featuring: Damon Young, Russ Green, Amanda Seales, Jamilah-Asali Lemieux, Ben Passmore, Kiese Laymon

FOUR   I'm Not One of Your Little Friends   87

Featuring: Niya Kenny, Delphine Adama Fawundu, Sidney Keys III, Saa Rankin Naasel, Rickell Howard Smith, Denene Millner

FIVE   God Is Good, All the Time . . .   105

Featuring: Darnell L. Moore, Haylin Belay, Pastor Michael McBride, Xia Gordon, Margari Aziza Hill, Rev. Dr. Valerie Bridgeman, Bishop Jacquelyn Holland

SIX   You Can't Tell Me Nothin'   143

Featuring: Michael Arceneaux, Tai Allen, Penny Wrenn, Beverly "Bevy" Smith, Diamond Stingily, Hanif Abdurraqib

SEVEN   Show Them Who We Are   161

Featuring: Harry Belafonte, Gina Belafonte, Mumia Abu-Jamal, Haki R. Madhubuti, D. Bruce "DJ Junior" Campbell Jr., Kierna Mayo, Shawn Dove, Ta-Nehisi Coates

EIGHT   Love Me or Leave Me Alone   183

Featuring: Dr. Yaba Blay, adrienne maree brown, Dr. Joy Harden Bradford, Aja Graydon, Ayana Byrd, Mahogany L. Browne

NINE   I Make Money Moves   211

Featuring: DeShuna Spencer, Dr. Kortney Ryan Ziegler, Tiffany Mikell, Bakari Kitwana, Jay Smooth, Tongo Eisen-Martin, Stefanie Brown James, Quentin James

TEN   Someday We'll All Be Free   239

Featuring: Imani Perry, Olalekan Jeyifous, Maori Karmael Holmes, Elissa Blount Moorhead, Robin D. G. Kelley, Mia Birdsong, Jasiri X, Wazi Maret, Alicia Garza

Acknowledgments   279

Contributor Photo Credits   281

Image Credits   285

INTRODUCTION

There was a time, when we were young, scrappy, and hungry, when fighting for justice brought to mind picket signs, linked arms, and raised fists. As our daily responsibilities multiply—and the folks who want to push liberty even further beyond our outstretched fingertips grab more unchecked power—it's harder to make it to the front lines. But we also know that's not the only way to fight. As we spend our days writing and editing stories about racial justice (and injustice), we are increasingly struck by all the ways Black people combat the physical and emotional wages of the system of White supremacy. Just as there are millions of us fighting, there are millions of ways to land blows.

The fact is, White supremacy defines our current reality. It is not merely a belief that to be White is to be better. It is a political, cultural, and economic system premised on the subjugation of people who are not White. That subjugation takes on an infinite number of forms and is enforced with varying degrees of physical violence, mental abuse, and robbery. White supremacy is the voice in our collective heads that says it makes civilized sense that one group of people gets to annihilate, enslave, incarcerate, brainwash, torture, sterilize, breed, and terrorize other people. White supremacy establishes, upholds, and normalizes hierarchy based on the premise that the less Black you are the closer you are to God.

We live in a country where law enforcement officers kill Black children and call them "thugs," the mainstream media calls neo-Nazis the "alt-right," and referencing "the African Americans" in discussions about urban crime is a sufficient credential to put a third-rate reality television personality in the White House. But the encouraging reality is this: Black people are working each day to inch us closer to collective freedom. We contain multitudes, and we are hammering at issues as varied and intersectional as police violence and body image and reproductive justice and lack of inclusion in the technology sector.

We're fascinated by those who resist and create despite the obstacles produced by White supremacy and its lackeys: sexism, homophobia, disenfranchisement, transphobia, colorism, ableism, and more. We wrote this book to document the people, from the unsung to the famous, who are doing good work right where they stand, fighting causes both sexy and pedestrian. There's the leader of a religious movement that holds up issues that impact queer people of color, the cartoonist who applies the Black punk aesthetic to the hard work of silencing White supremacists, the cofounders of a movement that made the world consider the worth of Black lives, and dozens of other freedom fighters who share their work and their dreams for a future that doesn't thrive on anti-Blackness.

Many people—both here and abroad—are considering the fragility of their freedom for the first time, and thousands of the newly "woke" need help with defining their own version of activism. Fortunately for us all, Black people can provide the key.

Black Americans have made a cottage industry of surviving, resisting, and fighting. From staging insurrections after being used as the literal capital that bankrolled the birth of this nation to arguing before the US Supreme Court in the face of codified racial segregation via *Brown v. Board of Education of Topeka*, to clapping back at the microaggressions that threaten to chip away at our humanity each day, we always find a way to stand rooted in the face of oppression. You want to talk about patriots? We honor the principles of democracy at every turn, even when the people charged with implementing those principles don't honor us. This ain't new to us. Whether we're singing, sitting, marching, researching, prosecuting, creating, laughing, studying, organizing, dreaming, building wealth, or drawing on spirit, we battle life-threatening forces as a matter of course. Why should this moment be any different?

What This Book Isn't

Although we sought out a diverse group of contributors, this collection isn't exhaustive: it does not apply an international lens, and it doesn't include Black "conservatives." We know that anyone who is truly interested and invested in dismantling the intricate system of White supremacy will learn from this book, but it's not here to tell you what to do, and it's not written with anyone but Black folks in mind (see no "explanatory commas" in the next section). It's also important to know that we began working on this book long before the election of the forty-fifth president of the United States. The acts of resistance it chronicles are not defined by the actions of one man, but by the collective longing for a justice that has so far eluded us.

What This Book Is

How We Fight White Supremacy is a curated, multidisciplinary collection that serves as a showcase for some of our most powerful thinkers and doers. It starts in the middle of a Black-ass conversation; you won't find any explanatory commas about our cultural mores here. Speaking of which, to reflect the permanence of our resistance, we organized the book according to Black conventional and contemporary wisdom, with chapters like "Laugh to Keep from Crying" (our gallows humor), "Get in Formation" (grassroots organizing), and "Love Me or Leave Me Alone" (how we love ourselves whole). Each chapter starts with our take on why a particular category of resistance is integral to the fight and ends with our (very) personal reflections on the matter. Seriously, this collection has everything: thoughtful interviews, "am I really crying right now?" essays, ridiculously relatable fine art, unexpected profiles, crying laughing emoji face funny fiction, reflections from everyday people on their everyday resistance, get hype playlists, and more—all breathe in these pages.

But most of all, this is a book about freedom dreams. We're well aware of the problems we're buried beneath. We can feel the weight of them on our limbs, the heft of them in our abdomens as our second brains gnaw on the indignity of it all. But what does it look like for Black people to claw our way to fresh air? What does freedom *feel* like? How does it taste on the tongue? For some folks in this book, it feels like raising kids who gleefully take up space for themselves. For others, it looks like providing the tools we need to triumph over race-based trauma. There's the pastor who envisions a day when following his radical, dark-skinned Jesus who always sides with the dispossessed will lift us out of this hole, and the organizer who can almost smell the sharp aroma of reforming the nation's political system. And we can't forget the professor who dreams of the day when we can bring our full selves to every table.

Although this book is not prescriptive—if we had a magic button we could press to end this nightmare, we would have leaned on that bitch long ago—it *is* thoughtful and hopeful and bursting with agency. In immersing ourselves in the work of others, we can define and refine our own work; in reveling in the freedom dreams of our beloved, we can labor to make them lucid. The reality is this: if we don't make time to close our eyes, breathe deeply, push beyond the binds we're in, and visualize a day when they don't exist, we can never truly be free.

Our hope is that by the time you read the last page, you will have your *own* strategy for making our collective freedom dream a reality. We'll see you on the other side.

Peace, power, and joy,
Akiba + Kenrya

CONTRIBUTORS

Hanif Abdurraqib

Mumia Abu-Jamal

Tracy M. Adams /
DJ Monday Blue

Tai Allen

Michael Arceneaux

Gina Belafonte

Harry Belafonte

Haylin Belay

Mia Birdsong

Dr. Yaba Blay

Elissa Blount Moorhead

Reverend Dr. Valerie
Bridgeman

adrienne maree brown

Stefanie Brown James

Mahogany L. Browne

Tarana Burke

Ayana Byrd

D. Bruce Campbell Jr. / DJ
Junior

Ta-Nehisi Coates

Shawn Dove

Tongo Eisen-Martin

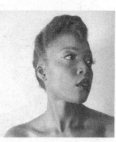

Delphine Adama Fawundu

Alicia Garza

Quinn Gee

Xia Gordon

Aja Graydon

Christopher Rashad Green

Russ Green

Dr. Joy Harden Bradford

Margari Aziza Hill

Bishop Jacquelyn Holland

Maori Karmael Holmes

Rickell Howard Smith

Quentin James

John Jennings

Olalekan Jeyifous

Robin D. G. Kelley

Niya Kenny

Sidney Keys III

Patrisse Khan-Cullors

Bakari Kitwana

Kiese Laymon

Jamilah-Asali Lemieux

Haki R. Madhubuti

Constance Malcolm

Contributors

Wazi Maret

Kierna Mayo

Pastor Michael McBride

Shane McCrae

Tiffany Mikell

Denene Millner

Darnell L. Moore

Ben Passmore

Imani Perry

Marlon Peterson

Tef Poe / Kareem Jackson

Saa Rankin Naasel

Amanda Seales

Beverly "Bevy" Smith

Jay Smooth

Asali Solomon

Patricia Spears Jones

DeShuna Spencer

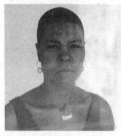

Diamond Stingily

Penny Wrenn

Jasiri X

Bianca Xunise

Damon Young

Dr. Kortney Ryan Ziegler

ONE
GET IN FORMATION

Although Second Wave feminism declared that "the personal is political" and Black feminists did the work of expanding "the personal" to include people who were not White, straight, or middle-class, the idea that "I'm not free until we all are free" has always been a major one for us. This explains how both Blacks who were born free and those who became free acted as conductors on the Underground Railroad at great personal risk. How Black folks throughout the African Diaspora toiled to defeat the murderous system of South African apartheid. It's our way of thinking, our cultural value, that provides the scaffolding for our drive toward universal equity.

As the Combahee River Collective put it in "A Black Feminist Statement" in 1977:

> The most general statement of our politics at the present time would be that we are actively committed to struggling against racial, sexual, heterosexual, and class analysis and practice based upon the fact that the major systems of oppression are interlocking. The synthesis of these oppressions creates the conditions of our lives. As Black women we see Black feminism as the logical political movement to combat the manifold and simultaneous oppressions that all women of color face. . . .
>
> We might use our position at the bottom, however, to make a clear leap into revolutionary action. If Black women were free, it would mean that everyone else would have to be free, since our freedom would necessitate the destruction of all the systems of oppression.

This belief that collective action brings about collective solutions underpins organizing in social movements. We are the informal and self-described strategists who refine tactics passed down from our previous tries at liberation, and we are the patient participants in the slow-going project of freedom. At our best and most holistic, we act as advocates for every Black person, regardless of gender, sexuality, class, immigration status, record of criminal charges, education level, quirk, or kink. As long as you don't act all the way up and out, our instinct is to claim you. This is what pulls activists out of bed each morning—the way we instinctively understand that "Black Lives Matter" is a rallying cry, not a threat to the humanity of others.

There's a reason you use your fists and not your individual fingertips to fight. From one of the minds behind Black Lives Matter, to a formerly incarcerated man working to restore the voting rights of others, to the woman who first encouraged survivors to say, "Me too," the organizers featured in this chapter are knockout artists.

<hr>

Patrisse Khan-Cullors on Why "We've Got to Tell a Different Story about Blackness"

Patrisse Khan-Cullors is best known for cofounding Black Lives Matter (BLM) in 2013 in response to the exoneration of George Zimmerman, the White self-appointed neighborhood watchman in Sanford, Florida, who followed seventeen-year-old Trayvon Martin as he walked home from the store and fatally shot him. But Khan-Cullors was a Los Angeles–based artist and organizer long before then. Her award-winning work with the Labor Community Strategy Center and her performance piece "Stained: An Intimate Portrayal of State Violence" were early shots fired in a career that has focused on making the lives of Black people truly matter. Her first book, *When They Call You a Terrorist*, was released in 2018. Here she talks to Akiba about the genesis of her community organizing.

How did you get into organizing?

Aww, the good old days. Let's see. I grew up in Van Nuys, a working-class suburb of LA made up of mostly undocumented Latino immigrants, some Black folks, and some poor White people.

I was very concerned about the environment in elementary school and middle school. I think I adopted a whale in elementary school, and I was concerned with animals going extinct. At the time, the environmental movement had the best stronghold on messaging around organizing and activism.

I learned my actual organizing skills at a social justice camp up in the mountains of California when I was sixteen. The camp was run by National Conference for Community and Justice. We had seven days of training in a "tolerance" curriculum. But I wanted an action component to that. At one point during my training as a youth leader, I asked a group I was working with, "Do you take on the police?" They said, "No, we're an environmental justice group." I said, "Okay, I'll take it."

Still, no matter how much I tell people I've been a skilled strategist for fourteen or fifteen years, people don't see it. I think it's because I'm a woman, am Black, and it's a more exciting thing to imagine, "Oh, you popped up out of nowhere!"

People don't understand that organizing isn't going online and cussing people out or going to a protest and calling something out. That's the most visible shit; we're not putting our boring-ass meetings on social media.

How do you define an organizer versus an activist?

Organizers are strategists. We are a part of producing and building the campaign. Activists are showing up to the things that organizers plan, signing the petitions, going on social [media] to promote the action. Sometimes organizers are activists as well—they can be out front *and* work behind the scenes.

Can you talk about the importance of telling your own story?

As Black Lives Matter—the brand of BLM—grew, it didn't follow us. God forbid Black women are behind something huge. So I made an executive decision when the *Melissa Harris-Perry* show did a panel about BLM without inviting me or [cofounders Alicia Garza and Opal Tometi]. It was like, "Nah, that's not going to work this time. We're Black women; we know the story of being erased."

We're forty years in and just now really talking about Ella Baker. That's no dis to MLK, but goddamn. Hundreds of Black women did work for the March on Washington. And after women did that work, [male organizers] decided that women weren't going to speak. So I decided that this time patriarchy was not going to rule the land. Or at least we were going to compete with it.

Why do you think patriarchy is still so appealing to us?

We are wired for patriarchy. It's how our bodies work. It's not even in our minds. It's in our belief system. We still believe in Black men more than Black women. That's how you get a man as a "leader" of BLM. At least MLK actually was a leader! We need a culture shift.

How do you cope with being forward-facing when people take shots at your work?

This work takes an extreme amount of restraint, and it's very lonely, very isolating. Sometimes I want to go on social media and go the hell off, but then I go call somebody. It takes community support, a commitment to what's bigger. And I try not to feel sorry for myself. I literally have a centering practice, Jordan somatics. It looks like being able to wake up and sit on the edge of my bed, standing up and taking deep breaths and healing into the deepest parts of me. I remember that I'm human and doing the best that I can. I keep it in perspective by keeping my oldest homies close, people who aren't a part of the movement. That gives me grounding and perspective.

What makes you proud about the work of BLM?

That we did something different than I would say the old guard did. We were talking about trans Black people, about police violence against Black women. We were looking at harm and violence inside of the Black community. For us, every victim is special and important, no matter their past. We've got to tell a different story about Blackness.

~~~~~~~~

Redemption Song

For Christopher Rashad Green, organizing is about redemption.

He was sixteen years old the first time he was arrested.

"At fifteen, I was an honor roll student attending a college prep program on the campus of Rutgers University. On my sixteenth birthday, I was locked up. Six months. That's how fast it happened," says the Plainfield, New Jersey, native. "Looking back now, I still ask, *How did that happen?* Some of the members of my clique turned south, and I went south with them. Trying to fit in, I was making poor decisions, shooting heroin. And then I was locked up. Altogether, I've put about fifteen years in on this installment plan."

After more than a dozen years in and out of prisons in New Jersey, New York, Texas, and Virginia for a series of addiction-related infractions, he'd had enough.

On May 20, 2010, at 11:00 a.m. Eastern Standard Time, police took Green into custody, and he decided that it would be his last time behind bars. "I can't explain it, but within forty-eight hours I just had this resolve. I just knew that I would never come back," Green says of his last three-year bid. "I said to myself, *My reentry program starts now. I'm not going to wait to get to the end of my bid, I'm going to start it right now.*"

And so he did.

He connected with mentors, joined a rehab program, started journaling—anything to prepare himself for the task of getting out and staying out. As he worked on himself, one word kept coming back to him: "service."

"I would only be successful in life if I served other people. That was the message I got. I didn't hear any voices or anything like that. But that, within my studying, that was the word that jumped out," he said. "I tried to dissect it, and it came to me. I would never be successful, anywhere in life, until I figured out a way to serve."

These days, Green is an organizer with the progressive nonprofit New Virginia Majority. He first attended a meeting in the fall of 2015, just as he was toying with the idea of getting his voting rights restored. "I hooked up with New Virginia Majority, and *they* were addressing the restoration of rights. It was just a perfect fit," he says. "From that point on, I became pretty much the face of restoration of rights for New Virginia Majority."

After volunteering for two years, he was hired as an organizer, focusing primarily on voter registration and restoration of rights, which means he does everything from knocking on doors to lobbying the state's General Assembly members. "The role seems like it was carved out for me," says Green, who is now based in Richmond, Virginia. "It keeps me alive."

He sees his biggest task as helping Black people in his community push back against the idea that they don't matter. "So many people, when we try to register them, say, 'It's not going to change anything. My vote's not going to matter.' And I say, 'No, it does matter, brother. Because it's not just about voting. It's about being involved.' I share my story with them, try to encourage them to jump in," he says. "And then look what happened here in Virginia last year: the balance of power in the General Assembly was decided by one vote. One vote."

Green estimates that he has helped thousands of Black people regain their right to participate in the democratic process. And on August 15, 2016, he secured his own. "I got to register and vote for the first time in almost thirty years," says Green, who is fifty-eight. "When I first started working with New Virginia Majority, I heard this term: 'political currency.' Your vote is political currency. That kind of struck me as like, 'Wow, my voice is like currency. Let me get my rights back.' What could I lose for doing it? It's my right. I'm a taxpaying citizen. I did my time."

Green's organizing work makes him feel like a new man. "I'm really trying to redeem myself. There's no excuse for all the bad things I did over the years. But as my people say, 'That's old, that's done. That's the old Christopher. This is the new brother Christopher here.'"

~~~~~~~~~~

The Makings of #MeToo: A Q+A with Tarana Burke

Tarana Burke is a veteran organizer, writer, and survivor of childhood sexual abuse. She has worked for nonprofits around the country, including Selma's National Voting Rights Museum and Institute, Philadelphia's Art Sanctuary, and New York City's Girls for Gender Equity. She's also an accidental celebrity.

Burke became famous in late 2017 after investigative reports confirmed sexual violence accusations against Hollywood producer Harvey Weinstein. That moment—which saw the toppling of Weinstein as well as TV hosts Matt Lauer and Charlie Rose, among many others—didn't have a name until the White actress Alyssa Milano suggested that all survivors should tweet "me too." What Milano soon found out, owing to a Black feminist Twitter outcry, was that Burke had founded a #MeToo movement in 2006 as a multiplatform initiative that provides refuge for Black survivors of sexual abuse and exploitation.

Milano gave Burke the credit she deserved, mainstream media caught on, and the organizer ran with the whole thing. Burke has been on billboards and on CNN. She has dropped the New Year's Eve ball in New York City and been named a *Time* Person of the Year. And she has forced the influential *Tom Joyner Morning Show* to stop playing R. Kelly's music.

Akiba sat down with Burke for a candid dialogue about movement-building.

Let's start with Tarana as a youth organizer.

I started when I became a member of the 21st Century Youth Leadership Movement, in Selma, Alabama. It was founded by people who came from the Civil Rights, Black Power, and labor movements. They wanted to make sure there was another generation to carry on their legacy. So we went to a summer camp and took all kinds of classes. We were also expected to do something during the school year. The first thing I ever organized around was Donald Trump.

Really?

Yeah, via the Central Park jogger case. Isn't that some full-circle shit?

It is! How old were you?

It was spring 1989, so I was fifteen. Yusef [Salaam, one of the Central Park Five] was dating a friend of mine. She came to the program, like, "They arrested my boyfriend, and I know he didn't do it."

When the story hit the newspapers, it was ridiculous. Donald Trump took out that full-page ad in the four major New York papers—the *Daily News*, *Times*, *Post*, and *Newsday*—calling [the accused] animals and calling for their heads. He really doubled down on this notion of the oversexed Black male out here preying on innocent White women.

So what did you do?

We held a protest in front of the *New York Daily News*, and we wrote letters to the editors of all the major newspapers. We were trying to make the point that they were criminalizing Black youth when there were plenty of examples of us doing positive things. The other point was that Donald Trump was racist.

Where were you raised?

In the South Bronx, not far from Yankee Stadium. My grandfather was a self-professed Garveyite: he *believed* in Marcus Mosiah Garvey. I was raised Catholic, but he told me that the only thing he wanted me to do was read a history book alongside the Bible so that I could learn what was actually going on in the world.

What did you learn?

When I was in seventh grade, he gave me *They Came before Columbus* and *Roots*. I was conflicted because I was a very good Catholic girl. At the same time, my mother had participated in the Black Power Movement in the '70s and was a Womanist in the early '80s because of Alice Walker.

That sounds like a well-rounded education!

It was. On the one hand, you had my mother with all of this Black feminist literature, and then you had my grandfather, who used to take me down to 125th Street to buy cassette tapes of John Henrick Clarke. We always had a birthday cake for Martin Luther King's and Malcolm X's birthdays. My granddaddy was like, "We don't need no goddamned United States of America to tell us when to celebrate our people!"

[laughs] So you were primed for Black activism.

Yeah, I was primed. But in some ways, my mother and my grandfather didn't [show] me how to make what they taught me useful for the community. I was a really conversant twelve-year-old, but until I found 21st Century, I didn't have a way to put that into action.

How did you find out about this Selma-based movement as a kid from the Bronx?

21st Century's New York chapter came through an organization called Jobs for Youth. I was the little assistant in the office. I made $3.10 an hour. One day the head of the office said, "Hey, you wanna go to Washington, DC?" and gave me a flyer. I took it home to my mother and asked, "Mommy, can I go to DC?" She was like, "How much it cost?" I said, "It's free!" If that trip had been $50, I might not have been a 21st Century leader!

Ah, the trip to DC was such a staple!

Yes! So a bunch of us go to DC. It's like eighty rambunctious-ass New York City high school kids. We get off at the 4-H center in Chevy Chase,

Maryland, which I thought was a joke. I was like, "How does Chevy Chase have a whole city?"

Anyway, we get off the bus and see these Alabama-ass kids singing and dancing. They were joyous fucking kids. And we were some ornery New York kids asking, "What the fuck are they so happy for?"

So what did you do there?

We did a three-day leadership program. Although I was still crotchety, I was low-key, like, *I love this!* So when I got back to New York, I helped start our chapter. 21st Century is where I first learned that fighting White supremacy didn't always have to look like what it looked like in history books. We had songs with lyrics like, "We are the ones we've been waiting for!" It was all geared toward us working for the community that we wanted to live in, in spite of White supremacy.

You were sold!

Yes. I became a complete and utter convert. It was like being in a sorority, and it was an escape from dealing with sexual abuse. I didn't have to confront my own demons. Becoming a fighter and then an organizer allowed me to shield myself from this part of my life that was really torture.

So how did you go from being a 21st Century leader to founding the #MeToo movement?

The concept of "me too" had been bubbling under the surface for a long time. As an adult, working for 21st Century, we would have community meetings, and I was seeing [evidence of sexual abuse] everywhere. I was trying to figure out how to talk about it so it didn't pathologize Black people or demonize the South. But living in Selma in particular, it was so pervasive. We had elders naming community problems, but not sexual abuse. I *knew* I wasn't the only one who had been abused. I was like, "What criteria do you have to meet before something [rises] to the level of a community fucking problem?" A big part of this had to do with how James Bevel, the civil rights leader, was found to be a serial abuser. Before he died, he was convicted of molesting one of his fourteen daughters. What's missing from the stories on the internet is how he was protected by the civil rights community. Some of my elders went mute when it came to sexual violence. They even allowed him to interact with kids. Even the accusation alone should have been enough. The adults should have said, "We don't know if it's true or not, but we can't have you around our young people." Their silence was it for me.

That is so awful.

I was being retraumatized. So that's what sparked #MeToo. My elders and people who I respected did not take sexual violence seriously, but they had also given me all the skills I needed to do it myself.

Because the movement has a Hollywood component, I've heard whisperings among Black folks that #MeToo has been Whitewashed. How do you deal with that?

What I've been saying to Black people when I'm traveling around is that it's not enough for y'all to celebrate me as an individual. Black people are not responding from that place of, "This is ours, a movement that started for us." We're still whispering. We are private. And we are still allowing this narrative that Black people can't say "me too."

I feel like we're still trying to protect us, whoever us is. I don't think we actually want CNN to do an exposé on abuse in the Black community. Somebody would be like, "But they fired Soledad O'Brien!"

It's always going to be like that. Look what happened when [editor-in-chief] Kierna [Mayo] put that picture of the Huxtables under broken glass on the cover of *Ebony*. [Black] people lost their fucking minds. People were saying, "You can't do that!" like it was a betrayal. And because of all of the uproar, we couldn't have an honest conversation about sexual violence and Black men, or the way that we idolize fictional characters and protect them over human beings. At this point, you can get a large group of people to agree about R. Kelly [being a pedophile and sexual abuser], but that's still a debate in our community.

We have to fight White supremacy and [how] it permeates our lives as Black people in America. But we've also been co-opted by it. I know I sound probably like my grandfather now, but we doing the work of the White folks ourselves. [*laughs*]

So let's talk about what you started. I remember you having a "me too" curriculum, a website, and T-shirts.

Yes. That work was focused on young people I was working with in Philadelphia. A friend and I cofounded an organization called Just BE Inc., that came out of a rites of passage program that we had previously created called Jendayi Aza. [*laughs*] It meant, "You are powerful. Give thanks." We put girls through twenty-one weeks of training. It was modeled after pledging a [Black] sorority with a little bit of Girl Scouts and African rites of passage. The girls loved it. We did it with high school–age girls for two years. Then a middle school asked us to create something for their girls.

So how did you get to "me too"?

When we first started our program, we didn't include sexual violence in the curriculum. But the girls were always coming and telling us some new shit. We found out that one of our seventh-graders was "dating" a twenty-one-year-old man. We chased his ass away. And then we had another girl who had been left back so she was fourteen in the seventh grade. She had one child and was pregnant again. We found out she'd had her first baby when she was either twelve or thirteen, at the hands of her mother's boyfriend.

That's a lot, Tarana.

She and another little girl who I met in Selma were two of the saddest cases I ever had. The girl in Selma used to fight all the time. She was in foster care because her mom's boyfriend had molested her and she got pregnant. She had the baby at twelve or thirteen and she and her child were in foster care together. When I met her, she was fourteen and pregnant again at the hands of another adult who assaulted her. These girls were so, so, so vulnerable.

So how did you deal with all of this given your own trauma?

After a few years, I needed to sit down. But back to the program: One night, I wrote out all of the concepts that became "me too." Then my partner and I built a workshop around it. We would start with language, giving the girls legal definitions for what they were facing, because they just didn't know. Most people don't know.

No, they don't.

The next part involved [the sexual assault stories of] Gabrielle Union, Mary J. Blige, Fantasia, Queen Latifah, Missy Elliot, and Oprah. The workshop would start with an icebreaker conversation that would lead to me saying, "I'm a survivor," and telling them parts of my story. Our acronym was SAAE, which stood for Sexual Assault, Abuse, and Exploitation. We wanted a way to name exploitation in that gray area that people don't really deal with.

So after you shared parts of your story, what would you do?

We had pasted a picture of each of the celebrities I named on a sheet of black paper and wrote the words "me too." On the other side, we'd pasted a [stock photo] of a Black girl that we'd pulled off of the internet, wrote "me too" under her picture, and added some statistics. While the girls looked at the side of the paper with the girl's picture on it, we would tell a story. Then we'd say, "Turn your page over." And the girls would be like, "Oh, it's Oprah!" It was so dramatic, but it worked for kids.

After going through that process, we would ask, "What do you think about when you think of Oprah?" They would write a whole bunch of [positive] words like "smart," "rich," and "pretty." Then we'd ask them what words they thought of when they heard the phrase "Black girls." And for the most part, they'd write down negatives: "loud," "nappy head," "ghetto."

I know it's problematic in some ways to base it around celebrities because I don't know what their healing journey was. But what they represented to those girls was a different life. We were trying to show them that there's a trajectory toward healing and joy. We wanted them to understand that trauma was part of their journey, but not where they lived. To make sure the entire program wasn't depressing, we used music and arts and crafts and we took them on trips.

So did it ever get personal?

The way we ended the workshop was to give each girl in the class a sticky note and ask her to write down three things she'd learned. Then we'd say, "And if anybody wants to share more, you can write that on this piece of paper too. You can say 'me too.' You can write down your phone number or email address if you need help." That was our way of making sure nobody was singled out. We also handed out resource sheets with the number of a local crisis center and counselors they could call. At the end of the first workshop, we collected all of the slips of paper and gave each girl a hug. There were about thirty-five girls in the class. When my partner and I got back to our room, we dumped all of those folded-up pieces of paper out of a manila envelope. There were like twenty-five "me toos" in there. My partner and I sat down and we cried and cried and cried.

Okay, so, how do you take care of yourself while you do this work?

[*laughs*] I feel like I don't. I mean, I do and I don't. Early on, I just felt like this was the price I had to pay and that I should just soldier on. Eventually my partner and I stopped working together, so it was literally just me doing these workshops. Then I had to put it down because it was a lot to handle.

So you just said that you "do and don't" take care of yourself. In what ways do you take care of yourself?

The way I take care of myself in a bigger sense is the same way I take care of myself as a survivor, which is, I have to rejigger my thinking. I spent most of my life hyperfocused on the fact that I had been through these things. I was so protective of my brain and my body that I was always thinking of how to stay safe. That meant learning how to not think about the shit that happened. But I was still in a fucked-up place.

How did you change this?

When [my daughter] Kaia was born, I was panicked. I was like, "Okay, I gotta think of something better than this." When I found out I was having a girl, I became obsessed with the idea of crafting a world where this child has access to joy. People always say she's a great kid and ask me what I did. I tell them that I was incredibly intentional. I've failed in a lot of ways, and failed to protect her in some ways. But in terms of who she was as a person, it became really, really important to me from pregnancy on that she knew joy in her life. The only way I could figure out how to do that was to change my own life into one that would lead into the joy.

Okay, Oprah!

[*laughs*] With survivors of all kinds of things, it becomes such a part of your identity that you almost feel uncomfortable without it. Unless we are intentional about retraining our brains, we can end up leaning into the trauma because it's what we know.

So what did you do specifically? Did you have a technique you used?

My overthinking Virgo brain was like, *There's gotta be a solution! I need to understand how to do this differently.* So say I had a great day. I would think, *This is wonderful! I'm so happy today!* But then, when I had a minute of quiet, a memory of the trauma would come back. And so I would say to myself, *This is not who you are!* The ball and chain would come out, and I would be like, *Get back to being this other thing!* That became the routine, remembering who I actually am. Kaia became the touchstone.

How did that hold up when you were working with the young survivors?

Well, the kids became the other reason why I had to do things differently. I used to think, *I'm already a lost cause, but let me help y'all get there so somebody can survive.* But kids see through that. That's when I knew I had to practice. I read self-help and affirmation books and wrote stuff down on sticky notes and put them on the mirror. And I would stand in front of the mirror every day and say, "I love myself!"

So you talked yourself out of negative thinking? That's amazing.

Not really. I also felt like it was bullshit when I was saying it. I think I'm too much of an asshole to really believe some of that shit. But then I realized that it wasn't just me being a pessimist. There just wasn't enough there to help me.

What ultimately happened?

This remains part of the work of #MeToo. What drove me to healing was that I didn't want to give these kids empty platitudes. Ultimately, I had to find something that was going to fill me when I wasn't in 21st Century, doing Just Be, or whatever else. Do you know what I'm saying?

Yes. I know what you're saying.

I wrote in a joy journal for a while. I would document what process I went through to feel joy because when I felt like shit, I needed something to refer back to.

One last question: did you study child development?

No. Political science. [*laughs*]

Well, okay. [laughs]

That's the reason why it took me so long to do this work with both feet in. I felt comfortable with leadership development because I had come from 21st Century and had been through training programs. But I was hesitant about the #MeToo work because I didn't want to mess up these kids. I'm not a social worker.

But in the end, I just forged ahead based on what I needed at their age and what I saw as their needs. They needed attention, somebody to make them understand their sense of self-worth despite whatever happened to them. And they needed to understand that there is possibility beyond this place. You don't have to study nothing to do that.

~~~~~~~~~

I fight White supremacy with my money by boycotting businesses that discriminate against people of color not only through how they treat customers of color, but in the products they choose to carry, the politics they support, and the way they treat their employees of color.

—Paulette Martin, finance executive

~~~~~~~~~

AND REGARDLESS OF 6% OF VOTERS IN 2016,
THIS COUNTRY HAS UNDOUBTEDLY BEEN BUILT BY THE
SUPPORTING HANDS OF BLACK WOMEN FOR GENERATIONS

EVEN IF OUR VOICES HAVE HISTORICALLY
BEEN MARGINALIZED AND IGNORED

LIKE MY GREAT GREAT
GRANDMOTHER WHO COOKED
YOUR MEALS

OR MY GREAT
GRANDMOTHER WHO RAISED
YOUR CHILDREN

AND MY GRANDMOTHER
WHO WORKED IN FACTORIES
DURING YOUR WARS

PLUS MY MOTHER WHO
FOUGHT FOR CIVIL AND
WOMENS' RIGHTS

WITHOUT QUESTION, BLACK WOMEN
WILL CONTINUE TO BUILD AND RESTORE
PEACE IN OUR COUNTRY

BIANCA XUNISE

"Generations" by Bianca Xunise (2017)

"'Generations' explores the decades of unrecognized labor Black women have done and continue to do for the benefit of all American people. This excerpt was a response to Black women pulling together and voting en masse to protect the American public." —Bianca Xunise

Bianca Xunise is an illustrator and cartoonist based in Chicago. Her work focuses on the plight and daily struggles of identifying as a young Black feminist weirdo in modern society. Her storytelling can range from simple, relatable slice-of-life content to complex, nuanced narratives like police brutality, and it garnered her an Ignatz Award for Promising New Talent.

Think Globally, Act Locally: A Q+A with Tef Poe

St. Louis rapper, activist, and writer Kareem "Tef Poe" Jackson was already a community activist when Darren Wilson, a Ferguson, Missouri,

White police officer, fatally shot eighteen-year-old Michael Brown. Brown's killing—and the fact that authorities allowed his bleeding corpse to lie in the street for hours—pushed area people to protest daily. They were met with police, tanks, tear gas, and rubber bullets.

Tef was among the cadre of young organizers who made up the Ferguson movement. In 2015, he cofounded Hands Up United, a local organization that offers tech and small-business training, the free Books and Breakfast Program, healing circles, and spaces for political dialogues.

When Akiba interviewed Tef in November 2017, he and the movement were in a different place. He was in his second year at Harvard University as a Nasir Jones Hiphop Fellow, and the local movement had splintered. Tef is a self-described revolutionary and revealed himself to be a young Black man with one foot in the movement and the other in the streets of St. Louis.

Why do you put such a strong emphasis on local organizing?

It's important because, when you look at history, it's really the most effective. When street gangs organize a truce, that's local organizing. Single mothers leaning on each other for resources is local organizing. All too often, we expect organizing to be this grand type of thing. The "we" in this scenario is the more academic, financially stable people that run the nonprofit sector. They intellectualize the issues and have grown into the face of the movement, and that would include myself sometimes. There is a disconnect between the people that do this professionally and the people who do this to live.

It can be difficult for people who aren't indigenous to an area or who are poor to organize without money, though.

I'm not against the nonprofit sector. But I'm thinking of what it's actually going to take to liberate Black folks in America. We use the word "revolution" all the time, but the fulfillment isn't going to come through the nonprofit sector. It hasn't for the last thirty to forty years. It's like, when somebody gets killed by the police. We see mass mobilizations that come through the nonprofit sector that are usually more docile and less about a long-term stance of revolutionary conflict with the people we deem as our enemies. There has to be a space for more radical voices. We also have to trust the creativity of poor people.

How did Ferguson affect how you think about organizing?

I'm in a weird space after Ferguson. Before, I believed more in the power of legislation. I believed in political power with a voice at the table. I still believe we need to be at the table, but I've sat down with FBI and Department of Justice folks and police chiefs [and] the next day I'm getting arrested by these people. Literally, one day I went to a meeting with [law enforcement officials] and the very next day they killed a boy. I got arrested after *they* killed somebody!

Are you still active in Hands Up United?

Very much. Hands Up is coming up on three years in existence. We're reassessing what we're going to be. We spent most of 2017 trying to stay out of jail because a lot of the charges that we had accumulated during the Ferguson actions came to knock on our doors. They might have been petty cases, but the state wanted to push each and every one of them. We spent a lot of energy, money, and time trying to stay out of jail.

Talk about what Hands Up does.

Our Books and Breakfast Program has served more than twenty thousand people. We've given out over twelve thousand books and graduated three classes of Black technologists ages fifteen to thirty-five that we pulled off the streets and taught how to code and build websites for Black businesses. We started a food and clothing pantry. That gave us a different ability to show up in the community. We can show up and tell the shooters like, "Yo, today we're out here giving away this food. There won't be no shooting from this time to this time." If we were to come to that community with just a clipboard, they may not necessarily listen.

You talk a lot about being poor and what that means in the movement. I'm interested in hearing more about class.

Not every Black person in America is poor, but they still Black. That carries its own type of mental, spiritual, and physical trauma because we have to rely on capitalism to, essentially, grant us our freedom papers. But poor folks are the most marginalized. If we're gonna have a revolution, it's gonna come through them first. Those are the people that are already shooting. They're already living with socialist values whether they know it or not. We just have to figure out how to turn it into something more substantial.

A fundamental problem that I've observed is that some of our organizing promotes toxic masculinity among Black men under the guise of taking care of them. How do you address that?

I think we have to lead by example. I don't shy away from the fact that women are soldiers. When we're going into these 'hoods, we're working with poor women for the most part. I struggle with the fact that a lot of brothers use negative language toward women. I've had conversations where I've lost friends. At the same time, I have an obligation to meet people where they're at.

How do you do that? Pushing political stances in interpersonal relationships can be so complicated.

I don't think that we can throw away humans if we're claiming to be in the revolutionary space. I've met brothers fresh out of prison who are like, "Yo, I want to be a part of the revolution, how's it going down?" They are comfortable because they can just be real. But there is some homophobia, sexism, and patriarchy involved. Some [movement] people go, "Fuck them. Forget them." But they just got out of jail! We gotta address them with love. Some of my friends in the movement have died and we weren't together because of them saying shit like, "Fuck these bitches. I don't like these hoes." I felt strongly about not being aligned with them when they passed. I felt as if I had shifted myself away from those brothers into a political body that didn't embrace me and my identity. When I'd go to the meetings, I would be the only straight man in the room. So what that tells me is that [this movement] was not willing to struggle with people that don't agree with us, even amongst ourselves.

Talk more about straight masculinity within a movement that is very steeped in Black feminism and queerness.

I am a person who is actively trying to purge myself of toxic masculine ways. I'm trying to show up not as an ally, but a straight up coconspirator with radical Black feminists. . . . I also will self-identify as an artist before I self-identify as being a Black man. That's important to me. I'm going to use the art, and I'm going to be in the art in every capacity of my existence. I am a Black man, but I'm a lot more than that as well.

~~~~~~~~~~

I fight White supremacy by reminding myself and everyone I can that race is fallacy, a divide-and-conquer strategy that will kill us all.

—Hank Willis Thomas, artist

~~~~~~~~~~

QUESTION, ANSWERED

Neither of us identifies as an organizer, but we're really interested in what makes people join movements and the groups that propel them. Here we each answer the question: "Are you a joiner?"

Akiba

People have often, as a compliment, called me an activist because I strive to create ways for people of color to say important things to one another and the rest of the world. But I deny this identity because it is not an informed assessment of my personality.

I am the child born in the mid-'70s of Philadelphia Black nationalists. Although my family has been improvisational and expansive in its activism, I somehow internalized the message that a narrow set of behaviors constitutes "real work." These behaviors are of the ready-to-die or at least ready-to-seriously-suffer variety. And no matter what anyone has said since I heard at a young age that real revolutionaries had to be ready to subsist on rats and pigeons while hiding out in a sewer, my soul just can't leave purism alone.

Without the drama and machismo of enforcing Black revolutionary purity, I can say that I believe that the most effective activism doesn't happen without committing to something besides your paid work, sticky social media posts, and private acts of service. Practically speaking, and what I believe so far, is that you *should* join an organization that has agreed-upon values, transparent ways to resolve conflict, applied codes of conduct, political education, credible leadership, and a decent legal defense fund.

I get these (not-that-revelatory) ideas from years of observing how change works through journalism. On a personal level, I have come to this conclusion after people I believed in acted a complete fool and fucked up what could have been a good thing.

In a piece that she was kind enough to allow me to edit at *Colorlines*, the Black feminist scholar Barbara Ransby made a cogent argument for joining groups even as today's decentralized movements spread through social media. In a June 2015 piece called "Ella Taught Me: Shattering the Myth of the Leaderless Movement," Ransby wrote:

> In my thirty years of working in many different groups, campaigns, and movements, I have been a part of efforts, not always successful, to strike the balance between mass mobilizing and organization-building; between inclusivity and accountability; and between strategic actions and spontaneous ones. Groups I've worked with have formed rotating steering and

coordinating committees instead of electing officers. They've met regularly and devised ways for there to be lots of talking, learning, processing, and thinking out loud together. Communication was always key and accountability has been crucial.

I have found that without organizations, coalitions, and leadership teams, there is no collective strategy or accountability. An independent or freelance activist may share their opinion, and it may be an informed one, but if these words are not spoken in consultation or conversation with people on the ground, they are limited as a representation of a movement's thinking and work.

At the time of writing this, Ransby was reflecting on the work of Black Lives Matter, Black Youth Project 100, the African American Policy Forum via the #SayHerName campaign, and the ascent of social media stars claiming ownership of the movement.

But all of this doesn't explain why I'm not a joiner.

I think it comes down to romanticized childhood notions of movement work. Throughout the years, I have developed a set of defense mechanisms that make me a questionable-to-undermining member of non-work-related groups.

One, I don't take actions that risk my livelihood unless I fully agree with the strategy and leadership. (In some dialects, that's called "being a punk." In others, it's called "being smart.")

Two, I have extremely high standards of individual accountability and become embittered when people, particularly those in leadership, don't meet them.

Three, I don't really trust anyone outside of my family and close friends.

I have no firsthand experience with COINTELPRO. I wasn't even a zygote as that murderous disgrace ripped through my people's work. Even more odd is that my biological and extended family have a deep organizing history. My late grandma, Mamie Nichols, an incredible community servant and organizer, has a freaking social service building named after her in her beloved Point Breeze South Philadelphia neighborhood.

My mother cofounded a group called Sisters Remember Malcolm and the Philadelphia Black Women's Health Project. She was on the board of a local Black organization called Art Sanctuary. She worked in the parent organizing and school reform movement before right-wing operatives hijacked them. Even in retirement, this woman fantasizes about getting arrested doing her volunteer work with a multifaith grassroots network called POWER.

Meanwhile, my father was in the Kwanzaa Cooperative, was a principal member of an R&B band called The Company, and today works with the Philadelphia Jazz Project, Philly Cam, and an unnamed group of retired Black men trying to do something with coding and math. Like me, he doesn't consider himself to be a joiner.

My late uncle, Richard Nichols, was the longtime manager and architect of The Roots, a group he helped hold together with revolutionary business acumen and duct tape. My late aunt, Yvette "Kinyozi" Smalls, had her own braid-based gang called Positive Hair Design. They didn't bang on anything but unhealthy Black hair, but they kept it hot at the annual Odunde Festival and changed the minds of little Black girls who hated their kinky hair.

And what have I done?

Become someone who asks questions and then fact-checks, cross-checks, and triple-checks things people say for a living. Basically, my job privileges skepticism and my well-documented paranoia.

That paranoia, which one of my best friends stops me from flippantly calling "crazy," is indeed justified by what I know of history. An informant destroyed Denmark Vesey's 1822 revolt in Charleston, South Carolina. Ernest Withers, the Black photographer widely praised for taking some of the most intimate images of the Civil Rights Movement, turned out to be a paid FBI informant. William O'Neal, an FBI plant who became head of security of the Chicago chapter of the Black Panther Party, set up twenty-two-year-old chairman Fred Hampton to be murdered in his bed in a Chicago police raid. Those police also murdered twenty-one-year-old Mark Clark, and they sexually assaulted Hampton's pregnant wife, then known as Deborah Johnson, by opening her robe and exposing her naked body auction-block style.

Besides scaring me, betrayals like these make me nauseous. A double agent in a trusted space of struggle rips apart our culture of survival. Betrayal makes us hypervigilant in unhealthy ways.

So while my inability to be a joiner is a source of frustration for me, I know to keep my mess to myself. Visceral paranoia and defensive what-ifs are not the best foundation for the kind of inspiration and faith that I believe people fighting White supremacy together need. If someone nice with their words (like me) always reserves the right to speak or change their mind, that does not make them a brilliant strategist. It makes them a critic—or a potentially toxic distraction. And yet, I know I am part of a greater project and legacy. I stay in my lane, yes. But I will never, ever, in my little smidgen of the world, let my folks be ground into dust. My position is not ideal, but it *is*. I believe that is enough.

~~~~~~~~

Kenrya

It's 1:00 a.m., and the mirrors are sweating.

Five of us are half-asleep in a surprisingly well-appointed room at the Embassy Suites in Romulus, Michigan, and it is hot and humid as hell, as a sixth woman makes clear after she quietly walks through and shuts the heavy door to the room, dropping her carry-on bag to the floor.

"How are y'all sleeping in here?" she asks as I stumble out of bed to help find the thermostat so we can turn off the heat.

We are so ragged from traveling that we haven't even noticed it's sweltering. It's been years since we crowded so many bodies into a room, though at least on this post-college voyage everyone actually has a bed to share. But we didn't hesitate to form like Voltron for this trip, purchasing last-minute airfares, renting a gleaming white Suburban, and piling into a hotel room just beyond the edge of Detroit Metropolitan Wayne County Airport. We are in town to help our linesister bury her father.

I am not one of those girls who grew up knowing she wanted to pledge. Hell, I didn't even grow up knowing that I wanted to attend an HBCU. I applied to several colleges for undergrad, but when I hit the yard for a visit one warm April day, I knew Howard University was the place for me. It was my first time on an airplane, and I had never set foot in Washington, DC, before that day, but being on that campus felt like being in my Black-ass home.

We were *everywhere*! And we came in forms and fashions I had never encountered, with paper-bag test winners laughing beside moonlight that dared you to bring that colorism shit over here. The Jack and Jill set whose families owned homes on Martha's Vineyard sat on the steps of Douglass beside those of us who had never heard of the enclave until Larenz Tate graced its beaches in *The Inkwell*. Brooklyn dudes in Timbs who thought a lazy two-step was the height of movement glared at the Atlanta cats who pulled all the chicks with their carefree twerking.

And among the crowd, joined at the hips, were the ladies of Delta Sigma Theta Incorporated's Alpha Chapter. They threw the best social action programs, ran the key campus organizations, raised the most money for charity, and laughed the loudest in the caf. And I wanted in.

The average prospective member will tell you that she is seeking membership because of the organization's long history of social justice advocacy and commitment to uplifting the Black community. And that makes sense: after the twenty-two founders broke ties with the first Black sorority to do their own thing, their initial official act was to participate in the Women's Suffrage Parade in March 1913. My "power to the people" brain was drawn to the "say no more, fam" of it all—they didn't think their original organization was doing enough for Black folks, so they threw up two fingers and did it themselves.

But the thing that captured my *heart* was seeing how the women on the line before mine interacted on campus. They were, in a word, sisterly. I could do community service beside anyone, but I was drawn to these women who came to the District from all over and found each other. They worked together, played together, fucked shit up together. And I too wanted a group of like-minded baddies to run the world with. So I pledged.

To this day, when anyone asks me about my Delta journey, I skip over the stuff I'm sure they want to know (Delta business is Delta business), and I tell them the most important part: my linesisters are the very best thing about this lifetime commitment.

I've worked with many groups over the years, organizing voter drives with my NAACP youth chapter, serving as chief of staff for HU's student administration, teaching Saturday school for Black and Brown kids in New York City's Alphabet City, helping Black co-eds develop their leadership skills. But for me, no group has illustrated quite as clearly the importance of working toward a goal—be it to stop responding when that fuckboy texts or to loosen the grip that Whiteness run amok has on our lives—with arms linked. My linesisters, you see, have shaped me.

We bonded on campus, but it was in the years after we graduated—as we found and lost and found ourselves many times over—that we became each other's limbs. These ladies have been with me when I was at my lowest (propping me up as I processed the trauma of my marriage and subsequent divorce) and highest (watching my cooch intently as I pushed my kid out on all fours).

And then there are the funerals. We've gotten to an age where we are nursing our children while we bury those who first taught us to love. One day they are here, cooking oxtails for their grandchildren, musing on their days playing professional baseball, buying us crystal-encrusted elephants. And then their bodies are gone. But their souls abide.

And so does our sisterhood.

TWO
THE STRUGGLE IS REAL

Can we take a minute to acknowledge that it has been a fucked-up few years? Like we're perpetually having a sock slid down in your boot, bonnet came off last night so your twistout is fuzzy, "Why do people refuse to learn the lessons of our abundant history of racial oppression?" kind of Groundhog Day. You can't even get lost online to escape it anymore; these days, social media is mostly a doomsday delivery service for the kind of breaking news that reminds us daily just how shitty things are.

For many, the current state of the world feels like abstract unease. It causes low-level dread, but it doesn't impact your ability to sleep, work, or otherwise adult. For others, it feels like craning your neck to scan the sky for a glimpse of the next bomb before it flattens you: your back hurts like hell and you're not at all confident that you can get out of the way quickly enough.

But for some, it's like someone dropped a wall made of solid shit directly in their path. It cuts off all routes to a quiet, peaceful life (and smells like, well, shit). For those people, there is no navigating around the obstacles manufactured by rotting systems. Whether they lost a child to state-sanctioned violence or were taught from an early age that their humanity wasn't guaranteed, they have been thrust into fights they did not necessarily choose. So when the wall blocks their way, the only thing to do is lace up their Timbs, pull back their hair, and get to clawing. For them, my friend, the struggle is real. Real dirty, real heartbreaking, real personal.

Whether battling the accumulated trauma of microaggressions or fighting police violence, the people in this chapter turned personal tribulations into work that seeks to dismantle the elements of White supremacy.

<div style="text-align:center">~~~~~~~~~~</div>

Constance Malcolm: "I Joined a Club That I Never Knew I'd Be a Part Of"

On February 2, 2012, three weeks before George Zimmerman killed Trayvon Martin, a White police officer named Richard Haste fatally shot Black eighteen-year-old Ramarley Graham in his Bronx apartment. Graham's maternal grandmother, Patricia Hartley, was close enough that some of his blood landed on her chest. His brother, then six, was only a few feet away. His mother, Constance Malcolm, arrived home a half-hour later to yellow tape.

The initial police version had Graham exiting a bodega under the surveillance of an undercover drug unit, "walking with a purpose" and fidgeting with his waistband, an alleged sign of gun possession. Haste, according to a police spokesman, followed Graham into the house, struggled with him in front of the family's bathroom, and then came the shot.

But cameras.

Cameras on his building's exterior showed Graham walking to his front door, quickly glancing over his shoulder, and entering. Moments later, there's Haste running up to the door, trying to yank it open, and kicking it repeatedly.

Haste eventually went to the back of the building, where a neighbor let him in. What the cameras couldn't show is how the officer unlocked the apartment door for two other cops, kicked in the door to Graham's unit, and shot him.

Unlike in so many other cases, Haste actually went before a grand jury. During the hearing, attorneys for the police called Graham "the perp" and declared him an "imminent threat." The grand jury indicted Haste for manslaughter, but a Bronx County Supreme Court judge overturned the decision on the grounds that the jury had received improper instructions. A second grand jury failed to indict Haste.

The family eventually settled a civil case against the city for $3.9 million. But Haste and the officers in his unit were still on the job. In March 2017, facing dismissal, Haste was allowed to quit with dignity. Another officer involved, Sergeant Scott Morris, reportedly resigned after settling departmental charges in December 2017.

Malcolm, a certified nursing assistant, has become a leading voice in police reform. She was one of the leaders of a 2015 campaign that compelled New York governor Andrew Cuomo to issue an executive order authorizing the state attorney general's office to act as a special prosecutor for police killings.

At the time of this interview, Malcolm was awaiting the NYPD's response to a Freedom of Information Act (FOIA) lawsuit. If the force is cooperative, it will reveal what all of the other officers involved in the killing and its aftermath did that day. While she waited for the outcome of the suit, Constance talked to Akiba about how she wakes up every day.

One of the things that really stands out to me is that over all of these years, what police tried to tell you about what happened doesn't make any sense. Frankly, it seems you would get burnt out and quit. How do you continue to do this work?

When this happened to me, I didn't know anything about activism. But I knew that I had to tell the story of my son—not what they [portrayed] him to be, like he had a gun and was selling drugs. That wasn't so. He was meeting a couple of friends to see some young ladies. This was at the height of stop-and-frisk, and Black men were disproportionately stopped. It was like, "We have to bring our numbers up. That's how we make our money, by incarcerating these young men."

So my son fell in that category. But they never found a gun. They started to backtrack and say that they saw a drug transaction. There was none. So I started organizing rallies every Thursday. I did eighteen on that day of the week because Ramarley died on a Thursday and he was eighteen years old. Then I was like, "Okay, this is bigger than just the precinct where the police officers came from." We had to start from the top. First we pushed for the DA to charge this officer, Richard Haste. They charged him with manslaughter one and two. On the day he was arraigned, I saw this man was just laughing, as if my child didn't matter.

I'm sorry—Haste was in court laughing?

When he got bail, he came out of the court laughing. And one of his fellow officers was cheering him on, saying, "You the man!" And I'm like, *Wait a minute. What is "you the man" about? You killed a young man that posed no threat to you.*

Who did you rally with?

I had a group of people from the community. I had one young lady I didn't know, [Black Lives Matter cofounder] Patrisse Kahn-Cullors. She said, "This could be my brother." She was at the court organizing. Then other organizations started coming in, like Justice Committee, Police United for Reform, Moms Rising, and Make the Road. These were young people. When I saw them, I saw my son. And this is why I fight so hard. There was this one young man, Darien, who would always come to anything I did and bring a whole bunch of other young kids with him. He just reminded me so much of Ramarley. Up until this day, I cry when I talk about it.

How are your mom and your other son doing?

My mom is angry, but she doesn't talk about it. I worry about my son. He was six when it happened, and now he's twelve going on thirteen. He watched this whole thing unfold, and I don't know where his headspace is right now. What if a cop decides to stop him and he decides, like, *I don't want to talk to you because I don't trust you. I remember what you did to my brother.* These are the things that go through my head. I remember when we were living on the block where the precinct is. He was like, "I want to blow up the precinct." I was like, "Not all cops are bad." But how can I tell a child that when he watched what happened to his brother?

Has your activism ever felt like a burden to you?

There are times where it gets very heavy, when I want to be home. But I've got to be in the street. When things like this happen, you're in a hole. There's no handbook on how a mother should react after losing a child, how to go pick a casket out and how to go pick a hole to bury your son in. When I go to talk to a person that lost a loved one, I let them know to bury their child first, before everything else, because your mind is clouded right now. Get that over with. Once your loved one is well situated in their resting place, then you can deal with the fight.

I read that you're active in the union at your job. Is that right?

Yeah, I'm a nurse's assistant and an 1199 member—1199SEIU United Healthcare Workers East. They've been supportive from day one.

Wow. So you take care of people for a living too?

Yes, I take care of the elderly, people with Alzheimer's, everything. In and of itself, it's a very stressful job. There have been times when I'd go to work with people I didn't know and they would say, "I saw you on TV, what's going on?" But my job is my job. It's very complicated to explain that to people sometimes.

I interviewed Tamir Rice's mom once, and she shared how people would walk up to her out of nowhere and try to hug her. She would get blindsided. Have you had that experience?

I get it a lot, but I know they don't mean any harm. The only thing that gets me really pissed off is when people come up to me like, "Oh, but you got a lot of settlement money." I'm like, "You think I'm in this for money? They could have the money and give me my son back."

So before Ramarley was killed, did you think much about race and racism?

No. Honestly, I didn't. I came to this country from Jamaica when I was thirteen years old. Back then, I used to see cops playing with the kids in the neighborhood. We used to have block parties and they'd come.

But as the years went by, you see cops beating up people. Kids come from school and they'd throw them against the wall and harass them. They just started beating on the kids as if they don't have a right to ask, "Why you stopping me?" I would see kids, when the cops came, automatically face the wall and put their hands up. You don't see this happen in neighborhoods like Scarsdale, where you see ten little White boys together and it's okay. But in this neighborhood, you see ten Black boys walking, it's a gang. The game is so unbalanced, it's not real.

What do you think would have to happen for things to be equal?

We'll never have change until cops actually get the time that they deserve for the crimes they commit. We've got to keep organizing, keep doing all this stuff that we shouldn't have to do to get basic answers for our loved ones.

For you, does talking to media and having press conferences help?

It helps me because I'm telling the story about what happened to my son. And another mother will look at me and say, "You know what? She's been fighting. I can do the same thing if it happens to me." But the reason why I'm in the fight is because I wanted to fight. You've got to want to fight. A lot of times, when I'm in bed, I think, *I can't do this anymore.* But I owe it to my kids.

Do you ever get to go on vacation?

Actually, I'm going on vacation for a couple of days, away from here. I never even wanted to because when I was fighting, I felt like if I left, the story would just die. We had to let the Department of Justice know, "Listen, we ain't going nowhere. You might as well just meet with us and let us know what's going on." I'm always going to kick a door down. You're gonna give me answers. I see myself as a winner. Because at the end of the day, I got two cops off the force.

What would you tell another parent who, God forbid, has their child killed by police?

You know, I joined a club that I never knew I'd be a part of. It's a club I would not invite anybody to be in. I know mothers who have been out here for twenty years fighting and nothing has changed. But I tell people, "We didn't get voters' rights overnight. We've got to continue to fight." One door closes, another one always opens. We just gotta keep fighting.

〜〜〜〜〜〜

I fight White supremacy by raising my daughter to take up space and make her voice heard in a world that wants to quiet her.

—Rochelle Rice, musician

〜〜〜〜〜〜

Conversations with Microaggressions and the Spirit World
Asali Solomon

1. Eating out with a large group of graduate students in the English Department of the University of California at Berkeley, an institution whose reputation for progressive thought was running on fumes by the early 2000s. "O" was younger than me, a twerp radiating the hostile energy that I associated with White male devotees of Literary Modernism. Back then, before they had to add Hurston, Larsen, and Hughes to the syllabus, Modernism

was the classic rock of English literature: White male–dominated, purportedly edgy, the pinnacle of post-Shakespeare achievement, a legitimate way to avoid the multiracial American literary reality of the 1960s to the '80s and Toni Morrison.

When these dudes weren't sitting around using Hegel to decode Stevens, they were spitting the word "diversity" and commiserating unselfconsciously about how hard it would be for them to get academic jobs because of being qualified White men.*

At the dinner we were talking about public transportation and agreed that the bus was the worst. The bus in Oakland evoked passages from Julia Kristeva's *Powers of Horror: An Essay on Abjection*. The smell could most charitably be described as deeply human. Some of the passengers looked like their skin hurt. Bugs were involved. Once, a drunk and disheveled man peed on the bus; I watched the stream roll slowly toward the front exit under my feet. When the driver kicked him off, he tried to blame "the fella that had just got off." I told that story at the dinner. I'm no saint. I'm a clown. But racism always has the last laugh.

I mentioned that I rode the 51 bus. "The 51," "O" chimed in enthusiastically. "You're lucky!" says "O". "There are White people on that bus!"

What I said is not even worth mentioning.

2(a). An elderly White person beelined down a hill toward me on the campus in the South at a university named for Robert E. Lee where, sadly, I was on the faculty:

"Are you a law student?"

---

* According to the US Department of Education, "In fall 2015, of all full-time faculty at degree-granting postsecondary institutions, 42 percent were White males, 35 percent were White females, 6 percent were Asian/Pacific Islander males, 4 percent were Asian/Pacific Islander females, 3 percent each were Black females and Black males, and 2 percent each were Hispanic males and Hispanic females" (https://nces.ed.gov/fastfacts/display.asp?id=61). In the late 1990s and early 2000s, when I was working on my PhD, listening to these guys fret and bellyache, the situation was even worse.

"I'm a professor."

"It's a compliment!"

What I said: "Thanks."

2(b). When we first met, the proprietor of the best thrift shop in town (a man who would later argue with me, claiming I was another Black woman) asked, "You a student at the college?"

"A professor."

"It's a compliment!"

What I said: "Okay."

2(c). Another day. Another White person: "You a law student?"

"Professor in the English Department."

"It's a compliment!"

3. A high school friend was concerned she wouldn't get into Brown, her top-choice college. "I mean, I'm a White girl," she wailed.

What I said, with a sinking feeling: "Right."

What I should have said: "Who do you think is at Brown?"

4. In the majority-White suburban private school I traveled to from the city daily, "H" fancied herself street-smart. (She was the kind of middle-grade girl in the 1980s who dropped the Viet- from -Nam.) There she was, asking me and my best friend, also Black, to poke out our lips.

What I did: poke out my lips and wonder why she was doubled over laughing.

5. One night as a graduate student in Iowa City, a place where insults were regularly leveled against my ancestors in the form of fiction workshop discussions and literary bar banter, I walked into a party at an unknown house. A tall thin White man emerged from the shadows like Dracula.

"Hello, Black Angel," he said.

What I regret (fifteen years later) not saying: "Hello, White Devil."

6. A female voice screeched "nigger!" out of a car as it drove past me. I was standing on the corner after high school, waiting for a bus to go to therapy.
What I did: Go to therapy. For ten years.

Microaggressions are like wack lovers and even more wack than the word "lover." The memories linger like slobbery kisses and jabby little dicks and the shame that somehow wound up on you. When you repeat them to other people, the stories are dull and incomprehensible, like dreams. We want to respond exactly the right way, but we never do. Sometimes we don't even know what's happening until it's too late, but also, if we could have shut it down in the moment, none of it would have happened in the first place. We'd be in an entirely different world.

The master text of the microaggression is Claudia Rankine's monster of a book, 2014's *Citizen: An American Lyric*. It captures the unreality of the microaggression moment. When confronted with hot White inappropriateness, the speaker repeatedly queries, "Was this racist, or was I just being oversensitive?" Instead of (verbally?) backhanding someone, we get caught up in the moment, reconstructing the crime: he was standing over here, the dog was there, it was raining, she was born in 1956. . . . As of the writing of this essay there is no known cure for microaggressions; the only salve is time. But more time equals more microaggressions.

Maybe these incidents aren't the end of the world. They often occur in rarefied spaces: ivory towers and frivolous stores, outside the yoga studio in the gentrifying neighborhood, for fuck's sake, where some lady is bracing herself to ward off your panhandling even though you're clearly wearing yoga clothes and carrying a mat like everybody else. But microaggressions signal that the end is coming; after all, they happen for the same exact reason that seven-year-old Aiyana Stanley-Jones, sleeping in her home, was shot to death by an agent of the state. It's your hair, your skin, your ancestors. And peace and power to the late Chester Pierce, the brilliant Black psychiatrist who coined the term "microaggressions" in the 1970s, but now that everybody who doesn't watch Fox News knows what they are, it might be time to clarify that there's nothing micro about aggression.

Fuck that prefix.

When somebody follows you around a store, or makes a watermelon joke onstage before they hand you a National Book Award, they are offering you a look behind the gauzy veneer of "civilized" Whiteness into the massive, rotten, pulsing, monstrous reality that's always there.

Philando Castile, killed during a 2016 traffic stop in Minnesota, had been pulled over by police at least forty-nine times in the preceding thirteen years. Consider, if you will, the "micro" encounters he lived through. Consider instead that he was murdered. How many ways are there to say this? It might be happening in Rikers and it might be happening at Harvard, but a "microaggression" happens because White people and their allies want to kill you.

Writing in 2018, from the terrifying dystopian novel that is our reality, I'm prepared to forecast a 100 percent chance of a rising tide of microaggressions. And yet I'm still here reviewing trifling bullshit that somebody said to me thirty years ago, still looking for the snappy comeback that would have shut it down, knowing deep down that there was really nothing to say that could have repaired the psychic damage.

But there are conversations I would rather be having in my mind and in real life. I want to ask a Lenape woman in the area now known as the Delaware Valley about life before White people arrived. I want to ask Toni Morrison impertinent questions about her love life: who covers her with a throw blanket when she naps on the couch (and ask if she has ever in her life napped on the couch). I want to talk to the man with no gloves, in heavy work clothes in the freezing Thirty-Seventh Street trolley station, about his inspired decision to warm us up with creamy '70s Philadelphia music blasting from his cell phone.

I want to ask Madam C. J. Walker if she's cool with the pervasive Black hair care practice of wearing some other person's hair entirely.

I want to practice my Spanish with artist and fierce activist Elizabeth Catlett, who hauled off and went to live, not in Europe like many of her midcentury contemporaries, but in Mexico, where she promptly ditched her husband, met and married a Mexican artist, had three of what must have been the era's most interesting children, and got herself banned from Amerikkka.

I want to talk to some literary-minded escaped slaves who couldn't get their memoirs published, partly to see if they'll talk trash about Frederick, Harriet, and Henry "Box" Brown. I have questions for Assata, for my paternal grandmother, Carolyn Solomon, who died before I was born. My mother says she came to visit me one night, a spirit looking into my crib. Did she?

I have a surprising number of questions for Drake. Does he ever call any of the Degrassi kids, Spinner or Ashley, "late night" after he's done calling Outback Steakhouse hostesses and Hot Topic employees?*

I want to talk to my uncle Richard, who complained about everything while he was here on earth. I want to ask him what it's like over there where he's been since the summer of 2014. I want to ask him if there's a heaven for a G.

Asali Solomon is the author of the novel *Disgruntled*. She received a Rona Jaffe Foundation Writers' Award and was selected as a National Book Foundation "5 Under 35" for the stories in her first book, *Get Down*. She is an associate professor of English at Haverford College, where she teaches creative writing and literature of the African Diaspora.

---

* "I mean, how many songs can one person write about 'Amber' from 'Silver Spring' who 'worked at Cheesecake Factory' and 'hooked you up with extra jalapeño poppers' and how you always wished you could 'escape the world together,' but you're 'too infatuated with Houston strippers.'" Damon Young, "The Difference between 'Hungry' and 'Thirsty' Explained," *Very Smart Brothas*, February 6, 2018, https://verysmartbrothas.theroot.com/the-difference-between-hungry-and-thirsty-explained-1822774582 (accessed April 15, 2018).

> **I fight White supremacy by loving on my Black
> family, embracing my ancestry and heritage,
> and recognizing the beauty in us all.**
>
> —Akili Brown, actor and producer

~~~~~~~~~~

On the Trauma of Being Black in White Spaces

Quinn Gee

"We think you need to see a therapist, just to process," "J" said, looking at me over her glasses.

It was 2015, and I was sitting in the office of my clinical supervisor and her practice partner. I had just told them what it felt like to be the only person of color in a room of more than 100 White people for eight hours. I was completing my practicum for my master's degree in counseling, and we were in Memphis, Tennessee, for a reconstruction, which is an experiential therapy created by Virginia Satir that involves the telling and retelling of a life story primarily in a group setting that impacts all the people present.

A wave of anxiety had hit me the moment I walked into the great hall (admittedly late, 'cause, Black). I immediately scanned the room, searching for someone who had some tint to them, and I was quickly disappointed. I sat in the group circle, doing the required check-in with everyone else in the room and trying to ground myself. But I had to get out. I pretended to go to the bathroom, but instead escaped to my Chrysler Pacifica and cried for ten minutes. Over the course of the day, I was forced outside four times, never feeling like I could center myself emotionally or even identify exactly what the issue was. Despite being in a room full of my peers, I felt isolated, like no one there understood the physiological and emotional effect that being the only Black woman in that space was having on me.

So it didn't help when this White man and White woman told me that I should seek counseling to figure out why I was so emotional. I felt like they pathologized my concerns rather than addressing them.

"Go see 'M' and work out what's going on with you," my supervisor said. I walked out of that office and right back to the refuge of my truck. I kept thinking, *There must be something wrong with me if they want me to talk to another therapist about this.* I trusted them with my burgeoning career and looked up to them profoundly. They both had minority identities (one was Jewish and one was gay), so I assumed they understood how it felt to be othered. But that interaction made it clear that I was on my own, a Black queer woman in a White space that was unfriendly to my existence.

At the time of this incident, I didn't know that repeated exposure to microaggressions could cause post-traumatic stress disorder–like symptoms. Not only did I not have language to explain what was happening to me, but I couldn't even *identify* exactly what was happening to me. I did know that it was wrong, and that if I—a woman who prided herself on being comfortable and unapologetically Black in predominantly White spaces—could be made to feel that uncomfortable, then surely there were others who felt this way. I also knew that I couldn't go on in that environment. I resigned a month later and the next day founded my first clinic, Healing Hearts Counseling Center in Memphis.

Then I began seeking out information about how race impacts mental health. I discovered the works of Robert Carter, PhD, who coined the term "race-based traumatic stress injury" (RBTSI), which he defines as "an emotional/psychological response to racial experiences that results in functional impairment (makes activities of daily living difficult)."[*] Simply put, RBTSI is what happens to people of color after repeated exposure to microaggressions and racism. Working, living, and going to school in areas that are predominantly White can have some of the same long-term psychological effects as actual physical trauma. Think about what a testament that is to White

---

[*] Read more on the website for Robert T. Carter and Associates, https://www.rtca411.com/.

supremacy: merely *existing* in spaces with White folks can be permanently damaging to your mental health.

You can see the effects of intergenerational RBTSI everywhere, especially now that there are criteria to measure it. The high rate of PTSD diagnosis in Black people is the most prominent indicator. And some of the somatic symptoms that come with it are more prevalent in Black folks, including hypertension, heart disease, and other chronic illnesses. Yes, fatback may have strained your heart, but being subjected to White folks' prejudice daily is just as heartbreaking.

And RBTSI doesn't only kick in following overt racism. It can occur anytime your Blackness is not primary in the environment, which we know is linked to microaggressions that over time can have a long-standing impact on your self-esteem and motivation and often result in depression and anger. Just think about how you feel in these situations:

- ▶ Your coworkers drop by your desk to ask about your hair every time you change it.
- ▶ Someone asks any question that starts with, "Why do Black people . . ."
- ▶ A White woman clings a little tighter to her purse when you walk past.
- ▶ This bro at the bar keeps inappropriately using outdated AAVE.
- ▶ Randoms fetishize you sexually ("I only date Black") and culturally (also known as "Dolezaling").
- ▶ People who don't know you grant themselves unwanted access to your person (touching your hair, standing very close to you, performing exaggerated handshakes based on stereotypes).

Like PTSD, some of the symptoms of RBTSI include anxiety, avoidance, and arousal, and the symptoms can present suddenly, without warning.

Unlike PTSD, however, RBTSI does not involve direct physical threats to your person but is based on emotional pain.*

RBTSI is not recognized officially by the *Diagnostic and Statistical Manual of Mental Disorders* (*DSM-V*), the diagnostic tool used by all the major mental health organizations, but it has been widely used and referenced since its introduction in 1952. And let's face it, as with everything, there is racial bias within the mental health community. A White former colleague once fixed his mouth to tell me that "race trauma is just a smokescreen for psychosis." So of course it is highly unlikely that a diagnosis that *only* affects people of color and that is *caused by* White people will make it into any drafts of the *DSM-VI*.

But for mental health clinicians in the know, it is important to provide culturally competent support for our clients. White people aren't going away; we have to find a way to exist with them. So how do we combat the issues that arise from RBTSI? More specifically, how do we deal with White people when they are a source of trauma?

We lean into each other as sources of community and support. When we feel safe and equipped, we let White people know our boundaries. We hold proclaimed allies accountable around their actions. We refuse to discount each other's experiences. We reject the cry of "not all White people" as a tactic to diminish our experiences. We don't let them touch our damn hair. And finally, we go to Black therapists.

Quinn Gee is a licensed psychotherapist and owner of Magnolia Mental Health in Washington, DC. She specializes in LGBTQIA and women's issues and trauma. She lives with her partner, son, and two stepdogs.

~~~~~~~~~~

* Robert T. Carter, "Race and Trauma: Race-Based Traumatic Stress and Psychological Injury," http://www.ctacny.org/sites/default/files/trainings-pdf/race_%26_trauma_5.28.15.final_.pdf (accessed March 27, 2018).

"BLK PWR TWTR" by John Jennings (2015)

How do you describe your aesthetic?

My aesthetic could be called critical race design. I make visual artifacts that interrogate constructions of race.

What were you thinking when you created this work?

I created this piece after the Mother Emanuel shooting in South Carolina, where nine African American church members were senselessly killed by a White supremacist. I do some social media on Twitter, but it's not my usual space for commentary. However, I know that Black Twitter has become a powerful space of resistance, discussion, critique, and healing in the age of Black Lives Matter. I created this piece as a symbol of solidarity for everyone who uses Twitter as a space to fight against the murder and oppression of Black Americans. I was truly honored that it was selected for the permanent digital collection of the National Museum of African American History and Culture in the section dealing with virtual resistance and BLM.

How does this work represent resistance to White supremacy?

The piece samples and remixes the Twitter logo with a Black Power fist.

By conflating this cultural symbol of unity with a corporate logo used for communication, this image repurposes both. It represents resistance by its very construction and societal significance. It is an index of how Black Twitter has created a space of political power in spite of White supremacy and corporate control.

John Jennings is a professor of media and cultural studies at the University of California at Riverside. He is an award-winning, *New York Times* best-selling author, illustrator, and scholar who studies graphic novels, Black speculative fiction, and race.

~~~~~~~~~~~~

Maladaptations and Deportations

Marlon Peterson

During my ten-year journey on the slave ship of incarceration, I *never* had a dream that carried me outside prison. When I dreamed about family, friends, or rendezvous with old girlfriends (which provided me with much-needed wet dreams), they were always in prison with me. I brought free-ish people into my experience of prison; even in the depths of my subconscious, I could not fathom being unbound.

About a year into my bid, I consciously decided that I needed to put all of my focus into learning how to exist as a slave. It became my occupation. I broke myself in. I manufactured and perfected the normalization of my own despair. It was necessary to survive.

It seemed all the men around me had submitted to a lucid normalization of our lives in prison. We euphemistically thought of cuffs and shackles as bracelets. We referred to the visiting floor as the dance floor. We called letters kites, perhaps to signify that our communication with the outside world and with our comrades in other housing units and other jails could fly above the ground of despair to which we were bound. We asked our families to send us Timberland boots and gave each other fly haircuts. We created communities of Bloods and Crips and Ñetas and Lions and Latin Kings. We did dumb shit.

We've been doing this type of dumb shit for centuries. Our despair pre-dated our dumb shit, our euphemisms, our dancing. The cruelty of White supremacy is the despair. The depth of that cruelty is why to this very day I often talk about my prison experience in the present tense, despite the fact that it's been almost nine years since I left that ship.

Prison was hard. It was painful. It was horrific. There were days I wished I could die unexpectedly. It's where officers threw my family pictures in toilet bowls, stepped on the bed sheet I slept on, farted into my cell, searched the inside of my mouth after I gave my mother a kiss on her cheek at the end of a one-hour visit, kept me in a cell for twenty-three hours a day for forty-five days, and starved me when I didn't get dressed quickly enough. Prison is also where I mastered the art of hiding pain, horror, and fear.

Prison was where I lived Angela Davis's words: "Jails and prisons are designed to turn its residents into animals in a zoo—obedient to our keepers, but dangerous to each other." It was where I identified the genesis of my keepers' behavior—their job is the progeny of White supremacist ideology.

The lineage of White supremacy in the world's prisons is clear. There is a process to enslaving Africans: Present enslavement as a better way to cap-italize on human greed; capitalize on internecine conflicts; rationalize the inhumanity of prolonged imprisonment as a solution to human delinquency; capture; rename; send the captured far away; limit access to loved ones; in-vest in the idea of penitence; convince the captured that there is nothing to consider but individual accountability; starve; abuse; instill fear; encourage more internecine strife; never harm the captor; dress its perpetrators as be-nevolent saviors; manufacture a form of freedom that is reliant upon acting as if the harm never occurred (successful reentry is all that matters); create a new nigger.

Halfway through my bid, a prison counselor said to me, "You are not Mr. Peterson. You are Inmate Peterson." He tried to create a whole new nig-ger out of me.

And he did.

But I fought. I won small victories. I helped other men write their parole interview packets and win their freedom. I published stories of my colleagues inside who were innocent. I masturbated to pictures of old girlfriends and images of beautiful women I saw on television instead of engaging in the porn magazine trade. I never acted on my desire to do harmful shit to others. I responded to officers with respect no matter how much they disrespected me. I earned a college degree. I read Malcolm, bell, Maya, and Sister Souljah. I came home one month early.

I maladapted to docility.

But White supremacy still stung me. It deported me to a world that says that prison saved me. To a world where a smooth reentry is more important than a rejuvenation of spirit and dignity. To a world where the liberal vision for reducing incarceration is motivated by fiduciary concerns rather than moral ones. To a world where capitalism rewards Whites living in majority-Black spaces. To a world where people of color are the ones languishing on the street corners and overcrowding the prisons. To a world where allegiant subscribers to White supremacy get to exploit mental illness as an excuse for the dangerous behavior their ideology encourages. To a world where our radical Black imagination is funded by White institutions that we are convinced we can infiltrate for good.

Our modern-day heroes—Michelle, Oprah, Ava, Beyoncé—have mastered thriving alongside White supremacy. They create and invest in art that inspires us despite its clutches. I too have figured out what I can accomplish despite the presence of White supremacy. I earned a second degree from a top private university. Secured a decent credit score. Traveled the world. Shared my story with thousands of young people. Gave a TED Talk with more than one million views, asking people to experience me as a full human being. (White supremacy got me begging for humanity—how preposterous is that?) Lectured at several universities. Successfully completed state parole. Started my own podcast. Told my story on television and in *Ebony* magazine.

I beat the odds.

But the problem with my narrative is that there are odds to beat. This system has convinced us that overcoming strife is a necessary part of life. It has manipulated us into not recognizing that White supremacy *is* the odds.

Neither the splendor of our heroes nor our personal tales of triumph go far enough. A Newish America is still America—a place that has evolved from slavery to the creation of Black urban ghettos, to drug infestation, to mass incarceration, to deportation. So, while we have won measurable victories against America—citizenship, voting rights, and so on—we still have a long way to go on the road toward dismantling the system that forces us to fight.

Marlon Peterson is a criminal justice advocate, writer, organizational trainer, and educator who spent ten years in New York State prisons. He hosts the *Decarcerated* podcast and is the chief reimaginator of the Precedential Group, a social justice consulting firm.

~~~~~~~~~~

Jim Limber Sees People Get the Heaven They Want

Shane McCrae

Heaven is full of white   folks but they got
These glasses on that they don't know they're glass-
es they don't know they're wearing   but it's not
Glasses 'cause it's a wide   black blindfold 'cause
It wraps around their heads it's thick and covers
Their ears   and it ain't glasses 'cause they can't
See through it 'cept I know they see   forever
Felt like forever   I watched for my chance

I got it when a white boy fell asleep
In the cafeteria   I tiptoed o-
ver and I took his glasses I just slipped
Them on   my head even though

They were too small   I looked   and saw the white boy
Looked at my hands   but I had disappeared I saw   the white boy

Shane McCrae's most recent books are *The Gilded Auction Block* and *In the Language of My Captor*. He is the winner of the 2018 Anisfield-Wolf Book Award for Poetry, the 2017 Lannan Literary Award, a Whiting Writer's Award, an NEA fellowship, and a Pushcart Prize, and he was a finalist for the National Book Award and the *Los Angeles Times* Book Prize. He teaches at Columbia University and lives in New York City.

~~~~~~~~~

QUESTION, ANSWERED

The people in this chapter were driven to activism following personal experiences with racism and the people who perpetuate it. Here we answer the question: what drives *you*?

Kenrya

The politically correct answer would be "love." And sure, okay, that's true. I am passionately in love with my people, my kid, probably some dude I haven't met yet, and the idea that we can make that change (read: make racists cry) like Michael Jackson eliciting White girl tears at Super Bowl XXVII. But the real, I'm lightheaded because I keep holding my breath, why can I hear my heart pounding in my ears right now, ohmygod I need to go lie down on the soft gray rug in my living room and stare up at the twinkling lights on my Christmas tree until I get my shit together answer is, "Anxiety mostly."

Which is patently awful, but not unique. There is not a human breathing who has not experienced anxiety. It fuels the fight-or-flight response that keeps us alive when raccoons brandish their tiny, too-human, trash-digging hands at us. It makes us stumble over our words when a @TheRealTank lookalike gets close enough to breathe him in. Alerts us when we have to go off on a "well-meaning" White woman who just showered us with bullshit. And who among us has not been propelled across a finish line by the fear that we would pass out along the way? For every writer who says they can't function without a deadline, I'll show you an anxiety-ridden soul who lives in constant fear of waiting a little too long to step away from the procrastination and get shit done right now.

Recently, my daughter performed in her first violin recital. She played Shinichi Suzuki's "Mississippi Hot Dog" variation of "Twinkle, Twinkle, Little Star," and her little brown face shone with delight and the effort of concentration. But before she took the stage in the spare wood-paneled church sanctuary where her teacher had gathered us for the occasion, her face was scrunched with worry.

"Maaaama," she said, left arm slung around my neck. "I don't want to play. I have butterflies in my tummy, and I don't want people to look at me."

"Baeba," I said, planting a kiss on her soft cheek, then wiping it clean with my thumb. "I know you feel nervous. I feel nervous when I have to be in front of people too. Every time. But," I continued, smiling, "do you know what feeling anxious makes us do?"

She tilted her head—she'd heard this before.

"It makes us prepare," I said. "And you prepared! You practice your violin every day, right?"

"Yes, Mama."

"And you know how to play this song, right?

"Yup!"

"Then your tickly butterflies prepared you to do well tonight. And I'm so excited to see you on that stage. You are amazing, and you're gonna do a great job."

She grinned, spun away, then sat down on the pew between her home-girl and her cousin, ready to pick up her one-eighth-size violin, propelled by a weird feeling in her tummy and a tiny pep talk. What a blessing to have anxieties that a mama can soothe with an iridescent purple kiss and a reminder of who she is.

That's not my reality.

I move through the world as a "we." We need to tear down this system of mass incarceration that means us nothing but harm. We need political representation that actually cares about Black women every day, not just when our voting power can help them keep a sex offender out of office. We, the Black delegation, no longer fuck with that clueless actress who thinks people give a damn about her thoughts on politics.

While my personal issues keep me in therapy, it's my larger-scale "we" concerns that push me forward. They compel me to grab my phone at 6:30 a.m. to scroll through the news, looking for the events, voices, and campaigns I need to amplify for people of color that day. They push me to help organize anti-bias training for the staff and parents at my daughter's school. They require me to seek out Black folks to take my coin for everything from head wraps to dentistry.

I am propelled by an aching need to protect and elevate my people. To be sure, it's a "we" anxiety. But when I look at my little's face, I am reminded that none of us is free unless we are all free. Ultimately, I'm working so that my kid's worries can continue to be one-eighth-size.

~~~~~~~~~~

Akiba

In general, what drives me is human being 101: food, clothing, shelter, and health care. But once I push beyond the prerequisites, my biggest driver is boredom. I greatly fear being bored, and boring the people I find interesting. That fear drives my work, many of my relationships, and the way I move in the world.

The first time I bored someone it nearly killed me—at least emotionally.

I was a cute little Leo kid used to getting positive attention from adults and peers. My slightly older Aquarian sister was the center of everything for me; she was the smartest, the most inventive, the most fun.

My mother called us "professional players" because of the worlds we created. Our main site was Babyland, where our always-Black, factory overrun dolls had copresidents. This nation also featured a special dialect and a death that did not kill the physical body but destroyed your "Babyland Thought." When our play cousins and friends tried to do our Babyland slang, my sister and I would exchange smug glances and abort the game.

But at about seven, my sister decided that books were far superior to the cracking plastic dolls we'd obtained from a Santa who came to our North Philly preschool with a trash bag full of dreams. Also boring, according to Asali: spacemen, Memory, I Declare War, Uno, Simon, checkers, Hungry Hungry Hippos, Operation, Life, and Barbies. The passable games were chess, Monopoly, and backgammon, all of which required too much forethought and cunning for me to ever win.

I say that Asali's boredom nearly killed me because she was the only real friend I had. Growing up Black nationalist with an African name and natural hair, celebrating Kwanzaa, not playing outside with the conceited twins up the street, speaking "proper," having restricted television viewing, and never getting beatings made us bizarros in our working-class West Philadelphia neighborhood. I don't remember this bothering me until my sister and I entered an overwhelmingly White and rich all-girls school in the suburbs. We were there for the academics, to obtain the tools we would need to rebuild a postrevolutionary world, not to make friends. One consequence was that when Asali announced that she was bored with a game I'd pitifully wheedled her into playing, what I heard was, *You are all alone because you are boring.*

At open mics and karaoke birthday parties, I always sing Stevie Wonder's "Knocks Me off My Feet." The hook of that song goes, "I don't want to bore you with it, oh but I love you, I love you, I love you." I always get extra on the hook.

When you lose your first soulmate—mine being my sister—avoiding rejection begins to drive what you do and fantasize about. In the dream arena I was constantly planning the Black king I would marry, the watoto we would make, and the Black liberation we would help secure through our art and work.

I do get this honestly. At press time, my parents have been married for forty-six years and have had the same home and phone number for more than forty years. My sister is in her own marriage with my two fascinating nephews. My best friend is married to a man whom she met because he interned for my mother. She's the mom of a genuinely enjoyable toddler. Family is everything for me.

There's a line in one of my favorite films, *Paid in Full*, in which the girlfriend of a successful Harlem drug dealer, Ace, tells him that she just wants a nice, boring life with him and their baby. That line sticks with me, always.

Alas, I am unpartnered. I am without a child. I don't live in Philly, where all of the aforementioned people have homes. I'm in Brooklyn, New York, where being a grown woman means not heating up your Prego via just-strained hot pasta. Before I realized that this Black love writ large was not going to happen, I thought a husband and a kid would prompt me to run every morning, make vacation plans, do my affirmations, buy a home, be unselfish, get dental checkups every six months, go up to the school to talk to the principal, and always take my kid's call like my mom did.

In the absence of most of those healthy and domestic tasks, I have the work I do. I am driven to make, facilitate, and house things that have a good chance of enhancing the lives of people who look like me. Up until very recently, I thought of this as false martyrdom or a rationalization for why I failed at the life I imagined. Now I see it as the mission I did not consciously create but that is the result of what I continually say to the world.

My work quells my fears. And if I *do* bore you, I've secured a tomorrow where I can try again.

THREE
LAUGH TO KEEP FROM CRYING

Humor is among our toughest suits of armor against White supremacy. One-liners, irony, tall tales, impressions, satire, signifying, playing the dozens, and trolling are all tools that we've used to reinforce our culture, pass down mother wit, and vent our rage without getting lynched, fired, or otherwise destroyed.

Take one Brother Jourdon Anderson. In 1864, near the end of the Civil War, Jourdon, his wife Mandy, and his family escaped during a Union raid on the Big Spring, Tennessee, plantation of Colonel Patrick Henry Anderson. After they were good and free in Ohio, Massa Anderson sent them a bizarre letter begging them to return to the plantation to work, this time for pay.

We're pretty sure that Brother Jourdon did indeed want to go back to Big Spring—to slash ol' massa's face into ribbons. But instead of ending up in a noose, he got his revenge via sarcasm about reparations. He told massa to go fuck himself in an August 7, 1865, letter:

> *To My Old Master, Colonel P. H. Anderson,*
> *Big Spring, Tennessee*
>
> *Sir: I got your letter, and was glad to find that you had not forgotten Jourdon, and that you wanted me to come back and live with you again, promising to do better for me than anybody else can. I have often felt uneasy about you. . . . Although you shot at me twice before I left you, I did not want to hear of your being hurt, and am glad you are still living. . . .*

*I want to know particularly what the good chance is you
propose to give me. . . .*

*Mandy says she would be afraid to go back without some
proof that you were disposed to treat us justly and kindly; and
we have concluded to test your sincerity by asking you to send
us our wages for the time we served you. This will make us forget and forgive old scores, and rely on your justice and friendship in the future. I served you faithfully for thirty-two years,
and Mandy twenty years. At twenty-five dollars a month for
me, and two dollars a week for Mandy, our earnings would
amount to eleven thousand six hundred and eighty dollars.
Add to this the interest for the time our wages have been kept
back, and deduct what you paid for our clothing, and three
doctor's visits to me, and pulling a tooth for Mandy, and the
balance will show what we are in justice entitled to. Please
send the money by Adams' Express, in care of V. Winters, Esq.,
Dayton, Ohio. If you fail to pay us for faithful labors in the
past, we can have little faith in your promises in the future.*

That was 1865. Today Black writers, artists, barbers, activists, video
bloggers, Spades champions, and aunties continue to use their legal-for-now
voices to expose the lie of White supremacy, hype up our relatives who can't
really sing, and kick people out of the race for tomfoolery.

In "Laugh to Keep from Crying," satirists, stand-up comedians, and car-
toonists explore how we use humor to maintain our culture, sanity, creativity,
and safety, because laughing is one of our most important tools of war.

~~~~~~~

Laughing While Black

Damon Young

On February 1, 2018, the *New York Daily News* reported that Patricia
Cummings, a White teacher at Middle School 118 in the Bronx, instructed

three Black students in her class to lie on the floor, and then she *stepped on their backs* to teach a lesson about slavery.

If you attempt to reverse-engineer, you could find a series of not-all-that-terribly-racist rationales for Cummings's decision. This story was reported by the *Daily News* on the first day of Black History Month, which often manifests as a shallow and hysterical salmagundi of contextless tidbits about traffic lights, peanut butter, and Wilt Chamberlain. Cummings could have been trying to be creative. Kind of like when you start adding kale and broccoli to your morning fruit smoothie, except instead of "kale and broccoli" Cummings added "racism." Or maybe she planned to rent *Glory* from the school's library, it wasn't available, and she remembered that scene where Denzel was whipped because he left camp to find comfortable shoes and she wanted to show her students how even the most comfortable shoes can feel uncomfortable if Darth Becky is cartwheeling on your back.

The most likely explanation for Patricia Cummings's behavior, though, is that like millions of White people before her, she's lost her goddamn mind. The pervasiveness of White supremacy has made White people fucking crazy. Patricia Cummings is a natural and predictable consequence of what happens when the possession of Whiteness is so blinding and deafening that it transmutes White people into baby groundhogs unable to see or feel or think or smell or taste anything outside of their vacuums of Caucasity.

Sometimes this insanity materializes as boundless and preposterous entitlement, as was the case with Abigail Fisher, aka "Becky with the Bad Grades." If you recall, Fisher is the aggressively pedestrian White woman who applied to the University of Texas in 2008, was denied admission, and promptly stated that she was discriminated against because she was White. Her gripe that the University of Texas had the audacity to treat her Wonder Bread ass like Wonder Bread instead of a tasty pancake reached the Supreme Court, where she lost in 2016 as the court finally ruled against her. (According to court transcripts, an exasperated Justice Sonia Sotomayor said, "She think she a tasty pancake," when providing the rationale for the decision.[*])

---

[*] I have no proof of this happening.

And sometimes this insanity forces White folks to lie and spin and gas-
light so zealously that they no longer know where the truth ends and their
bullshit begins. There are myriad examples of this. America sits on a Jenga
tower of lies about its inherent goodness, godliness, and manifest destiny,
its "free market" economy, and its "exceptional" history. At the time of this
writing, my favorite recurring example of this happens when President Donald Trump does or says some demented fuckshit surpassing the demented
fuckshit he did or said the day before, and Sarah Huckabee Spicer Scara-
mucci Sanders squiggles out from the Incubus's lair to triple-speak their president's actions into something they think is honorable. This motherfucker
could shit on the White House lawn and wipe his ass with a Polaroid of the
Boys Choir of Harlem and within an hour one of his minions would hold a
press conference to state: "The president is just very serious about going green
and conserving energy. Which is exactly what you liberals and the media have
been asking him to do, right?"

Existing as a Black American while pressed against this force is terrifying.
Not consciously. At least not all of the time. But sometimes, when stepping
back and fully processing the vastness and the depth and the transcendence of
it, it's not unlike what happens when you accidentally glance at the sun. And
this condition is rage-inducing. It makes you want to fight sometimes and
duck and hide some other times. It makes you want to be sure you're holding
and hugging and loving the Black people around because you know they
need to be held, hugged, and loved because you do too, and they're Black like
you. It can, if you allow it, make you so consumed with a white-hot animus
toward them for what they did to you, and toward people who look like you
for what they did to you, and toward yourself for what they did to you—that
it swallows you. You become ensconced in it.

Resistance, of course, is vital. And sometimes that resistance looks like
what happens when you plug "resistance" into Thesaurus.com and scan
the most antagonistic results. It's defiance. It's friction. It's blocking. It's a
struggle. It's combat. But then sometimes you need to go to Facebook or
GroupMe and send an invite for a game night at your house this weekend.

And you invite all of your best and Blackest friends. And you lure them in with promises of properly seasoned and appropriately cooked chicken wings and an array of the brownest of liquors. Maybe you even name the games you'll play. Taboo. Cards Against Humanity. Mafia. Spades. And you ask them to bring nothing except maybe some chips, some juice, and even a thoroughly vetted friend. And they come, and you have a fucking blast. But even as you're playing an especially intense round of Spoons, the real reason for this gathering lurks beneath the surface and occasionally bubbles up:

"Nigga, did I tell you about what Susan in accounting did today?"

"I swear to God that if Conner brings another Caucasian casserole to the company potluck I'm gonna choke his Patagonia ass."

"White people age like bodega bananas."

"Don't you know this chick French-kissed her Shih Tzu and then tried to give me a hug? I told her my insurance doesn't cover White people dog cooties."

Sometimes these jokes turn into a morbid and numbing reminder of exactly how unwelcoming and dangerous it can be to exist while Black in America:

"Ayyiyo, who's on y'all's 'I Just Got Pulled over by the Cops for No Reason and I Need to Hurry and Put Something Nonthreatening on My Stereo' playlists? Mine has Taylor Swift, Creed, and the *Golden Girls* theme song."

One of the reasons that existing while Black in America can be exhausting is that it entails an endless search for safe spaces and opportunities to exhale. But once that space and that oxygen is found, perhaps at a game night or during a flag football outing or maybe just on a sparsely populated Twitter timeline, sometimes the best and only thing to do is make fun of these mindless motherfuckers with no worries.

There will always be time to be sober and serious. But sometimes finding a way to ridicule a Patricia Cummings, an Abigail Fisher, or a Darth Chad provides a necessary catharsis. A moment of respite when you recognize how you've been forced to be fully human in a way they'll never be, when you become tickled with the irony of them considering themselves to be the superior ones. And then sometimes the laughter itself becomes a weaponized tool, a vital piece of resistance-encouraging and Whiteness-withstanding hardware that allows you to love Blackness even harder and louder and longer than you did before. Maybe they've lost their goddamn minds. But our humor keeps that from being contagious.

Damon Young is a writer, critic, humorist, and satirist. He's the cofounder and editor in chief of *VerySmartBrothas*, a columnist for GQ.com, and the author of *What Doesn't Kill You Makes You Blacker*.

〜〜〜〜〜〜〜〜

Dismantling White Comfort Is Our Wakanda

Russ Green

If you come see me perform, we gon' talk about some shit.

As a stand-up comedian, when I walk onstage, my intention is to question everything. Why are we walking around acting like we have a government? Do Black lives *really* matter? How am I supposed to raise children when it's illegal to be Black in public? These questions need answers. I'm on a mission to find the truth, and I invite the audience to join me on the journey. If it goes well, it's liberating for everyone, and if not—at least no one got shot.

It doesn't always go well. I've been accused of being anti-White, which is absurd. I don't hate White people; I hate the idea of Whiteness, a social construct that entitles people to live rich fulfilling lives as long as their skin is absent of melanin.

The reality is that if jokes that call out the societal ills associated with White supremacy make you uncomfortable, you are probably complicit in upholding the institution. I would imagine the opportunity to elevate your consciousness and awareness would be cathartic, like a warm rain to wash away your obliviousness to your privilege. But my White hecklers say otherwise.

I hear people say all the time that comedians are fearless. I'll take it, I guess, though I'm not blocking highway traffic in protest, investigating corrupt police officers, or blowing the whistle on corporate greed or sellout politicians. People don't send me death threats or deliver explosive packages to my front door.

The bravest part of my evening is when I leave the comedy club, get into my car, and drive home in the middle of the night. The reality is, there is always a chance that I will never make it. Once, after a show, I made a pit stop at Taco Bell—the one true king of late night grub—and was pulled over by a cop who claimed I had a taillight out.

The moment the squad car started trailing me, I thought, *Fuck.* Then the dormant respectability Negro voice in my head started cataloging all the things I did wrong that night. First mistake: Leave home. Second: Drive car. Third: Be Black.

Driving while Black is scary. The fear of being pulled over is so extreme that when sirens go off during songs on my playlist, my heart races. I shouldn't be as afraid of police officers as I am of sharks, but to my ears, blaring sirens sound like the *Jaws* theme song. So when I looked in my rearview mirror to confirm that I was indeed being pursued by a known superpredator, I was equal parts afraid and furious—I was five minutes from my house.

The Bagger Vance in my head assured me that if I simply relaxed and remained rational as the officer approached my vehicle, the Dirty Harry in his head wouldn't be saying, "Go ahead, make my day." The officer opened with, "Is this your vehicle?"—standard-issue microaggression. I confirmed it was by handing him my license and registration. A beat passed, then the officer stopped blinding me with his Maglite and instructed: "Wait here. If everything checks out, you'll be on your way soon."

I'm fairly certain officers write 1,500-word essays while reviewing your driving record. In the time it takes them to figure out the perfect ending (will this be a comedy or dramatic thriller?), I'm usually playing through *Choose Your Own Adventure* scenarios, hoping I stumble on the right sequence of page turns that lands me safe in my bed. Turns out my third taillight, the one that's near the roof, was out and I found myself "fortunate" enough to go home with a warning.

My XXL Grilled Stuft Burrito with Fire Sauce was bittersweet that night, and the Wild Cherry Pepsi couldn't wash down the realization that things could have ended calamitously. Unlike Sandra Bland and Philando Castile, the patron saints of traumatic social media clips, I made it to my house, exhaled deeply, and kept breathing. I sat in my car, finished my junk food, calmed my nerves, planned my trip to AutoZone, and thanked God that I was pulled over and not my wife. She can't die—*somebody* has to take care of all these kids.

What compels me—a husband and father of four—to leave the safety of my house to tell jokes for strangers? I have no idea. What punchline is worth dying for? The risk of making people uncomfortable by telling my truths should be worth more than the reward of validation from people I will never see again.

But is what I do any more ridiculous than walking around pretending that we don't see the daily injustices Black people experience? Are White folks' ears too fragile to hear a narrative that differs from theirs? Are we only allowed to be free in our own homes, as long as those homes aren't in predominantly White neighborhoods? Not on my watch, fam.

We underestimate the value of Black joy; it should appraise much higher. It is imperative that we experience more than pain. Maybe that's why I'm drawn to perform. I get to be in service of Black joy in a communal setting, initiating boundless conversations where my premises construct new realities. It's straight up carefree, liberated hysterics—our own little Wakanda. Fuck the colonizer's feelings; I risked my life to tell these jokes.

Russ Green is a writer, comedian, husband, and father of four from Washington, DC. The Howard University graduate finds humor in the absurdities of life: White supremacy, race, and identity politics. Russ has performed at The Kennedy Center and the Knitting Factory.

I fight White supremacy by actively reminding myself that it's a man-made perversion. It's a real thing, but it's not the truth.

—Kimberly Shells Wilson, human resources adviser

~~~~~~

Comedic Actress and Producer Amanda Seales on How She Challenges the Concept of Whiteness

I fight White supremacy by existing in the unabashed way that I do, as a creative and as a speaker, and I encourage others to do the same. I also work to make White Americans denounce their Whiteness.

I always say there's only two kinds of White people: those who are White, and those who happen to be White. And so I challenge White people with that question on a regular basis: "Do you define yourself by your Whiteness?" And when they fire back and say, "Well, do you define yourself by your Blackness?" I say, "They're not the same thing. Whiteness was created for the purpose of oppression. Blackness was created *in spite of* oppression. We're not coming from the same place, so don't try to conflate equality where it does not exist." In my talks at universities, I'm inserting this real questioning of White people to no longer just question racism as a concept, but to question their own positioning within that and how that affects what they're doing. We have to start having conversations that are different than the ones we've been having. I talk about racism of course, because it's real. But I accompany it with what I feel could be possible.

~~~~~~

A Eulogy for the White Gaze: A Tale from the Future

Jamilah-Asali Lemieux

The year is 2080, and Black people are finally free. Yes, really. It's true! I know, *I know*.

You want me to tell you everything so you can go and get things started, but I can only give you these seeds to plant, the seeds that will grow the revolu—just listen.

Certainly, you recognize the absurdity of challenging the authenticity of someone's Negritude based on their particular dialect—or the absence of one. You know that "real" Black people can prefer rock (which is African at the root) or rap (which was decidedly African until around the late-aughts, when our folks gave the mic to every tattooed druggie who wanted a piece). You certainly realize that Black cannot be vanquished by an inability to dance or a dislike of soul food.

However, in your day, there were some cultural markers so linked to our experience in the Western world that, well, we couldn't rightly say you were really Black without having encountered them.

Prior to the, umm, *liberation*, it would have been virtually impossible to be a Black person raised in the United States who had never heard or uttered some variation of a common African American proverb:

Don't embarrass me in front of these White folks.

I talked about this with a group of kids just the other day, and they couldn't fathom the idea of being concerned with how they behaved in the presence of White people, let alone having that concern presented as a mandate from someone who loves them. They really don't know how good they have it.

Yes, I'm serious. We don't say that shit anymore, ever. Okay, no more questions or I'm done talking.

Back when I was young, the White gaze was often one of the most difficult places that a Black person could find themselves in, and God forbid you ever did something to make a Black elder who had lived through Jim Crow feel even more uncomfortable while there. As I explained to those kids, the DEMIFOTWF rule was so much more complicated than the language may have indicated. It's super-easy to assume that it was little more than older Black folks assigning undue value to the thoughts and feelings of White people.

Among some of the likely circumstances that might summon such a command:

- Acting like "you ain't never been nowhere before" at a nice restaurant, department store, gas station, city bus, or anywhere *they* may be watching—especially when you were in the minority in said location;
- Cutting up at school and forcing your mama to leave her job and be scolded by some White folks essentially telling her that she failed as a parent;
- Doing anything that was a painful reminder of racism, like ordering fried chicken and watermelon in their presence, or using terms like "baby mama," "ghetto," and the "n-word" in mixed company.

Yes, I said "the n-word." I can't say the real version because that word is totally banned now. No one says it and if you say it again, I swear I'm done talking.

Thus, "Don't embarrass me in front of these White folks" wasn't a plea; it was a universal rule that Black folks had better not run afoul of. The "me" most often was a woman (your mother, grandmother, auntie, play-auntie, godmother) or any other trusted authority figure. But it could be any other Negro on the planet. Hell, it could be *yourself*, your internal monologue cautioning you against setting everyone back by doing some totally human shit.

As you know, Black folks' obsession with decorum had its roots in being told that we were inherently broken. That we were three-fifths of a person. That we were unintelligent, unsophisticated savages in need of constant correction. If the people who had enslaved us had constructed an idea of Blackness vile enough to justify lording over us for centuries, what might they do when we provided actual evidence of some sort of shortcoming?

Our elders felt like they had no choice but to prove White folks wrong early and often. Absent the empowerment to go to war or simply say "no more," the best they had was to embody the goodness they believed we lacked.

They said we were dirty, and so we obsessed over the cleanliness of our homes and bodies, so much so that we'd put toxic shit like baby powder and douches in our most intimate places in order to refute that.

They said we were sexually deviant, so we policed our own desires so rigidly that our only release would come via shouting and hollering in churches built as monuments to White gods.

They said we were too loud, and so we tried to shrink in their presence, tried to speak softly and be less vibrant. Most of us never mastered this one, thankfully.

It wasn't until we truly recognized the hypocrisy of *their* gaze that we finally broke free of its cold, steely hold on our lives.

We were dirty, but compared to whom? Surely not those folks we saw kissing their dogs on the mouth at the park, the people who went on social media to defend taking showers without washcloths, that infamous woman on the internet cooking without the slightest bit of concern for the litter-caked cat paws that walked through her casserole pan just moments prior. (We still joke about these things, but dammit, it stings!)

If we were both sexually irrepressible and immoral, why couldn't they keep their hands off our bodies, in every sense of the phrase, for centuries?

Our women were beneath their standards of femininity, yet White mothers outsourced the rearing of their children to us from the moment we arrived on these shores—and would later begin to emulate our hairstyles, modes of dress, and even the shape of our bodies. Our men were somehow shiftless and lazy, but also terrifyingly powerful and strong? That math doesn't add up.

Around 2014, the term "respectability politics" ventured outside of the academy and entered the regular Black people lexicon. This was a good thing. Ideas that can improve our overall quality of life are pretty useless if they aren't made accessible to the masses. The better our people understood why they'd been taught to contort their humanity to weather the whims of White folks, the easier it would be for them to divorce those unhealthy habits, right?

However, as these things tend to go, it didn't take long for some young people to confuse having any sort of behavioral standard with "tap-dancing for massa" like a self-hating "coon." This caused some of our elders to suffer some serious discomfort as a number of Black kids willfully gave *them* their asses to kiss in an effort to, well, give *White folks* their asses to kiss. The rebellion against respectability politics was a complicated one, but ultimately it pushed our people in the right direction: toward a standard of behavior that centered our own ideals and identities.

Meanwhile, the Trump administration would inspire two very different reactions among our now-former oppressors that would power the beginning of the end to our traditional respectability politics—and set the stage for the revolution that finally saw us get free.

Scores of White kids proudly emulated the boorish behavior of the unapologetically racist, sexist, and charmless forty-fifth president of the United States. This was a pretty understandable reaction: if someone can make it to the highest office in the land by acting like a petulant child *and* claiming superiority over other groups, why not indulge in all the antisocial behavior you could ever dream of? White privilege is a hell of a drug.

Meanwhile, equally large groups of White young people were so turned off by Donald Trump and his ilk that they would form the largest group of progressive White folks that the United States had ever seen. Like, *for real* progressive—nothing like those "White moderates" that Martin Luther King Jr. identified in his famed 1963 "Letter from a Birmingham Jail" as "the Negro's great stumbling block in his stride toward freedom."

As a result, Black millennial and Generation Y parents were less inclined to caution their own children against shaming themselves (and their families) in the presence of the melanin-deficient because they had less to prove to them than ever. How self-conscious can you actually be in the presence of pussy-grabbers who don't even believe in truth, human rights, and washcloths? And the White folks on the other side of the political aisle were so deeply—and rightly!—ashamed of their own kind that they didn't dare parrot the sort of judgment and contempt that their parents had once used against Black folks.

Many of our people had started to resemble what Dr. King said about those White moderates, "more devoted to 'order' than to justice," so I gotta give some props to both the radical Caucasian defectors who sought to shed their privilege like dead skin and the MAGA-hat motherfuckers who clung to theirs for dear life. Without both, we might not have ever gotten to the point when we were ready for revolution.

Of course, it was young Black folks who actually led the charge, starting with . . .

No, no. I want to tell you, seriously. I wish I could say more about how it all went down, but I can't. And we're out of time. You have to go back home now. Don't cry! You'll be fine and we need you to be fine. We need you to get your folks ready so that this world exists someday. I can't tell you how to do that, but I can offer this one last bit of advice:

We move differently without our chains. Pretend yours are gone, and they will be someday.

Jamilah-Asali Lemieux is a renowned cultural critic and writer who focuses on issues of race, gender, and sexuality. The award-winning writer is a leading millennial feminist thinker and new media maven.

～～～～～

I fight White supremacy by teaching people that it is okay to embrace our culture and not just adhere to the norms of the dominant culture.

—Jamie Parker, entrepreneur

～～～～～

Ben Passmore Is Not Interested in Your Space Coffee Shop

Don't get him wrong—your café in the sky might be spectacularly rendered. But cartoonist Ben Passmore would much rather make art that pisses off racist trolls in all corners of the internet. Here, the *Your Black Friend* author talks to Kenrya about his creative foundation, why he puts himself in his art, and the tradition he'd like to see flourish.

When did you realize that you were an artist?

I guess I've always known. My mom paints and sculpts, and as far back as I can remember she had me drawing on placemats and scraps of paper. It's weird, but I started making my own toys at like six, seven, eight. Everyone wanted GI Joes and stuff, but we couldn't afford it. So I'd make my own. It was very sad, but I was super into it.

What were you making them out of?

It was napkins and tape at first. And then I was making them out of—you know those ties you get off bread? They come in lots of different colors and are very flexible. I'd make them out of those and pieces of plastic.

Word! So how would you describe your aesthetic these days?

Someone said that I was both quintessentially millennial and nihilistic, which maybe fits. I make Black punk comics.

Do you identify as a Black punk?

I did. I had already been disappointing women with my terrible haircut and ratty clothes for a while when Afropunk popped up. But it got sexy when I was in my late twenties. So I have some resentment about that. I don't identify as a punk now, though. I realized subcultures have a tendency to repeat the fails of the mainstream.

How do your Black punk comics fight White supremacy?

My hope is that what I do inspires people to act, or at least to think about contending with White supremacy in ways that seem intentional and sort of fun. It feels like we really need people out here just being brave, people who will go out and confront racists. There's a long history of punks chasing skinheads and Nazis out of their communities, and I feel like it's a good tradition. I would like to see it keep on going.

You often put yourself in your work. Why?

I think I did it at first because I didn't know a whole lot of people like me. I didn't know a whole lot of Black punks who squatted in abandoned buildings and valued living more freely rather than spending a lot of time working, people who lived outside of society in the same way. So it was self-affirming to write about myself and sort of process. And also, Black people are often presented two-dimensionally in comics. A Black man is just a big aggro man with a gun. I really wanted to make comics about someone who was complicated and not masculine in these very contrived ways.

You're talented, right? You can draw literally anything. So why do you do this work that brings racists to your mentions?

It doesn't really feel like a choice to me. I can't imagine going off and writing about, I don't know, space people operating a coffee shop or something. Or drawing Mickey Mouse. Even though I guess technically he *is* a Blackface character, so that would still be related, now that I think of it. We live immersed in White supremacy. And I'd rather not. But as long as it's something that we're subjected to, I want to write about fighting it in ways that feel inspiring.

～～～～～～

~~~~~~~~~

My Dad Loves Popeyes Organizations and I Love My Dad
Kiese Laymon

Ben Carson is not my father. Ben Carson is My Dad. Earlier today, My Dad was tongue-lashed by this *Golden Girls* cousin–looking White woman on national TV. My Dad said it's harder to make him the victim of a high-tech lynching if he doesn't have a neck, so he successfully made his neck the opposite of erect.

My Dad is hilarious. I love My Dad.

Right before the high-tech lynching, My Dad gave back over $30,000 worth of love seats, waterbeds, lotion dispensers, and butter knives he bought for Mama. Right after the high-tech lynching, My Dad told me that the entire political charade was an inevitable consequence of working for Uncle D to The. "It's a witch hunt," My Dad said from the passenger seat of his Lexus. "But niggas gotta eat, son. And we eating so good, son." This is how My Dad talks in his Lexus, the bedroom he shares with Mama, and the basement of our six-story home that is five stories bigger than yours.

My Dad's skin is so supple. I love My Dad.

When My Dad gets embarrassed on TV or in print, he likes to eat at Popeyes organizations. I stayed out in the car while My Dad walked into the Popeyes organization on the corner of Jackson Avenue and Highway 6. As soon as My Dad walked in, I could see My Dad get swarmed by Black folks fiending for selfies and autographs. The Black patrons of the Popeyes organization looked longingly into My Dad's eyes, surprised that My Dad was so handsome, so fine.

I love My Dad.

All of a sudden, I saw that something near the cash register had the attention of the Black patrons of this Popeyes organization. Three people ran out of the Popeyes organization yelling, "They shooting," and, "Chile, somebody 'bout to shoot Ben Carson up in Popeyes," into their cell phones.

My Dad was no longer in my line of vision, but I wasn't worried. I know from previous trips to other Popeyes organizations that when Black folk run out saying, "They shooting," and, "Chile, somebody 'bout to shoot Ben Carson," there are rarely shots and no one is ever actually attempting to shoot My Dad.

Still, I slid My Dad's semiautomatic weapon into the back of my waistband, got out of our Lexus, and burst through the doors of the Popeyes organization to see what high jinks the Black patrons in the Popeyes organization were up to.

Two cashiers, surrounded by at least sixteen Black patrons in the Popeyes organization, were six inches from each other, arguing loudly. Both held their left hand in their right fist until it was time to make their most effective points. I considered the hand gestures quite Negroid.

"You see that fruit punch?" the short cashier with the long ashy neck said to the tall cashier with wet lips. "That fruit punch ain't just make itself. See how that shit cascade up, down, all around that container? That shit ain't cascading 'cause it want to cascade. I made that shit cascade. When I got here, that shit was just sitting in basic white pitchers. No kind of style. Fuck is wrong with you questioning my Employee of the Week status?"

"Right, right," the cashier with the juicy wet lips said back to the cashier with the ashy neck. "You see that shine on them biscuits, though? Do you see that shine, nigga? That's all I'm asking. Do you see that shine? I ain't met nan biscuit that woke up this morning and said, 'Let me bathe myself in this regal-ass butter before I start my day.' I did that shit. And I learned to paint with butter interning at Red Lobster, Papa John's, and then at the movies. Ten years it took me to learn my craft. I brought that biscuit fashion here. When I got here, you know good and well that the butter was in the biscuit batter. Wasn't no kinds of shine. Am I lying?"

"She ain't lying," a few folks from the kitchen said to each other. "She did do that."

"Brothers and sisters," My Dad said to both workers in slow-bop public-talk style. "As I'm sure you know, I would never ever support a living wage, but please know how much I appreciate your labor. You are all Employees of the Week to me. That cascading fruit punch, there's nothing better when my throat is parched. That buttered coating on those rolls, it is really some kind of exquisite."

No one corrected My Dad when he called a biscuit a roll. I love My Dad.

Both cashiers came around in front of the counter. I thought My Dad and I were going to have to fight some Blacks at the Popeyes organization by the look of their eyes. But we didn't. The cashiers hugged My Dad's neck, took more selfies, and apologized. My Dad told the cashiers that strange things happened every time he entered a Popeyes organization. Then he made me go out to his Lexus and get his bag. My Dad calls his bag his "grip."

When My Dad placed the grip on the counter and unzipped it, I saw thousands of Amazon gift cards. "I'm going to leave these with you people on the condition that no one in here tells anyone in the media where you got these. If I hear on the news that I blessed your rusted working hands with these gift cards, I will be forced to immediately cut off service to these cards. Let's go, son."

On the way out of the Popeyes organization, the cashier with the wet juicy lips asked the cashier with the long ashy neck if My Dad was saying "rusted" or "rusty" or "rustic."

"Rusted," I told the cashiers. "My Dad called your Black working hands 'rusted.'"

I love My Dad.

My Dad and I were in the Lexus for fifteen minutes before either of us said a word. "You ever think it's strange," I asked him, "how Black working people call you all kinds of names on the internet, but every time we run into Black working people in real life, it's like they love you?"

"Niggas love me," My Dad said to me. "Why is that strange to you?"

"Yeah," I told My Dad. "I mean, why do you think they're so nice to you in person, but . . ."

"Because they know," My Dad said.

"They know what?"

"They know niggas gotta eat. They know a hustle when they feel one. They know a hustler when they see one. They know this is all bullshit. Same reason they loved Obama."

"What's bullshit? And Obama, he loved them, or at least acted like he loved them."

"Right. That was his hustle, son. Niggas loved that hustle."

"So Black people will love any Black person who hustles themselves to the national political stage?"

"You gotta be hated by White folks for us to really support you," My Dad told me. "We love a clean nigga hated by White folks. But even if you're loved by White folks like me, privately, niggas know the hustle. This ain't new, son."

"But if you could get love by loving Black people, why make hating, or hating on, Black people part of your public performance and hustle?"

"Two reasons," My Dad said. "One is that White money spends way better than Black love. Black love ain't buying us no leather couches, no leather coats, no leather pants, no fine cutlery. I been successful since you were born. Have we ever ate as good as we eating since I started really fucking with these racist-ass White folks? If all these brothers out here slanging little dime bags decided to use their little platforms to shit on niggas and hoist up White folks, do you know how much better they'd be eating?"

"Not really."

"Exactly. Second, it's all about suicide bombing, son."

"What you mean?"

"I mean, people think this political apparatus is about greed. Maybe. But it's really about old-ass White people not being okay with just harming themselves. Why is there a minimum age requirement for the presidency but no maximum age limit, son? These old wealthy White motherfuckers want to hurt themselves by applying for jobs that will kill them faster, but they want to hurt us too. They hate themselves. They hate us too, though. And then they hate the country by extension."

"Hillary Clinton?"

"Lackluster-ass suicide bomber."

"Biden?"

"Lazy-ass suicide bomber."

"Bernie?"

"Loud-talking, one trick pony-ass suicide bomber," My Dad said. "Look. Did you see a seventy-five-year-old working at Popeyes or anywhere you have to actually do work?"

"No, I didn't."

"Exactly. Do you see any niggas lucky enough to make it to seventy-five fiending to be president of anything? Niggas who make it to seventy-five with money are trying to sit they ass down somewhere, watch some *Family Feud,* and not lose they money. The last thing I want at seventy-five years old is the hardest job in the world."

"That explains them," I told My Dad. "But what explains you?"

"I'm a nigga. I look good, but I'm old. I gotta eat," My Dad said as we pulled into the driveway of our house that is five stories bigger than yours. "That explains me."

We sat out in the garage. I looked out the front windshield as My Dad finished eating the life out of his last Popeyes biscuit. My Dad asked me why I looked so confused.

"Don't be confused, son," My Dad said. "The question is how healthy can a nation be when its racial majority's appetite for Black, Brown, Muslim, and nasty women's suffering is literally insatiable? For real, this is really one of the only questions that matters. As long as that appetite can't be quenched, hating on niggas will always be a thorough hustle. And this," My Dad said, "is a question with an answer that will never qualify as Breaking News, son."

Earlier this summer, My Dad and I took a road trip across country in his Lexus where he told me everything that was going to happen to D to The's administration. While I was watching a fifty-four-inch television on the twenty-sixth floor of a Mississippi Gulf Coast casino, Boyz II Men were on television singing to a White woman with an apparent belly full of gas.

I felt so much shame for Boyz II Men. But like My Dad said, niggas gotta eat. When the commercial went off, there was Breaking News that My Dad already predicted.

A man who looks like an *American Psycho* remix of That '80s Guy from *Futurama* was enjoying telling reporters how much "respect" he has for Sean Spicer and how much "love" he has for D to The. The American '80s Psycho Guy kept saying, "One more question. Should we do one more? Let's do one more." My Dad said that American '80s Psycho Guy loved attention too much to be good at anything that required listening. Like D to The, he seemed to lack shame, humility, home-training. But unlike D to The, he could be fired. My Dad said he would not last a week.

Later that night, while I was on one of the beds looking up YouTube videos and My Dad was brushing his waves in the hotel bathroom, Ced the Entertainer came on the television over-enunciating every syllable while earnestly looking at the camera talking about My Dad's "diabetic nerve pain." I felt so much shame for Ced the Entertainer. But I understood. Niggas gotta eat, and My Dad has diabetic nerve pain too.

Near the end of our road trip, I asked My Dad how anyone who had ever seen the tens of thousands of empty United States miles could talk about building a wall to keep people out. "White folks love to keep darker people out of things, son," My Dad said. "And as long as this shit is true, someone will capitalize on that. This ain't new."

All of a sudden, there was Breaking News on SiriusXM. Mueller apparently convened a grand jury. I looked at My Dad and waited for him to say something. My Dad looked afraid. Eventually, he said, "Oh well. Guess this shit will be ending sooner than I thought. Barack Obama was the best president White folks ever had, son. He just was. The nigga was hired to clean up their mess. He cleaned that shit up. In way more ways than White folks on the left and right want to admit, he saved them. Saved their jobs. Saved their retirements. Saved their health care system. Saved their country. And what do most of them do? They despise him for it."

I asked My Dad if he felt that way, why was he working for Uncle D to The? My Dad just looked at me without blinking, and this was hard because My Dad blinks more than you. My Dad sucked his teeth. My Dad ran his palm over his waves. "My bad," I told My Dad. "Because niggas gotta eat, right?"

"What in the world am I doing?" My Dad said to himself. "What in the world am I doing?"

That was then.

Tonight we are home from a trek to the Popeyes organization on Jackson and Highway 6. "Donald is in trouble, and when this is all done, he will eventually be destroyed not because of what he's done to vulnerable Mexicans, Muslims, White women, queer folk, poor folk, and Black folk in this country, and not because his White ass conflates the health of his reputation with the health of the country," My Dad says as we sit in the Lexus. "That mediocre man is headed toward absolute destruction because of money laundering, conspiracy, obstruction of justice, and really because of what he dared to say about the media and the intelligence community while working with, and really for, Vladimir."

"Right," I tell My Dad. "But what about you? Aren't we eating good enough? Can't you walk away and spend the rest of your retirement at home singing and eating that dark meat with Mama?"

My Dad ignores my question and gets out of the Lexus. As we walk through the door, he says, "There is no clean work for any Black person in this country who wants to be rich."

"Is there clean work in this country for any Black person who wants to be free or healthy?"

My Dad is standing in the kitchen. He's looking me directly in the eye. I see My Dad thinking, wondering, wandering. "There is cleaner work at that Popeyes organization," My Dad tells me. "But who would you rather be? A clean, hungry, Black rusted hands–having nigga who works at a Popeyes organization, or a rich, sellout-ass nigga who stays full like us?"

I love My Dad too much to answer his question. My Dad loves me too much to wait for an answer. I look down at both of our hands. Our palms are not rusted or rusty. Our palms are actually quite rustic.

"Us," I finally tell My Dad while he is laying his head in Mama's lap eating that dark meat, tears sliding down his beautiful face. "Right," My Dad says. "I'd rather be us because we are eating. We are compromised, but so are all niggas. And so are all Americans. But niggas gotta eat. And we are eating so well."

I love My Dad.

Kiese Laymon is a Black Southern writer, born and raised in Jackson, Mississippi. A professor of English and African American studies at the University of Mississippi and distinguished visiting professor of nonfiction at the University of Iowa, he is the author of the novel *Long Division*, an essay collection, *How to Slowly Kill Yourself and Others in America*, and the memoir *Heavy*.

~~~~~~~~~

QUESTION, ANSWERED

Here we consider the question: how does humor inform the way you move through the world?

Kenrya

You know those sad clowns? The ones with the red lipstick smeared down to their chins, the painted-on furrowed brows, and the scraggly orange hair grazing their collars? The ones who make people cringe and titter uncomfortably as they recognize their own pathos in their downer one-liners?

I'm not one of those.

I'm more like: Where does she keep digging up these Black-ass gifs? Yup, she's right, that *is* a word, bitch, your auntie is hella shady funny. As my Bumble connects know, my hobbies include baking, reading, getting lost in Twitter black holes, and talking shit both inside *and* outside. My texts are full of side eyes, laughing so hard they're crying faces and skulls, 'cause I stay killing it in my "this seat's taken"–ass group texts. And I've been known to earnestly describe myself as a funny bitch, 'cause, Aries.

My sister Leena has been a victim of and party to my bullshit her whole life, and I'm more than happy to put on a show for her, my first and best audience. We were downloading about our day last night, she taking a break during her shift as an emergency medical technician, me cleaning my kitchen before bed.

"So we're sitting in the antiracist, antibias training that I helped organize at the school, and the facilitators are talking about the history of race, who created the concept, how they used propaganda to spread it, all that. And out of *nowhere* this old White dude raises his hand as they are presenting and just starts talking on some 'fuck yo' presentation' shit. He's like, 'But Black people have been enslaving and killing each other for years, all over the world. What does that have to do with White people? We didn't do that to them, they did that to themselves.' Bitchhhhhh. I couldn't have stopped myself from yelling, 'Are you kidding me?' if I wanted to; they're lucky I didn't cuss. Meanwhile, the head of the school looked horrified, a few folks near me fidgeted mad uncomfortably, and the Black mama sitting beside me was telepathically communicating that we might need to morph into the Dora Milaje and fuck shit up. And I was with her, but I was also thinking, *Lord, can you please tell me who this racist motherfucker is in case Saa wants to have a playdate with his kid?* Like, really, b? Your trash-bag ass might as well have stayed at home if you were gonna bring this shit in here. The fucking Caucasity."

It should be noted that Leena started tittering around the time I got to "old White dude," and was full on cackling when I lamented the Caucasian audacity of it all. The laugh helped her get through a long shift and gave me an opportunity to vent my annoyance and horror that my child might come across this man on the playground.

Because trauma—whether it's the type whose scars disfigure our bodies and psyches in an instant or over time—is a motherfucker, and I think we all know that comedy is often the show we put on to convince ourselves that we are "Dy-no-mite!" Those sad clowns know it. Our ancestors who made fun of massa in the moonlight knew it. But knowing that laughter is a mask for our agony doesn't shrink its impact.

In a world that gobbles up Black pain, there is something luxurious about spinning the blocked hair touches and outright bigotry into stories that start with "Niggggaaaaaaa" and end with your sister not being able to catch her breath because "How dare you?!" Those tears of laughter you're wiping away? They seep back into your body and heal the abrasions your heart collected during your morning commute that included the man who decided his bag deserved a seat on the crowded subway car more than you did. That scream laugh you let out when Kid Fury read the White man outside the expensive theater who assumed he must be waiting there to sell him weed? It clears your skin and fills in your edges. The joy that collects in your body when you hear "Harrison Booth" say that he wears "a thick brown leather belt" to express himself as a White man on that very special episode of *Atlanta*? It presses Pause on your anxiety and gives you permission to step away from your constant vigilance.

When we allow laughter in, we unfold, relax our shoulders, loosen our limbs, release our tongues, throw off the invisible cloak of respectability, and feel rejuvenated enough to head back into battle, heads high.

It lets us return to ourselves.

~~~~~~~~~

Akiba

One time I went on a magazine job interview where the Black guy doing the hiring asked me, "Are you even *funny*?" This was a trick question. First of all, a job applicant declaring that she is funny suggests that she is ready to bust out her best material over a haphazardly toasted conference-room bagel and tap water. Wocka, wocka nah.

Second of all, this dude had already made it clear that he didn't think I was right for the job. To him I was the constipated hall monitor, the sooty Tipper Gore, that bitch who would invade and neutralize the locker room atmosphere of his workplace. I don't remember how I responded to his question, but what I know for sure is that what I said was flaccid.

At the pre–social media time of this interview, there were next to no outlets for a droll Black girl to shine on her own terms. And I cared too much about what men thought of me. So young Akiba actually saw his question as a flaw in my personal brand. If this particular cornrock didn't think I was funny, that meant that the satirical and biting writing I was becoming known for didn't land right.

At this point I guess I should explain why being Black and funny meant and means so much to me. I do this with trepidation because I decided early in my career that I would never serve as a translator. This mapping-out is only okay because Zora Neale Hurston famously said, "I love myself when I am laughing . . . and then again when I am looking mean and impressive." Zora already told us the entire thing! Laughing? Mean and impressive? Same difference.

The long version: For a people who were seized and stripped of our bodily autonomy, our history, culture, language, and traditions, humor has always been a way for us to touch and care for one another. Laughing is an underground railroad for those of us lucky enough to ride its tracks, the vehicle through which we have mushed you in your savage face for murdering us because you are a land-thieving lazy ass who believed that something called God told you to kidnap, dehumanize, and torture other people into doing your fucking farming, child care, and nation-building.

In today's context, humor is how we tell our coworkers that we are code-switching rather than telling all the family secrets. From Jourdon Anderson to Moms Mabley to Donald Glover, Black humor that does not explain itself is the marrow of our tradition.

As I've written elsewhere in this book, I was raised Black nationalist in West Philadelphia in the '70s and '80s. If you've spent any time with these beautiful, committed, brilliant folks, you know that irreverence is not necessarily the goal. If Baba el-Something called everybody at the program a bunch of sellout Negros, that charge would be entertained.

Also, the fonts of the movement were very severe. This meant that 98 percent of the people who took the flyer about the program already agreed with us. Despite the near 100 percent buy-in, Mama Somebody was still going to deliver her 7,000-minute address about buying Black (we already did this) and learning who we were (that's why we were at the program). Then would come Baba Two Times telling us to throw out the White man's TV (no).

At one gathering, someone who very likely had PTSD from the Vietnam War, COINTELPRO, Reaganomics, or all three yelled at us children about how we needed to learn how to eat roaches and rats because that was going to be our diet during the revolution. No adult that I know of said, "N***a, this is the worst recruitment method ever." Or, "Do we really plan on losing that badly?"

This daunting thing could have flattened me, except humor is such a huge part of my family culture and resistance.

My mother, father, and sister, my aunts, uncles, and cousins, and my crazy grandma Mamie know (or knew, for the homies who aren't here) that real laughter is non-negotiable if you are to beat White supremacy. A major component of enslaving Black folks was keeping us terrified at the whims of untalented and ridiculous White people.

Part of how we survived lies in how and why we laugh. I'm not a sociologist, anthropologist, or psychiatrist. But I do know that Black hilarity heals. On lock, we have deadpan, absurdity, signifying, one-liners, tall tales, the dozens, silly faces, bizarre inventions, shit-talking, and pretending not to know the names of people we don't like, like your girl Whatsherface from that Rick Ross video who was in *Clueless* that one time.

My favorite joke from my father involves a family friend who always rocked his fraternity's paraphernalia at holiday dinners, including purple and gold beaded necklaces. Once, as my baba helped set the table, he asked, "Is Mardi Gras coming?" then pantomimed flashing his nonexistent breasts.

My favorite mom humor is her calling every talented Black male my age or younger a sibling. "Your new brother Hazim," she said of a Black academic who came to dinner after winning a prestigious prize. "Your brother Damon is hilarious!" says Mom of a popular writer from Pittsburgh. "I love your brother Ta-Nehisi's new book," she will say of a friend from Howard University. Really, she just wanted a boy.

My sister cracks me up so much, it's hard to pull up a good example. My current favorite is a text involving "unresolved feelings about Drake." Get it? Somebody who is not Aubrey Graham has a lot of feelings! Wocka wocka!

So no laugh-deficient hiring manager can stop my shine. I have a tribe that seems to find me amusing and understand why that even matters in the world. My 1,875 Oldbook and 4,273 Twitter followers indicate that at least 6,148 people could be chuckling at my cat jokes and pictures of my ugly writing socks. I do this for the people. It is the people who shall determine whether or not I deserve a pie in the face or a genuine laugh. The laugh is one of my life's best rewards.

FOUR

I'M NOT ONE OF YOUR LITTLE FRIENDS

Have you ever spent a substantial amount of time around a tiny human? Not "I'm the auntie who pops in for a couple hours once a year" time, but wiping butts, building castles, and catching sneezes in your mouth time. If so, then you know that those little people are positively aspirational when it comes to the art of not giving a fuck. They don't need T-shirts or memes that proclaim their willingness to do and say exactly what they want; their lives are testaments to their philosophy.

Not here for somebody's overdose of perfume at church? Scream that it's making it hard to breathe just as the choir finishes singing "Now Behold the Lamb." Incredulous that a man two parking spots over just swept garbage off his raggedy passenger seat and onto the ground? Gon' head and loudly tell Mama that "He needs to take better care of the earth!" Not feeling the guy in the White House? Inform your classmates over lunch that he doesn't like them because they are brown and offer up your strategy for making him be nicer. (Hint: it involves personally presenting him with a letter of advice and taking Mama along for backup in case he tries it.)

That drive to speak the truth typically evokes one of three responses in parents: rebukes, apologetic murmurs, and stifled cackles. But when we are intentional about cultivating this fearlessness in a way that balances children's innate bent toward justice with a strong sense of self, we can raise natural leaders who ease into their personal brand of activism. The young people in this chapter are proof that as Whitney—and Randy Watson—once put it, "the children are our future."

"I'm Not One of Your Little Friends" celebrates our children, spotlights those who are fighting for their lives, and highlights the work of the youngest activists among us.

~~~~~~~~

The Accidental Activist

In the fall of 2015, eighteen-year-old Niya Kenny shot video and spoke up when a school resource officer threw one of her classmates across a room, sparking the #AssaultAtSpringValleyHigh hashtag and amplifying the national conversation about the school-to-prison pipeline. Kenny was subsequently arrested and charged with "disturbing a school." She decided to leave Spring Valley High School and earn her GED: "I was ready to get this entire high school experience over with," she says. Now Kenny is working with the American Civil Liberties Union (ACLU) to challenge the South Carolina law that allowed her to be taken into custody and that sends disproportionate numbers of students of color to jail each year. Here she tells Kenrya about the day she became an activist.

What made you stand up for your classmate that day?

I can't really say there was a thought that went through my head before I stood up and started yelling. It was just my natural reaction.

Why do you think it wasn't a natural reaction for the adults in the room?

My guess is that maybe the adults felt they had to stick together in this situation, whether it was right or wrong. I mean, the administrator who came in before the officer, he was like, "I don't got time to play with y'all kids today." Like, we already different from him in his head.

What was going through your head when school resource officer Ben Fields put you in handcuffs after you stood up?

Honestly, *My mama is gonna kill me.* That was my biggest fear, because I was my mom's problem child. I would get into trouble with my teachers, and I was just like, *Dang, this is the first time that I never really did anything, and I just need my mama to believe me!* I was just so scared at what she was going to think, and sad because I knew it would be embarrassing for her to come get her child out of jail.

How did she react?

My little sister said that when she told my mom, her initial reaction was, "I'm gonna kick her behind. I send y'all to school to learn, not to be getting in people's business." Because the officer told my mom, "Oh, Niya got in someone else's business and now she's being arrested."

What a piece of shit. How did she react when she found out what really happened?

She was very supportive, just letting me know that everything is going to be okay. She wasn't really telling me like, "Oh, we're not gonna let him get away with this," but I could tell that was her attitude. "You're not gonna put my child in jail for no reason and then not suffer any kind of consequence." Her biggest thing was getting justice for me, because she felt like her child had been done so wrong. That's every parent's nightmare.

How long were you in jail?

I was there for between eight and nine hours. That's a full school day, in a holding area with men.

What was your first thought when you got out?

Thank God I didn't have to spend the night!

Why do you think Solicitor Dan Johnson ultimately dropped the charge?

Honestly, I feel like there was no wrongdoing on my end, you know? He had no choice but to drop those charges. This girl was assaulted, she was taken to jail. Yelling and cursing in the classroom is disturbing school, I won't take that away, but the environment had already been disturbed before I started protesting.

Why did you decide to challenge the constitutionality of South Carolina's disturbing school and disorderly conduct laws with this ACLU lawsuit?

Because it's regular kids whose lives are really affected by this law, and it's not fair. You can be arrested and taken to jail for anything that a teacher considers disturbing their classroom, like chewing gum loudly, passing gas, burping, whatever. This is a teacher, not a judge. Oh God, now I'm just thinking about it all again. Those people made me so mad.

With good reason. What do you hope the outcome will be?

We want this disturbing schools law completely taken away. No child should be charged with disturbing the school. Charging them with that is basically just charging a child with being a child.

Did you think of yourself as an activist before October 26, 2015?

No. Never.

Did you think of yourself as an activist after that?

Yes, but not until I was told that I was one. I never knew how significant it was until the video went viral. It was just me naturally reacting to what I saw in front of me. This whole organizing world was introduced to me after the incident. I didn't even know about the organization I intern for, African

American Policy Forum. Kimberlé Crenshaw reached out and asked me to come work for her. I didn't even know what intersectionality was before then.

What issues feel most important as you come into your activist self?

I'm definitely still focused on the school-to-prison pipeline because I have a personal experience with it. That's always going to be an issue that I care about the most, because I had to experience that myself.

Do you want to continue working in organizing?

I think I will do this work forever. But it won't be the only thing that I do, you know? I'm young. I want to experience everything that life has.

~~~~~~~~~~

I fight White supremacy by working with writers on the forefront of dismantling racist, sexist, homophobic, and classist ideology. Every book that envisions a truly integrated future while challenging narratives of oppression is a meaningful intervention with the power to change minds.

—Tanya McKinnon, literary agent

~~~~~~~~~~

"Cornrows, Afropuffs, and Joy"
by Delphine Adama Fawundu (2014)

"The goal of White supremacy is to make people feel less than human, to dehumanize us. As a photographer, I'm looking for the natural essence in things, something that gives you a peek into the humanity of people. This photo was part of a project called *I Am Here: Girls Reclaiming Safe Spaces*. But what does it mean to create and reclaim a *mental* safe space? There are some things that you have to be conscious of every day, or else you'll get sucked into this world of White supremacy and never see yourself. We have to fight it, but if it takes up your whole life, then when are you supposed to *live*? This photo shows the power in these young, living girls, which is the power in us. They are living in their element, and they possess so much. There is so much joy in who they are—in who *we* are." —Delphine Adama Fawundu

Delphine Adama Fawundu is a New York City–based multimedia visual artist whose work examines the theory of social constructivism within the development of identity.

Sidney Keys III Wants to Give the World a Book

When Sidney Keys III's mom, Winnie Caldwell, surprised him with a visit to the St. Louis bookstore Eye See Me, he had no idea that it would make him a digital star and an entrepreneur. Caldwell shot a video of her then-ten-year-old son reading *Danny Dollar Millionaire Extraordinaire* by Ty Allan Jackson, and it went viral, racking up more than sixty-five thousand views. "We were like, 'Maybe we can do something with this,'" Keys says.

That something was creating the Books N Bros club, which works to increase literacy among boys ages seven to thirteen, with a focus on African American–centered literature. "We started with this age group because boys are specifically behind in reading, and seven to thirteen is the age range where we typically stop picking up books," Keys explains. "I don't want reading to be something you get made fun of for doing, or something that scares boys."

It took just one month to organize the group's first meet-up in September 2016, where seven boys came together at the bookstore to read and discuss *Danny Dollar*. "I had my own lemonade stand there because in the book, the boy made a million dollars from a lemonade stand," Keys says. "We had snacks and then we discussed the book in a little circle. It was a really cool experience."

Keys says he was drawn to the book because Danny Dollar reminded him of someone he knew: himself. "I saw someone who looked like me. Usually that only happens with nonfiction things, like books about Martin Luther King," he said. "Don't get me wrong, those are good stories—but it's nice to see fiction, just regular stories, with people like you in them."

Keys quickly expanded Books N Bros to include a subscription service. Each month, subscribers get a book, a related worksheet, and a bookmark that nets them free treats in exchange for reading. But Keys has even bigger plans for Books N Bros: he wants to flex his entrepreneurial muscle and create an after-school curriculum so that kids can hang out and read books about Black protagonists.

"Boo, Donald Trump" by Saa Rankin Naasel (2017)

Imagine walking into an art space and seeing a group of small brown girls marching by, waving signs, pumping their fists, and chanting, "Donald Trump, Donald Trump, has no friends! Donald Trump, Donald Trump, smells like eggs!" That's the sight that greeted visitors to an art camp in Hyattsville, Maryland, where six-year-old Saa Rankin Naasel organized five other girls—ages three to eight—for an anti-45 march. Struck by inspiration after lunch on an afternoon in late December 2017, Rankin Naasel said she organized the march "because Donald Trump is bad. He doesn't like brown people." The pint-sized activist said that the way he treats people makes her mad, but that marching made her feel happy because she was doing something to push back against him.

~~~~~~~~~

The Fight to Free Black Children

Rickell Howard Smith

I am a civil rights attorney working to dismantle the school-to-prison pipeline and eliminate the mass incarceration of Black children in America. I represent children in civil rights cases and policy initiatives, focusing my efforts on reducing racial disparities in education and the juvenile justice system. I used to think my goal was to get favorable decisions in court, help children avoid expulsion, and reduce racial profiling of Black children and their subsequent contact with the system. But time, experience, and raising two children of my own helped me realize the true purpose of my work: I fight for Black children to be *free*.

Freedom is defined as possessing the power or right to act, speak, or think as one wants without hindrance or restraint. But my vision for Black children is more nuanced than that. They should be free to be children and do childlike things without fear. They need the freedom to be bratty, sad, confused, self-centered, and combative teenagers without fear that the system will punish their age-appropriate behavior with lifelong or life-ending consequences. The freedom to live without being subjected to race-based trauma. The freedom to throw a temper tantrum without fear that the cops will be called. The freedom to look at their phone in class without concern that a law enforcement officer will body-slam them. The freedom to play cops-and-robbers without being killed by one. The freedom to experiment and find themselves without the suffocating intrusion of institutional racism into their lives.

I became a mother during my second year of law school, and motherhood has guided all of my personal and professional decisions since the birth of my oldest child. For me, parenthood and civil rights advocacy have a symbiotic relationship. I am, without a doubt, a better lawyer and a better mother because I am both.

As a parent, I fight for my own freedom to teach my children that they have dominion over their own bodies, the freedom to teach them that they do not have to comply with a stranger's order. However, my ability to teach them how to be confident, strong-minded, and informed is restricted by the exhaustive list of lessons that I have to teach them to ensure that they aren't seen as threats. I am fully aware that these lessons chip away at their ability to be carefree, but I need them to make it home. I want to be free to raise my children with the lessons and guidance necessary for them to realize their full potential and be amazing people *without* fear.

Working in courtrooms has taught me that Black children are especially vulnerable to becoming victims of injustice simply because of who they are. They are simultaneously subjected to age-based prejudice *and* systemic racism. The American legal system does not afford the same constitutional rights to children as adults. They are taught to respect and comply with authority figures at home, in the community, and at school, to be seen and not heard. The system is designed to stifle and silence them. On top of this, Black children experience the same barriers to freedom as Black adults. They often feel powerless to self-advocate because their spirits are suppressed by systemic racism, and they lack the legal protections and opportunities to advocate for themselves.

Case in point: Even though the American juvenile justice system has been undergoing systemic reform for nearly twenty years, Black children have barely benefited from those efforts. National youth incarceration rates have dropped significantly over the last decade, but racial disparity in the juvenile justice system continues to grow as Black children are victimized by systemic racism. They face harsher school discipline consequences, at higher rates, and they are more likely to be arrested, charged, and punished severely for engaging in the same age-appropriate behavior as their White counterparts.

Of course, this is no secret to Black folks. We don't need data reports to tell us what's happening in our own communities. But being entrenched in this work reminds me that no matter how well they were raised, or how wealthy or educated their parents are, our precious kids are not immune from this. This understanding shapes the way I advocate for all Black children and raise my own. Rearing children as a civil rights advocate makes me view everything through a dual lens. As an advocate: how do I use the outcome of this court case to help Black children be free? As a mama: how will this make things better for my babies?

I once thought that being a Black woman civil rights attorney was the height of my personal revolutionary action. Now I know that parenting my children is the most revolutionary thing that I can do in this world. Parenthood transformed me from a lawyer to a freedom fighter for Black children. They need all of us more now than ever. They need our collective love and support. They need us to see them as children. They need the change agents in the world to focus on their voices, needs, and desires. They need us to create space and opportunity for them to advocate for themselves. They need us to tear down the suffocating force of systemic racism so that they can be free. So they can *live*.

Rickell Howard Smith is the litigation and policy director at a nonprofit child advocacy organization. She specializes in civil rights litigation aimed at reforming the criminal and juvenile justice systems and was a 2017 Youth Justice Leadership Institute Fellow of the National Juvenile Justice Network.

<center>~~~~~~~~~~</center>

I fight White supremacy by teaching my children about Black power, excellence, and magic. The same way that White supremacy is a learned behavior, our children need to learn that their ancestors were great leaders and innovators whose contributions impact the world in a major way.

—Khalfani Walker, dentist

<center>~~~~~~~~~~</center>

Author and Journalist Denene Millner on Why She Has Dedicated Her Career to Making Books for Black Children

When I got pregnant with my first baby, I promised that my child wouldn't have to spend the most impressionable part of her life longing for herself in literature. The books I publish through Denene Millner Books all celebrate Black children. What I love about these books—including *Crown: An Ode to the Fresh Cut*, *There's a Dragon in My Closet*, and *Early Sunday Morning*—is that they shine a light on our babies and their everyday lives. There's no focus on civil rights icons. No big-ups for famous jazz singers or sports figures. No nods to slavery. There's no overcoming or struggling to get by, or Black "firsts" we force children to revere. They are just good old-fashioned tales about the lives of little human beings with brown skin—my love letter to children of color who deserve to see their beauty and humanity in the most remarkable form of entertainment on the planet: books.

~~~~~~~~

QUESTION, ANSWERED

Much of who we are starts when we are tiny humans. So we explored the question: what's your activism origin story?

Kenrya

A play in four acts.

Act I

It's 1989 at Aurora Road Elementary School in Bedford Heights, Ohio. I'm in the third grade, and I am decidedly my father's child. He had settled into paycheck-to-paycheck-class life in a suburb across town from my cousins where we could get a good public school education and still see Black people, but before I was born, he was a beret-wearing, rifle-toting, school breakfast program–starting Black nationalist. And though his strong moral compass meant that he left that organization when internal corruption surfaced, he never stepped away from his love for his people and contempt for the system that brutalized us. Accordingly, he was very honest about what it meant for my sister and me as Black children growing up in a nation that has, from the very beginning, treated us as less than human. So after I learned from him while I was still in single digits that this supposedly "indivisible" country was fueled by disregard for our lives and that the actual words of the Pledge of Allegiance were drafted with xenophobia and White supremacy in mind, I decided that I was not pledging my allegiance to shit, thanks. Every morning the entire school says the pledge as someone recites it over the intercom system. Every morning I stand, hands at my sides, mouth closed. No one says a word to me about it.

Act II

It's seven years later, and I join the NAACP because my friends are in the youth chapter and it looks fun. We hold a ton of voter registration drives at skating rinks and parks, but the first time I feel like an actual activist is during a national convention. That's when I participate in my first sit-in. The details are hazy—I'm old, y'all—but the national board is planning to reduce funding for youth field coordinators, the folks who provide training and support for local youth chapters like mine. Being a kid in this elders-dominated space feels like engaging in a never-ending game of Mother May I? The organization is granted giant steps forward for publicly holding up young people as the next front in the movement. But when it withholds the support we need to actually lead, it feels like we're bounding backward when no one is looking. So we use the tactics of those who came before us and hit the floor outside the boardroom, vowing to stay there until they make it rain. I go on to hold leadership positions with my college NAACP chapter.

Act III

The summer after my freshman year at Howard, I spend my afternoons interning at an advertising firm in Cleveland where I am, of course, the only Black person in the entire office. One Friday, my supervisor, a young White woman, gives me a task. "Can you please take this box of client contacts and put it in alphabetical order?" I cheerfully accept the box of maybe one hundred notecards, sit at my desk, and proceed to put them in order in a few minutes. When I arrive back at her cubicle with the cards, she looks confused. "Do you have a question?" she asks. "No. I'm done," I say, handing her the box. "Done?! How?" she asks, still puzzled. "It was alphabetical order," I say, eyebrow raised, also puzzled. "Wow! You're amazing! Thanks so much for doing this so quickly!" she says. I squint at her, then walk back to my desk, wounded, but not really understanding why. The soft bigotry of low expectations is some insidious shit.

Act IV

It's 2014 and I'm somebody's mama. Police shootings of unarmed Black men and boys like Eric Garner and Michael Brown are forcing us to beg the world to assign value to our lives, and the National Action Network holds the Justice for All march in Washington, DC. I hit the ground with a couple of my linesisters and our kids and try not to cry as they march—literally, because my three-year-old isn't fucking with you if you're not high-stepping it through the streets—holding handmade signs that read, OUR LIVES MATTER. I tell an interviewer that day: "I wanted her to know, even at her young age, that we are our most powerful when we are united. I wanted her to see what it looks like when thousands of people come together to advocate for themselves. I wanted her to feel the energy that is generated when people have had enough and decide to do something about it. So we took to the streets."

<hr>

Akiba

I did a decent amount of community service growing up. I participated in walkathons, collated stuff for my mother's meetings, served as a peer educator at Planned Parenthood, and took part in an "Africentric" curriculum effort called African Youth for Education. On the get-shine side, I sang the Negro National Anthem at an anti–Desert Storm rally. And because I was "conscious," I was also quoted in the newspaper, once for citing the fatal flaws of an all-White newsroom and once for pointing out that "a dangerous psyche of materialism" explained why a Black girl had been shot over a pair of gold earrings.

Still, it wasn't until my senior year of high school that I attempted to organize people to fight White supremacy.

The public school my sister and I attended was considered the best in the city and one of the top in the state of Pennsylvania. Coming out of a pre-dominantly White, single-sex prep school, this elite public school I will call Super Selective College Preparatory Magnet Academy (SSCPMA) had many appealing features: boys, boys who were Black, and a bevy of Latinx, Asian, and South Asian kids.

But in this public school, where I desperately wanted to fit in, I was incensed by the racism of some of the teachers.

First, there was a phrase I only saw Black kids being disciplined with: "This is not your neighborhood school! This is SSCPMA!" Within this context, "neighborhood school" was coded language for an inferior "ghetto" institution that accepted just any old person. The trope suggested that Black students should go back to their natural habitat—a school with low standards.

In another case, an elderly White teacher who I was told had tenure would routinely make blatantly ignorant mistakes about Black history. No, sir. Malcolm X was not murdered in 1950. And slavery didn't end after a "few decades." When I tried to clarify, he would kick me out of class.

Another teacher, we heard, was overtly racist. He once told a Black student eating an apple that she should be eating a banana instead. Another time he told a Black girl wearing a headwrap that she looked like Aunt Jemima.

My headwrap-wearing, conscious Afrikan crew had been commiserating about the subtle racism of the school, but the Aunt Jemima comment compelled us to do *something*.

I truly don't remember whose idea it was to distribute daily anonymous flyers demanding that racist teachers be fired or at least forced to undergo diversity training. I also can't recall whose idea it was to tell students to wear black armbands in solidarity with our movement and come to a speakout we'd be holding at the end of the week.

I do remember writing the text for our missives, which I photocopied on hundreds of pieces of colored paper at my mother's job. Each installment included a subversive quote that could be read as empowering, vaguely threatening, or a declaration of race war, depending on your vantage point. Apparently White students into neo-Nazi punk culture took our movement as a war cry—we heard they were planning to bring knives to our speakout.

After we promoted it with a week's worth of flyers secretly dropped in various locations throughout the school, the speakout was lit!

As planned, we in the vanguard of the movement sanctioned our racist teachers and called for them to be fired or retrained. But somehow the discussion drifted to interpersonal racism among students. (This is my adult retelling. I didn't know the phrase "interpersonal racism" until I was like forty.) One of the Nazi girls started an impassioned speech about how scared she was about what "you people are doing here."

"*You people?*" we vanguards hissed.

"Let her explain!" said unaffiliated centrists of color in the room. The girl got to make her point about how "we" wouldn't get anywhere if we focused on race so much. People clapped. I felt sick, then checked out.

After our speakout ended, I found myself enveloped in the arms of a non-vanguard brother who had helped us set up the chairs. "We did it!" he said joyously.

"We did not do it at all," I said. "We let that racist White girl disrespect us."

He looked at me strangely and said, "You're never satisfied."

A few days later, it got back to me that at least two girls in our little Afrikan organizing crew were calling me full of shit and saying that I only "did this to get famous." I was so crushed by their betrayal that I got sick with flulike symptoms.

I was out of school with the flu and what was very likely a bout of depression so long that I missed the school gospel choir's big performance at the Gallery Mall downtown. I was a soloist and had been plotting for weeks how I would impress this college-age gentleman who designed and sold conscious Black T-shirts at the mall. Not only had organizing made me sick, but it ruined my (imagined) chance with T-shirt jawn.

Months later, the four White Los Angeles police officers caught on video camera savagely beating Black motorist Rodney King—Stacey Koon, Laurence Powell, Timothy Wind, and Theodore Briseno—were found innocent. It was an early '90s precursor to today, when ubiquitous cell-phone and police video footage of officers beating, Tasing, choking, setting up, sexually assaulting, and fatally shooting Black people ensures the trauma of both victims and viewers—and too often leaves the apathetic justice system unmoved.

As Los Angeles burned, students of all races held a walkout. School authorities accused me of orchestrating the protest, but it certainly wasn't me. It *was*, however, the moment when vanguard and oblivious alike agreed that there was something very, very wrong with America.

FIVE

GOD IS GOOD, ALL THE TIME . . .

When she was five, a kid we know and adore discovered Siri. Every morning she pressed the home button on her iPad and kicked off the day's conversation, which usually revolved around one of two things: jokes and questions about Jesus. For the record, Siri is too bougie for the former and clueless about the latter, bringing up random Wikipedia pages with Jesus's name sprinkled across them like she's really doing something. The kid's perennial favorite Siri question was, "What is Jesus's favorite color?" but she saved the tough religion questions for her mama.

On the way to school on 45's inauguration day, she asked the question that troubled the minds of many: "But he doesn't like people who look like us. Why did Jesus let him win?"

Yeah.

It's heartbreaking that kindergarteners are already contemplating why bad things happen to good people, but for people of faith, this illuminates the often-complicated relationship between religion and justice. We all have an auntie who consistently answers the question "How are you?" with "Blessed," and says the Black Lives Matter activists need to pull up their pants and get out of the street. And her leather-bound Bible is full of verses that excuse earthly injustice and encourage the oppressed to pray for the souls of their oppressors.

> But I tell you, do not resist an evil person. If anyone slaps you on the right cheek, turn to them the other cheek also. . . . You have heard that it was

said, "Love your neighbor and hate your enemy." But I tell you, love your enemies and pray for those who persecute you, that you may be children of your Father in heaven. He causes his sun to rise on the evil and the good, and sends rain on the righteous and the unrighteous. (Matthew 5:39, 43–45, *New International Version*)

But religion has also formed the core of righteous movements and works of art, from Phillis Wheatley's poem "To the Right Honourable William, Earl of Dartmouth," to the formation of the Southern Christian Leadership Conference, to the advancement of the Woke Vote movement. And there are people organizing right now around the idea that faith—combined with good works—is strong enough to push away those who seek to use the word of God to oppress a people.

From the pastor who challenges the prevailing characterization of Christ to a witch who celebrates the divine in us all to the Islam convert who revels in the ways Black Muslims around the world unite, this chapter explores how a connection to the spirit can be a catalyst for change—especially among those who have been disabused of the notion that they have to wait until the afterlife to be free.

~~~~~~~~~

Black Grace Is Not Cheap

Darnell L. Moore

On the morning of August 31, 2014, the pews at St. John's United Church of Christ in northern St. Louis were full. It was the final day of the Black Lives Matter Freedom Ride to Ferguson. At the beginning of that Labor Day weekend, nearly five hundred contemporary freedom riders from across the United States and Canada had arrived to provide support to local organizers. Our presence in the church that morning was a sign of our collective resistance, not a reverent, forbearing acquiescence to extrajudicial killing. Black grace, after all, is not cheap.

The streets of Ferguson were still hot when we arrived. The rage of the local Black activists swelled because one of Ferguson's young, eighteen-year-old Michael Brown Jr., had been fatally shot by White police officer Darren Wilson.

Justice seemed to be an illusion, but local organizers and their allies were determined that there would be no peace in the absence of perceptible, material amends in response to Brown's killing. During one of a few marches held that weekend, it seemed that many of the people in attendance had dispensed with grace. Some of the younger marchers were rightfully angry because not only had their neighbor been killed by a police officer, but his bloodied body had been left in the street on public display under the heat of the summer sun for four hours. They were less interested in offering solemn prayers calling for peace. They wanted Wilson's job. They demanded an end to the abuse and killing of Black people by law enforcement. They were prepared to disrupt a local law enforcement unit whose bloated financial coffers were full because of unjustified and biased fees imposed upon Ferguson's mostly Black population.

But offerings of Black grace, without any hint of justice, are exactly what some church leaders have preached. Biblical scriptures like Ephesians 6:5—"Slaves, be obedient to those who are your masters according to the flesh, with fear and trembling, in the sincerity of your heart, as to Christ"— have been rendered as the calculus for Black servility, and the authoritative proof that enslaved Africans' submission to White slave masters was akin to them submitting to Christ. But these are different, and not so different, times.

Throughout the history of the United States, Black people have been expected to forgive. We have been asked to extend charity in advance of the "freedom dreams" so many Christian leaders preach as manifested realities to be experienced in heaven only. Forget the police shootings and the officers who kill Black people with impunity. Forget the incessant conditions of overpolicing, surveillance, and incarceration in Black communities—whether rural, urban, or suburban. Forget the economic policies and voting systems that continue to disenfranchise Black people. Forget housing markets established to diminish Black ownership and economic well-being, the urban renewal plans created to keep Black people locked within ghettoized zones and gentrification and educational inequity. Forget White racists marching under the banner of Confederate flags on Southern streets and a sitting White racist president who called Black nations "shithole" countries while refusing to call White nationalists racists.

In some ways, the "when we all get to heaven" understanding of justice makes sense. Black preachers' insistence that we will someday ascend to a far-off plane beyond our present world that's free of anti-Black racism, economic disparity, and social death is a commentary on the state of our present realities. It's their way of saying, "Shit ain't right in our here and now." Yet any theology that is disconnected from the material evils impaling Black bodies, Black communities, Black life, is not indicative of liberation at all.

The message we received during that weekend in St. John's was different. What was preached was not the typical word offered during Sunday morning services for Black Christians, who are often imagined as too benign or caricatured as people befuddled by a colonizer's theology.

Rev. Starsky Wilson preached a sermon titled "The Politics of Jesus." He did not sermonize a White Jesus, the Christ with blue eyes and blond hair deemed divine in Renaissance paintings and the racist imagination. There was no preaching of a gospel that demands that the downtrodden, Black people included, throw up weary hands and resign themselves to the torment meted out by individual actors and anti-Black institutions who do them harm. His sermon was peppered with words like "radical" and "revolutionary," not "moderation" and "restrained."

The state, in Wilson's estimation, should be the target of Ferguson organizers' critique. Whether the cross, the lynching tree, the bullet from a police officer's gun, or the unjust judgment of a court, the Black body, like Christ's tortured frame, figures almost always as an enfleshed target at which the state and White racist vigilantes (and sometimes they are one and the same) aim their weapons. And as the congregation of the affected leapt from seats, swayed arms in the air, and cried out affirmations, it was clear to me that the spiritual pulse of this particular iteration of a long-standing movement for Black lives, like freedom struggles of the past, would be one electrified by a fierce rejection of the status quo, not tamped down into submission.

The movement for Black lives has presented contemporary Black churches and professed Christians with a necessary task, namely, a push to reconsider the contexts of a faith system steeped in patriarchy, sexism, militarism, xenophobia, rape culture, homophobia, Zionism, and anti-Blackness. Black people have critiqued dogmatic, anti-Black Christian theologies that have been used to douse Black rage in the past. But now it is time to consider the ways in which some churches have perpetuated perverted ideas of grace— the type of twisted, unmerited favor granted by some Black Christians who prefer praising Jesus alongside racist rape apologists like Donald Trump and Mike Pence while condemning and disposing of other Black people.

In the past, too many of the organizers had been told by some Black Christian leader that Black feminism, transness, and queerness, our liberated gender expressions, our unconventional Black politics, our roots in African traditional religions, our disbelief in deities, our lack of faith in the state, the ways we love, the ways we fuck, the ways we resist, are all counter-Christian. Some leaders have even preached that "hell" would be the lot of many of the Black activists in that sanctuary because of their beliefs, political views, or ways of being.

The Black people assembled in St. John's that Labor Day weekend showed up because of their profound love for Black people. The sermon, which was emblematic of the politics of the people, insisted that we must fight for liberation for *all* Black people—even those who have preached words of hate condemning us. The appeal to resist the lure of Black disposability was, to me, Black grace as practice.

Black people must never do to each other what the system does to us, and we must never acquiesce to the iniquity, the evil, the collective sin, that is White supremacy. Black grace is expensive. And its cost is the end of the violences that do us harm. Its consequences are transformative justice and a remaking of the world as we know it. And it won't be granted for White tears. Or White guilt. Or White self-invested liberalism. But for Black freedom.

Darnell L. Moore is a journalist and the author of *No Ashes in the Fire: Coming of Age Black and Free in America.*

~~~~~~~~~~

> **I fight White supremacy by being Black as fuck and staring White people in the eyes while I do it.**
>
> —Erica Young, administrator

~~~~~~~~~~

What Matters Is What Is True

Haylin Belay

You are a being of immense power. So am I.

"Magic" and "witchcraft" are umbrella terms used to describe a diverse collection of religions, belief systems, spiritual practices, and superstitions. Some of these systems, like santeria and voodoo, are culturally bound, developed by specific groups. Others, like wicca, cobble together existing practices from various disciplines, philosophies, and ideologies and codify them into a single dogma. Some forms of witchcraft involve god, goddess, or saint worship; some are highly structured, with clear hierarchies of power; some are both of these things; and some are neither. My witchcraft is solitary, nondogmatic, nontheistic, and highly eclectic. But it is only one of many ways to be a witch.

There is one unifying thread that ties all of these beliefs and practices to magic. Imagine that there is a universal energy outside of our current scientific apprehension that helps to shape our world. You can envision that energy as a named deity or group of deities, as color, as light, as feeling; I personally see it as the divine. When we brush up against this energy, we often describe it as fate, synchronicity, or "the universe."

To believe in magic is to believe that in our mundane world—where the things we can see, feel, measure, and touch reside—the divine is ever-present, explaining the inexplicable. Most importantly, the divine is present in individuals. To believe in witchcraft is to believe that, with intention, we can intuitively access our personal divinity and harness that energy to enact change in the world on both the energetic and mundane levels. In this imagination, in this belief, you are a being of immense power, and so am I.

Whether I'm on a first date, chatting with coworkers, or mingling at a cocktail party, people invariably ask the same question when I describe myself as a witch: "Do you think it's *real*?" To which I reply: "It doesn't matter if it's real, it matters that it's *true*."

And it is. Witchcraft is one of the most true things that I have found—not only as a spiritual practice but as a political one, a reclamation of my personal power as a woman, a Black person, a Black woman.

There is a mundane argument for the "reality" of witchcraft. The antimicrobial, antibacterial, and adaptogenic properties of basil are well documented by science, for example, and the reality that many cultures worldwide have used basil as an herb of protection and healing suggests that the medicine and magic of our herbalist ancestors had some basis in "scientific fact." Similarly, research on mindfulness seems to support the idea that mantra, meditation, and prayer—intentional thought—can have a profound effect on our emotional, mental, and physical well-being.

But the, well, *magic* of magic is that it does not need to be rationally explained to be true. The "validation" of herbalist and spiritual practices of centuries past means little to its historical and present-day practitioners. Much in the same way, sociological and psychological studies "documenting" the weathering effects of racist microaggressions, or "revealing" the challenges that Black bodies face, mean very little to Black people, who know and feel these things to be true. A woman who has been abused by men does not need incontrovertible proof of a man's character to recognize the way she feels in her body when she is around a man who is untrustworthy. This is what we call intuition: when we do not need something external to prove to us what we know to be true.

Whether or not you consider yourself magical, or a witch, or even esoterically inclined, you have intuition. It is the gut sense that tells us truths our conscious mind alone cannot explain. These feelings also have a basis in scientific fact, in the cranial nerves and autonomic nervous system, but you do not need me or anyone else to explain to you that it is true. You are a being of immense power, and so am I.

I had been doing magic for a long time before I ever called myself a witch. Not just doing it—I was steeped in it, though no one ever called it that. When I was a child, my nineteen-year-old mother took me to an Eastern Orthodox Church whose practice approximated the tradition she was raised in back home in Ethiopia, the most ancient Christian empire. In that church, shrouded in thick incense and golden ornaments, I learned about God, sin, and ritual. God and sin never followed me home—those concepts lived in the church, where sermons about harlots and the evil of single motherhood eventually drove us out. But ritual was everywhere around me, like the very air I breathed, or the water of the womb.

Ritual was the way my mother walked around the house roasting coffee beans, allowing guests to waft the smoke into their faces, to cleanse their bodies with the rich and comforting smell. Ritual was the way my mother laid her hands on my belly, or my head, wherever it hurt, to "take the sickness out" of me. Her hands were a better remedy than any pill or ointment. They held the power of intention and the power of my mother—the greatest power my child's mind could imagine.

One of the most important sites of ritual in my young life was the kitchen. It was there that my mother poured homemade *kibbe* and love into clay pots and served up a platter of *injera* and *wot* for the household to share, always eating it with our right hands. It was where we fed each other *gursha*, the Amharic word for the heaping handful of food that friends, family members, and loved ones feed each other, hand to mouth, as a sign of love, respect, and devotion. Feeding someone, nourishing their body, is the purest and simplest act of love.

For most of my life, my mother was a God-fearing woman who would have collapsed to her knees in prayer if she ever heard her daughter say she was practicing magic. Now she holds her love for God and her clairvoyant visions in the same body, without apology, because she knows her intuition is of God and from God. Much as I bought my first Tarot deck in the aftermath of an abusive relationship, seeking a way to rebuild my sense of self and worth, my mother's transformation happened after she was released from a marriage that robbed her of agency. In her rejection of that oppression, she embraced the personhood that she had been denied for decades.

So it is not surprising to me that our paths wound in the same direction; in fact, my mother is the one who taught me magic. After all, what is magic if not the way that a kiss on the forehead becomes a seal of protection? What is magic if not the way that food from my own hand tastes different from the food my mother placed lovingly into my mouth? These physical motions took on special significance because of their intention, because when a human being acts in the mundane realm, their intention ripples through the energetic world. That ripple is magic.

For me, claiming the name of "witch" is an active reclamation of the ways of knowing and being that were denied to me by White supremacy, by patriarchy, by capitalism, by abuse on institutional, interpersonal, internalized, and ideological levels. To call myself a witch is to call myself a being of power, to honor the ways in which I know things and my capacity to effect change in my world. My practice brings me closer to the intuition that systems of oppression have sought to beat out of me. It helps me to heal my own personal trauma, my familial trauma, the intergenerational trauma and mass-scale gaslighting that fights daily to splinter my spirit and the spirits of people who look like me.

On a functional level, it helps me get through my day. Ritualizing my own self-care (cleaning becomes a ritual of cleansing and protection, bathing becomes a spell for calling in self-love and acceptance) helps me maintain my physical body—the body I have been told, implicitly and explicitly, is only useful for giving pleasure and receiving degradation from others. When I imagine my body as a vessel for my divinity, my humanness, I reclaim myself. They tell me Black bodies are worthless; I tell them this Black body is sacred.

On a spiritual level, it helps me heal and find purpose. Centering my own intuition, my own pleasure, my own boundaries, as not only parts of myself but parts of myself that are undeniably divine shows me a path forward when the path behind me is littered with reasons I am wrong and do not matter. Every time I come to my altar space and craft spells with intention, I remind myself that I am a being of divinity, a divinity beyond apprehension, and that no one and no thing can take that from me. What they say about me, about us, isn't true. *This* is true.

I am a being of immense power. So are you.

Haylin Belay is a sex educator, holistic health expert, public speaker, and witch living and working in New York City.

~~~~~~~~~

Pastor Michael McBride on the European Bastardization of Jesus and Why We All Need to Stop Aspiring to Whiteness If We Are to Be Free

As the lead pastor at The Way Christian Center in Berkeley, California, and the director of PICO National Network's Live Free Campaign to end mass criminalization and gun violence, Pastor Michael McBride spends his days attacking White supremacy from the pulpit *and* on the streets. He was on the front lines in Ferguson following the death of Michael Brown; cofounded New Nation Rising, which operates a political action committee that supports the strategic engagement of young Black religious voters across the country; and helped create the Woke Vote program, which mobilized Black folks in Alabama to save the state from an alleged sexual predator.

In this talk with Kenrya, Pastor Mike, as he's known, shares the conversation that forever changed his practice, the ways the American empire hijacks the Jesus he serves, and why the world needs to stop reaching for Whiteness if we all are to be free.

In one sentence, what do you do?

I organize faith leaders and people of faith to dismantle White supremacy and structural racism through the power of representing voices and practices.

What's your origin story as a pastor?

Well, our family is four generations of Holiness Pentecostal Christians, and we have a deep tradition of ministry in our family. When I was born, there were certain words of prophecy—or at least encouragement—that I would continue in that projection of ministry. I was called into the ministry at the age of sixteen, licensed around twenty-one or twenty-two, had my master's of divinity at the age of twenty-nine, and started pastoring at the age of thirty. My ministry vision was honed and shaped out of an experience of injustice and violence, at the hand of the police, and certainly pastoral care, engaging with congregation members and communities that were experiencing perpetual violence at the hands of the state. All of those things informed my ministry call. My theological formation at Duke helped to create a "theo-practice"—both theology and practices that are liberatory. It helps to inform much of the work that we do.

Now tell me your story as a racial justice organizer. It sounds as if they overlap.

I would say that my racial justice lens, and tipping point, came when I was a youth pastor in 1999. I was physically and sexually assaulted by two White police officers while I was in Bible college. That experience crystallized the need for my ministry to be about more than just saving souls. I was moved by my own abuse at the hands of the police, but also by the testimonies of the young people in my congregation who told me that it happened to them all the time. And when I asked why they had never mentioned it to me, they said they didn't believe that this part of their lives was something to bring into the church.

That conversation was just as disjointing as my experience with the police, as I realized that my young people could trust me with their souls, but they couldn't trust me with their bodies. It really forced me to have a totally different orientation as to my responsibility as both a survivor of police violence and a minister. That catalyzed me to enroll in Duke Divinity School, and it introduced me to a number of powerful mentors and theologians who had a history of Black resistance and theological reflection that continues to inform the way I imagine ministry.

Why do you think they didn't feel that church was a place to bring their concerns?

They didn't see us actively addressing it from the pulpit. Most of our conversations were around personal responsibility. We had about a hundred young people showing up regularly, so it wasn't as if the space wasn't welcoming for them. But we sent both implicit and explicit messages that what happened outside the church was not something that we put a priority on addressing. What we were really trying to address was their personal, moral formation—maybe building resilience for whatever came their way. But the idea that we would try to change the actual realities of their day-to-day lives—much less the systems that guide them—I would say, in hindsight, was totally absent from my ministry practice and vision. They obviously understood that, and it forced us to think differently about who had power and what that power could be used to accomplish.

I once heard you paraphrase Black theologian James Cone as saying, "Too often, American Christianity has become comfortable being a chaplain to White supremacy." What does that mean to you?

The United States has figured out a way to bend a false interpretation of Christianity to undergird, and make sense of, a logic of White supremacy and racial hierarchy. It means that they turned Jesus of scripture into a champion of empire. The Jesus who was actually murdered by the state, they turned that Jesus into a war hero who wants to lead imperialistic projects all across the globe. I think Cone rightly named White supremacy as a project of the American Empire, which requires religious underpinnings to help it make moral and political sense. Too often the church has allowed itself to be seduced by that project. The Black church serves as a departure from that.

Now, of course, the Black church is imperfect. We still have so much growing and learning to do around issues of misogyny and gender, around justice and LGBTQ issues, and making sure we're resisting and critiquing capitalism and racial hierarchy. But I think it's an enduring institution that deserves the continued investment of Black people because it continues to be a life-giving place. I hope that's our biggest legacy: reintroducing a vital institution for Black people to continue to draw moral, spiritual, political, and cultural power from.

What's the biggest misconception that people have about the Jesus that you serve?

The Jesus I serve is a dark-skinned Palestinian Jew who was born to an unwed teenage mother in the 'hood of His day called Nazareth. He was unjustly arrested, racially profiled, and convicted for crimes that He did not commit, and was killed by the Roman Empire of His day. That Jesus is a Jesus who sides with the poor and dispossessed; that Jesus is a liberator of the soul and the body; that Jesus is never siding with the rich, the powerful, the elite; that Jesus offers salvation to all who would renounce the ways of oppressive death and dominion. The Jesus that *I* serve says, "I've come to disrupt, I've come to confront." The Jesus that I serve is one who is not silent in the face of oppression. That Jesus is very self-sacrificial and puts Himself in harm's way, and that Jesus is a victor—He overcomes evil.

How does reaching for Whiteness impact the fight against White supremacy?

Whiteness is a constructed identity in the United States. As people show up to the United States, they have to forgo a certain kind of historical and cultural point of value and try to fit into a destination that leads nowhere. Whiteness, then, robs everyone of their ability to actually be their full person and their full humanity. Because if you're not White, male, wealthy, and Christian, then you're consistently reaching for something you can never become.

I believe that this is the greatest task for faith leaders in this season: to help individuals stop reaching for Whiteness. Even White people have to stop reaching for Whiteness. Because there are a lot of folks who identify as White now who, in this country's history, used to not be considered White. It's a creation that we all have to resist. Only then can we effectively address the systems that oppress us all.

So when we're not resisting, we need to be building, right? What does that freedom look like in your eyes?

I go to images that come out of my faith. The garden is a fascinating frame that is used in scripture. It's a place where there's abundance; a place where there is life; a place where there are notes of tranquility, peace, and interdependence; a place where you feel safe. To me, liberation is about human flourishing. It is about creating systems that do not limit the ability of human beings to flourish, to reach their highest potential. It is not overly punitive. It takes into account that to be human is to also be one who makes mistakes, that to be perfect should not be the prerequisite to experience life. We need systems and modalities and processes for redemption, for second chances. Liberation is where a difference is seen as an asset and not a liability. We need an economic system that is not exploitative. One that is almost utilitarian in a sense that economics are a means to create a common good—not a tool to drive exploitation or hierarchy.

～～～～～

"The Ease of Being" by Xia Gordon (2016)

"This work was an exercise in loosening up and drawing from impulse. I thought about what images I tend to shy away from and why, then I confronted that with drawing. I think a depiction of a Black body existing easefully and comfortably is resistance." —Xia Gordon

Xia Gordon is an illustrator and cartoonist based in Brooklyn, New York. She graduated from the School of Visual Arts and has worked with folks at the *New York Times*, *BuzzFeed*, and *VICE News*.

~~~~~~~

The Pilgrimage
Margari Aziza Hill

We were a spectacle in the Old City of Fez, Morocco: my White classmates, our white-haired professor, and me, a Black woman, straggling behind as we moved through the ancient streets. Someone shouted, "*Belek!* Watch out!" and we moved in time to avoid being knocked over by a delivery man barreling through with his cart. Another "*Belek!*" and we dodged a mule loaded with goods. Bustling residents coagulated at shops and haggled over goods, while others squeezed by, hurrying to their destinations. My classmates' Whiteness drew attention. The children playfully announced our group to shopkeepers ahead, shouting, "*Al-Amerikiyeen!*" My brown skin and long frizzy hair contrasted with that of my classmates, and a Moroccan child ran up to me and asked, "*Anti-Maghribiyyah?* Are you Moroccan?" No, I wasn't Moroccan. And unlike much of the Moroccan population, I didn't grow up as a Muslim. My path to Fez, to learning, and Islam, was intertwined with my struggle to resist White supremacy.

As a teen, like a typical Black hipster from San Jose, I made regular pilgrimages to Oakland. After graduating high school in 1993, I took a trip to the Lakeshore district, where I read two books that changed my life's course.

The first was Chancellor Williams's *The Destruction of African Civilization*. Williams was notedly anti-Muslim in tone, calling the Afro-Berber Almoravid tribes "fanatic" and "semi-barbarous," but his contradictions piqued my interest. The Almoravids established an empire that stretched from Mauritania to Andalusia, and African rulers embraced Islam and tapped into trans-Saharan trade routes. That same day I read Clayborn Carson's *Malcolm X: The FBI File*, in which agents and informants tracked the leader's journey from prison to Africa and the Middle East, where he visited heads of state.

I began wondering what it was about Islam that transformed Malcolm and led him on a journey to transnational liberation. And what roles did trade and Islamic learning play in connecting the three precolonial West African empires: Ghana beginning in the eighth century, thirteenth-century Mali, and the Songhai from the fourteenth through the sixteenth centuries? What did the world look like outside of a system of White supremacy?

I embraced Islam that fall as an act of self-definition and rejection of my internalized racism. Believing in an omnipotent god without human form short-circuited the White god I'd been taught to worship.

Ten years later, I finally graduated from Santa Clara University. In the admissions essays I crafted when I applied to nine graduate programs to study the history of Islam, I wrote about my personal struggles to finish school, as well as my informal and traditional Islamic learning. On Valentine's Day 2004, the director of Stanford University's history department called with news of my acceptance. In preparation for graduate work, I enrolled in a six-week summer program to study Arabic and learn about Morocco. It was my first trip abroad, one that opened up a world beyond books, rhetoric, and semantics.

My experience in Fez gave me a new context to explore being a Black woman of faith—it forms the core of my resistance. Through ritual, communal worship, and movement, my *ziyara*, or pilgrimage, marked a connectedness that shapes all I do. My acts of worship have everything to do with fighting White supremacy, and I am still exploring issues around resistance, faith, racial oppression, and community formation fifteen years later. The oppressed in every Muslim society struggle for liberation through religious interpretation and the creation of new ways of being in community. That includes women like me.

While addressing inequality in Muslim-majority societies, the marginalized among us draw on Islam's antiracism ethos to critique power. I resist by believing, learning, creating, and connecting with others to be free within our communities and in society at large. Working in antiracism education allows me to name the system that seeks to alienate me from my Black female body, my sense of connectedness, and my yearning for transcendence.

Black Muslims in the United States resist anti-Muslim policies and narratives, while addressing anti-Black racism from within *and* outside our faith community. In the years following 9/11, the Federal Bureau of Investigation developed a network of more than fifteen thousand informants, many of whom were tasked with infiltrating an estimated twenty-five hundred mosques.[*]

---

[*] Trevor Aaronson, "The Informants," *Mother Jones,* September/October 2011, https://www.motherjones.com/politics/2011/07/fbi-terrorist-informants/ (accessed April 1, 2018).

Meanwhile, the NYPD mapped out twenty-eight "ancestries of interest" that were all linked to Muslim-majority societies and included "American Black Muslims."* Law enforcement detained my husband for the innocuous act of taking a picture of a train for an art class; the FBI interviewed him at work. We are deeply aware of profiling from the Transportation Security Administration when we travel, we are subject to no-fly lists, and we were even prevented from entering the country under the Muslim ban. Black Muslims also feel the brunt of overpolicing and state violence. The criminalization of Black Muslim communities makes me deeply aware that I live in a White supremacist, Christo-centric society that spends billions to bomb, drone, and surveil people who look like me and pray the same way I do.

From Nabra Hassanen to Stephon Clark, Black Muslim bodies are vulnerable. State policies targeting Muslims embolden White supremacists to commit hate crimes and attack our women. Yet in movement spaces, Black Muslims are often marginalized. And the media erases the role we play on our streets, reaching over us to amplify the voices of non-Black Arab and South Asian activists. My work centers Black Muslims while maintaining a transnational lens that explains how neoliberal policies and the military-prison industrial complex cause mass suffering. I have organized forums, convenings, and Twitter town halls exploring the linkages and exchanges on what we have termed the "Black Muslim Atlantic." Black Muslims bridge continental divides and cross oceans to form a distinct culture. We connect through migration, travel, exchanges of ideas, and borrowing and inspiration in dress, music, and art. We find intertwined roots and routes to connect our struggles. While the criminal justice, national security, and immigration systems target us, we forge shared futures and spaces where we can be free. This has been central to my work in antiracism education.

---

* Matt Apuzzo and Adam Goldman, "The NYPD Division of Un-American Activities," *New York,* August 25, 2013, http://nymag.com/news/features/nypd-demographics-unit-2013-9/ (accessed April 1, 2018).

And the seeds of the embodied work of connecting were sown that day in Fez almost fifteen years ago. As my classmates and I walked with our tour group through neighborhoods that predated Western ascendancy, I felt the full measure of what it meant to be Black outside the United States *and* a Muslim in a Muslim-majority nation. Morocco's ancient palaces and heritage sites evoked an era outside the reach of White supremacy. We wound through old neighborhoods, including the Andalusian area, where the Moors and Jews resettled after their expulsion from Spain in 1492. It wasn't all lost to the Reconquista or French colonialism or neocolonialism. There was still beauty there, even as we faced the crushing effect of neoliberal policies on Black and Brown bodies.

My professor introduced me to a caretaker of the shrine of Saint Ahmed Tijani. French colonial law's mark remained, forbidding non-Muslims from entering mosques. Leaving my classmates behind, I became more than a tourist when I walked alone through that large keyhole-shaped doorway. I became a worshiper.

The space opened into a courtyard with a prayer hall facing east. I went to the fountains to perform my ritual washing to prepare for congregational prayers, and I encountered beautiful West African women with ebony, mahogany, and chestnut skin tones wearing jewel-toned gowns. It was the season for the annual pilgrimage of West Africans to the shrine. One woman assisted me as I clumsily made my ritual ablutions, not from a water faucet like at home, but by dipping a cup and pouring the water over my extremities. I washed the dust away from my face, my arms, and my feet, feeling refreshed after hours in the hot summer sun. We walked to the prayer hall, and the African pilgrims gestured to the tawny and beige Moroccan women. We synchronized to form straight prayer lines, shoulder to shoulder, foot to foot. White supremacy seeks to divide us, but in Fez, those of us who spoke English, French, and Moroccan *Darijah* raised our hands to our shoulders in an act of surrender and said, together, "*Allahu Akbar*, God is the Greatest."

Margari Aziza Hill is cofounder and managing director of Muslim Anti-Racism Collaborative (MuslimARC). An educator and freelance writer, she gives workshops, and lectures about faith and social justice at universities and community centers around the country.

~~~~~~~~~~

I fight White supremacy by expressing and doing what is right, not what is popular.

—Imani Samuels, marketing director

~~~~~~~~~~

Building a New Community
Rev. Dr. Valerie Bridgeman

The sermon that I offer here was preached on March 3, 2018, at Alfred Street Baptist Church in Alexandria, Virginia. As a Hebrew Bible/Old Testament Womanist scholar, I usually preach the Hebrew biblical text, and so I didn't "choose" the text during that third week of Lent, so much as I wrestled with the Revised Common Lectionary text to the point where I could make sense of something that is "common" to people. I mean, even people who don't know the Bible know the Ten Commandments. But for it to be a liberating text of resistance, I needed to put it in the context of a formerly enslaved people who were trying to figure out how to be a liberated community.

Part of the genius of the Black preaching tradition is finding new ways to approach old texts. I find naming the questions, and siding with those who have them (both in the word and outside the word), part of the liberating work of preaching. As I say in the sermon, this particular approach was a first for me. Reading it again, I don't think I would say that they didn't know God in Egypt. I would say that they knew God under the duress of bondage. That's not the same thing, because I believe divine wisdom is with us no matter what. I would also do more resistance of those verses about slavery. If I have a regret for this sermon, *that* is the biggest—I didn't push back in the proclamation moment against the presumption that slavery was a given, or that wives and slaves and donkeys were all property not to be coveted. That needs to be roundly resisted in a new community. That too is the genius of preaching: you get to correct yourself.

I am, in my mind, always destroying and building as I go—by which I mean destroying commonly held beliefs that do not foster anything but pacified religion in order to build bold and bodacious faith that questions and demands dialogical faith. For me, that is the very nature of resistance.

The Sermon

Let's turn our attention now to the text for tonight. We're reading what I believe is familiar to all of you today. It's Exodus 20:1–17. You may not know how familiar it is, but it ought to be familiar to you. Listen, I'm reading from the New Revised Standard Version. See if in the listening of this word you will not hear from God.

"Then God spoke all of these words. I am the Lord your God who brought you out of the land of Egypt, out of the house of slavery. You shall have no other gods before me. You shall not make for yourself an idol whether in the form of anything that is in heaven above or that is on the earth beneath or that is in the water under the earth. You shall not bow down to them or worship them.

"For I the Lord your God, I'm a jealous God, punishing children for the iniquity of parents to the third and the fourth generation of those who reject me, but show a steadfast love to the thousandth generation of those who love me and keep my commandments. You shall not make wrongful use of the name of the Lord your God." (I think the King James says, "You shall not take the name of the Lord your God in vain.")

"For the Lord will not acquit anyone who misuses His name. Remember the Sabbath day and keep it holy. Six days you shall labor and do all your work, but the seventh day is the Sabbath of the Lord your God. You shall not do any work, you, your son, or your daughter, your male or female slave, your livestock, or the alien resident in your towns.

"Well in six days the Lord made a heaven and earth, the sea and all that is in them, but rested the seventh day. Therefore, the Lord blessed the Sabbath and consecrated it. Honor your father and your mother so that your days may be long in the land that the Lord your God has given you. You shall not murder. You shall not commit adultery. You shall not steal. You shall not bear false witness against your neighbor. You shall not covet your neighbor's house. You shall not covet your neighbor's wife or male or female slave or ox or donkey or anything that belongs to your neighbor."

Prayer: God, the lion has roared. Who will not fear? God has spoken. Who can but prophesy? We come again to this time and to these texts, and we ask that you speak a word to the listening of your people so that we may hear what the Spirit is saying to the church. Arrest our attention and help us, oh God, to hear you clearly and to respond to you with our whole hearts, our whole lives. I pray this in the name of all that's holy, in the presence of all of our ancestors, and in the strong name of Jesus. And the people of God say amen.

You may be seated.

Now I know you know these words as the Ten Commandments. You may have heard them called the Decalogue. My Jewish friends call them the Ten Sayings or the Ten Matters. But it turns out that if you really read this text closely, there are really only three things in the text. Before I tell you what they are, I want to back up in time and take you back to before these words were spoken.

They are standing right now at Mount Sinai, but before they get to Mount Sinai, you may remember that they had been in bondage in Egypt. These ancient Israelites who make their way—three months after the last plague, standing at Mount Sinai—for generations had been told that they would be delivered from Egypt.

They had heard from their parents that there was a God who listened to their prayers and loved them. But imagine, if you will, how many generations you are in and people are still saying, "God will deliver us." And you are now the fortieth generation. The God of your parents, Abraham and Isaac and Jacob, and the women who came along with them.

Not just their wives but their second wives and their concubines, and everyone that they gave birth to, had been told that God would give them a land of their own. And had been told that they would live in freedom, but it's been four hundred years. And they had not heard from God. And it wasn't for lack of trying, for the scripture says that they had cried out to God many times and that they had cried out to God under the burden of slavery. That in the heat of the day and under the whip, they had cried out to God. They had said the prayers that their parents had taught them. They had cried out to God.

I don't know, maybe you know something about this. We have domesticated this text and we have made it easy. We make it sound good that they've come so quickly and so easily to Mount Sinai, but it had been four hundred years of crying out to God.

As far as they could tell, the heavens were brass, the heavens were silent. God was not listening to them. They didn't know, they didn't know that Moses would one day go and run into God out in Midian. They didn't know, while they were crying out, that the murderer Moses would become the deliverer. They didn't know.

In fact, if you remember the story right, they didn't even like Moses. They didn't trust him. It is not uncommon that the people that God lifts up to lead us are often folk that we don't know whether we're going to trust them or not. That's not uncommon, but it had been years. And so, when Moses showed up and said that "the God of your ancestors has spoken to me," and says to go and "set you free" and that "I'm going to go to Pharaoh on your behalf," they were like, "We don't know this God." Think about that. The people who had been crying out to God did not know the God they were crying out to.

And so, you know the story: There were plagues and there was praying; and there were plagues and there was praying; and finally, on that last dreadful plague where death overtook the land, they were set free to run for their lives. Oh, I know they plundered the people, including taking some of the people's slaves. God didn't say nothing to them about taking nobody's slaves, but they did. Because you understand that when you are under oppression, the only thing you know is how to oppress. And so they had learned from Pharaoh that they needed some slaves.

It didn't occur to them that they could build the community where everybody was free. It didn't occur to them because they had been under slavery. You learn what you have been under. You learn that. And so they took slaves and they took bangles and bobbles and they took animals and they went running for their lives.

They didn't go skipping out of Egypt. They weren't sure what Pharaoh was going to do and they were right to not trust Pharaoh because the next morning they found themselves between Pharaoh and the Reed Sea,* and they needed a way out of no way to survive. They needed a path through the waters, an escape route. I really want you to get a picture, a sense of what they must have felt: slaves running for their lives and Pharaoh on their tracks, right? Like you really have to understand, because I think we have domesticated this text so much that we can't feel the terror that they felt.

And so there they are at the Reed Sea and Moses is hearing from God, but they are hearing nothing. And they are looking at Moses like, "It would have been better to die, we were going to die in Egypt anyhow, but now you gonna bring us out here in the middle of nowhere." And I know, I know we're so saved that we say we would have never said that, but I'm with them. I'm with them. They don't know. It's been four hundred years. They have not heard God speak. They've only heard the stories of how God works.

Maybe it works like this in your life: your grandmama, your mama, your daddy, your granddaddy, your auntie, and your uncle, they all got great

---

* As a Hebrew Bible scholar, I go with the dominant text and not the misreading from the King James Version that people are accustomed to. Thus, I always call it the "Reed Sea" because the words frequently translated as "Red Sea," *yum suph,* mean "sea of reeds."

stories of how God has been in their life, but here you are in your twenties and thirties and forties and you ain't never heard God say nothing.

And life has been hard for you. "Life ain't been no crystal stair." And you smile at Thanksgiving dinner while they're telling those stories. But in your mind, you are like, *If God loves us so much, how come? How come?* Four hundred years and all they had were the stories of God. And then God shows up. Yes, God shows up.

Three months after this deliverance, they have had to eat manna in the wilderness. Manna, you may know, means "What is it?" It is not anything deep. Like they actually asked, "What is this?" There's no deep revelation in it. They were just like, "What is this?" Moses was like, "Y'all complaining about food, I've given you food. Eat the food." Bread. The Psalmist would later call it the bread of angels. But they didn't know anything about what angels ate. It was just something on the ground that they had never seen. It didn't look like the onions and the leeks of Egypt that they were familiar with. It didn't look like something they knew what it was. You all know what it's like when you are in a situation where God is doing something new and it doesn't look like nothing you've ever seen. You are yourself, running around going, "What is it?" So, "What is it?"

And then they got thirsty and they were like, "You brought us out here to die." Now I know we've got hindsight, so we're like, "We would have never done that because God had given them manna from heaven. We would have known that God will still give us water from the rock." Nooooo.

I grew up in Alabama. When it hits 105 and you count the days in hundreds, not in, you know—we're on day five, we're on day forty of 100-plus degrees. If anybody grew up in the South, you know what I'm talking about. You're like—water is better than most anything else. (I can't say what I was really thinking. But use your sanctified imagination—or not sanctified!)

They had manna, and now they were thirsty, then God provided water. All of this happens in three months and now. Now. They are standing at Mount Sinai, the place that Moses said that God was going to bring them, to bring them to worship, and to hear from God. And they actually hear from God and it's terrifying.

Most of us—if we tell the whole truth—want a mediated voice from God. We want somebody else to speak on God's behalf. We do not want to hear from God ourselves, and I ain't mad at you. Let me just say, I'm not mad at you about that because the voice of God terrified them. Terrified them.

And what God spoke was literally three things. I know it's ten, but it's really three. The first thing God says, "No other gods. Don't make graven images, don't take my name in vain." That's one thing that we made into three.

Basically, God says, "Get to know me. I know you don't know me. I know you know *about* me. I know you have heard about me. I know you've got stories about me, but what I really want is for you to get to know me. I don't want you to talk prepositionally about who I am. I really want you to get to know me. I'm the God who brought you out of Egypt. I am the God who bore you up on eagle's wings. I am the God who brought you onto myself. Get to know me."

The first part of the Ten Commandments, the first three, are "get to know me." Get to know me. I don't know where you are in your journey and maybe your faith is still tethered to somebody else's story of how God is, but God is inviting you to get to know God for yourself.

My pastor when I was growing up used to like to say—growing up in both the Baptist and the Holiness church I was really confused—but let me just say, I believed this. My Holiness growing-up pastor used to say to us, "God has no grandchildren. God only has children."

You get what he's saying? That our faith is not inherited like we inherit money. Our faith is not inherited like we inherit the quilt that our grandmother is handing down to us. What we get to know about God we have to get to know for ourselves. "Don't put anybody else in front of me, get to know me for yourself."

We like mediated space between us and God. Sometimes we mediate that space with drinks, sometimes we mediate that space with sex, sometimes we mediate that space with the work we do, sometimes we mediate that space with our family and our friends. But God is saying, "I want some unmediated space between me and you."

"Get to know me. Get to know me." God knew, God knew, God understood that, all those years in bondage, what they knew about God was really kind of fantastical in their mind. They had not seen, they had not heard for themselves. They had not experienced God for themselves. They had prayed, but they had not had experiences.

And maybe they had assigned to some other deities, some other entities, some other energy, what only belonged to God. Maybe you are doing some of that yourself. Maybe the church is doing some of that. The way in which we in community find a way to mediate between us and God. Get to know me for yourself.

The second thing that's in this text that literally, before I started trying to think about this sermon for us, I had missed—the second thing is get to loving yourself. Now I know you don't think it's there because it doesn't say that, but what it says is observe the Sabbath and keep it holy. Six days God worked and did everything and then rested.

God theologized rest, otherwise known as self-care. God theologized for them self-care. Do it because I do it. Do it because I did it. You need to learn to love yourself enough to rest. Now imagine being a slave where you worked eighteen to twenty hours a day every day and you never got a Sabbath, and to hear at Mount Sinai, "Take a rest." You deserve to rest. You deserve it because the God who called you created you and created rest.

Imagine what it's like. Sister Andrea James helped us today when we were talking about women and girls in incarceration and she talked about how, when mothers get out of jail, that the first thing they want to do for a long time is sleep. Because they have spent all that time guarding themselves against sexual assault and physical assault and working from sunup to sundown in our carceral state and what they want is rest.

And how about God wants that for them. And God wants that for us. So, if you find yourself working so hard that you can't think, you are not loving yourself and God calls us, in these words, to love ourselves with rest. And theologizes it; God theologizes it. "I did it. I did it. I did it, and if you get to know me like I'm telling you to get to know me, you will understand that getting to know me means I want you to rest like I rested." You all with me? Get to rest.

And then the third thing that's here is pretty obvious, which is love your neighbor. Love God, love yourself, love your neighbor. That's it. It ain't that deep. It really is not that deep. How do I know that God is calling you to love your neighbor?

Well, honor your father and your mother: those are the nearest neighbors you've got. Your close kinfolk, the people that you've got to live with every day, they are the hardest people to love. Go on and say amen, everybody, so won't nobody feel bad. Your nearest kin are the hardest ones to honor and treat right.

I remember one time my mother, somebody was telling her, "Oh, Mrs. Bridgeman, you would have been so proud of your daughter." And she was telling her what I'd done. And my mother—as only my mother could, may she rest in peace—said, "Are we talking about the same Valerie?" You know, because you do right out in public.

Your parents have taught you to act like you got some home training. You better act like you know what your name is. These are the things I grew up with. You better remember who your mama is. So when you went out in public, you took that with you. But you didn't always act as well at home as you did in public. Okay, well, *I* didn't always act as well.

Some of you are better than me in this area, so maybe you have always been just as good at home as you are out in public. Well, for me and my house and my children when they . . . the notion of longevity connected to honoring our parents . . . of course it is a part of their culture that you honor the elders, you honor your parents, but it is also the way in which you monitor your regrets and your resentments.

When we honor people, we learn how not to hold on to resentments and regrets. Some of us are dying from the inside right now because we are still holding something over the head of our parents or over the head of our children, over the head of our siblings. Something they did and they have long forgotten, but you are still nursing that thing and not honoring them.

Learn to love your nearest neighbor. The rest of it is pretty self-evident. Don't kill nobody. I don't think I need to say anything else about those. Please don't do it. Stop touching people! Don't do it. Just don't do it. This adultery piece needs a little bit of explication. Don't get quiet. I used to worry about this in the Decalogue, not because I think you should commit adultery, not that, but because I know us.

We always reduce things to sex. But Professor Esther Acolatse, who teaches pastoral theology—now at the University of Toronto, used to be at Duke—says, "Adultery is wrong, not because of sex." I know that's the way that we have filtered it out, particularly in the Pauline epistles, but it's wrong because of the way in which it breaks company in community.

It's wrong because of what it does, not just to the two people involved and their spouses or partners, but to everybody connected in that eventually, it hurts everyone. I hope I don't tell too much of this story so that the person recognizes themselves, but if they do, you do the deed . . . I'm just saying.

This brother had not one, not two, not three, but four on-the-side chicks. Now, I don't even know how they do that. Don't tell me, I don't want to know, because then I'm going to wonder how you know. And I don't want to have that in my head! Right? And his children knew. His wife suspected a couple, but she didn't know about all of them. The children knew. And other people knew, most specifically, his boys knew.

And he had a heart attack, not at home. Yeah, I see you all got a picture. And let's just say he was not dressed for the ER, right? So he gets to the ER and dies, and they called his next of kin, who is his wife on the paper. Where's his clothes? Where is his car? His boys knew. That broke relationship not just with her and him.

She thought they were his friends and they're her friends too, but they were covering for him. So at the time that she needed them most, she couldn't trust them. It wasn't about the sex. It literally was about the broken community. Sex is incidental. Even if you're really, really good at it, it doesn't take that long. But is it worth what it does to community? (I'm a woman of a certain age, what can I tell you.)

Love God, love God, love God. Get to know God. Love yourself. Rest, rest, rest in the assurance that God loves you, and rest enough to know that you don't have to perform to be loved. And then get some do right in your spirit. And love your neighbors. Treat them well.

This, as it turns out, would become the sum total of the law and the prophets. These words were aspirational, they were not even written in stone at this point. That doesn't happen until four or five chapters later, and even when they are written in stone, the people are so flaky that they get broken.

These words are not written in stone because God knows humans and our propensity to idols and our propensity to try to work our way into being okay. God knows our propensity toward nursing grudges and treating people wrong, but to build a new community, these people stood at Mount Sinai and listened for words that would help them try to figure out what being free folk would look like; what it would take to build a relationship with God and with one another that is beyond the terror and the trials they lived for generations in slavery. These Three Revelations that we call the Ten Commandments—love God, love yourself, love your neighbor—are the foundational building blocks for a new community, a just community. They are words of life to a people fresh out of bondage. They are words for life for us if we are going to build a new community, one built on justice and love. Let's build a new community. May it be so.

Rev. Valerie Bridgeman, PhD, has been ordained for more than forty years and teaches Hebrew Bible and preaching at Methodist Theological School in Ohio. She is an activist, an advocate for human rights, and a member of The Movement for Black Lives.

The Calling

It was the music that brought her back.

Before she was a bishop, Jacquelyn Holland was a little Black girl splitting her time between the Pentecostal church and a home that was ruled by the Pentecostal church. "My mother raised us in the church, and I was taught from a young age how to pray and to believe in God," explains the native of Charlotte, North Carolina. "It was very orthodox. You weren't supposed to listen to any music besides gospel, you weren't supposed to wear pants as a woman, you weren't supposed to party. We basically went to church most of the time—and bowled. We were allowed to bowl for some reason."

She felt a calling even then; her teenage self organized other young people from the church to visit their peers' homes and pray with them. But she was never encouraged to go into the ministry. "Women were able to preach, but we weren't able to be pastors," Holland says. But she *was* encouraged to get married, so she did that at the age of twenty and settled into life as a junior high school teacher and mom of two boys.

Six years later, she separated from her husband, came out as a lesbian, and left her church, despite the constant pull she felt toward the ministry. "In the Pentecostal church, we were taught that to be gay was against God," Holland says. "I never gave up my relationship with God, but I decided I wasn't going to go into ministry because I wasn't going to lie, I wasn't going to be in the closet anymore. If God didn't accept me, there was no reason for me to try," Holland says.

And then came the music.

She started singing with a group called Lavender Light, and it was full of people of color who identified as queer. "When I started singing with the choir, I felt for the first time that I could connect with God and be gay at the same time," she says. Her new family introduced her to the Unity Fellowship Church Movement (UFCM) in 1992. "There, I was taught that God loves everybody—lesbian, gay, bisexual, all people—and that God does not discriminate based on your sexual orientation," she says. Her calling validated, she quickly became assistant pastor in the UFCM's New York City church, and later she started a new congregation across the river in Newark, New Jersey.

These days they put a "Bishop" before her name at UFCM, which describes itself as the "oldest open-and-affirming, progressive Black Church founded to reach primarily Black queer, same gender-loving and LGBT Christians." Founded in a Los Angeles home in 1982, the church now has fifteen sanctuaries dedicated to being a refuge for people fighting for justice under the mantra "God is love and love is for everyone." In her role, Holland helps manage the movement, counseling the pastors, setting policy for the denomination, and making sure it meets its mission.

Her big-picture goal is to create a space that feels inclusive. "Unity is based on this message of love, the love that Jesus talked about, loving God with all your heart and all your mind, and loving your neighbor as yourself," Holland says. "We created these spaces because we were not welcomed in other spaces. But a real, freeing worship experience should be so powerful and so welcoming that *everybody* should feel included. I want my legacy to be one where Jesus's message of love is a lived experience. I want the world to say we made a difference."

~~~~~~~~

QUESTION, ANSWERED

The question we tackle here is: how do you keep the faith?

Akiba

The question "How do you keep the faith?" assumes that I know how to do it. It assumes that I have the strength to resist feeling defensive and exposed about the matter, or that my conscious mind even works this way. I wish I had a less clichéd way to say it, but the jury's still out on faith for me.

How I came to this particular kind of heathendom has all of the markers of growing up Black and "political" in the '70s and '80s. I never, ever, not once looked at that drawing of White Jesus with the flat-ironed blond hair and the Scope-colored eyes and believed that Black folks had any business praying to "Him." That wasn't even Him.

I knew that slavers and other genocidal motherfuckers used some fuck-shit that Ham did eons ago to justify some of humanity's worst crimes.

I grew up saying grace, but a Swahili one that my father and mother created. I was and am Kwanzaa-only. Never did a cross, a tree, or a sugarplum fairy enter our home.

My mother's general theory of humanity is that we are a failed experiment. She often quips that if the people at the Episcopal church she went to as a kid sang better, she might still give it the time of day.

Meanwhile, my poor father has always been uneasy about and, I suspect, resentful of the irreverence my sister and I inherited from our mother, who is hilarious and brilliant and perfect, thank you very much. But at most, he behaved as a closet Christian with an affinity for liberation theology during our formative years.

Still, I am an adult. I have had plenty of opportunities to figure out a practice that cultivates and sustains my spirit, the lynchpin of faith as I understand it. I did try and fail at Buddhism. Islam never called my name. Culturally speaking, Christianity is the default. There's a huge amount of pressure for us to "draw on the faith of our ancestors." We're taught to put the dramatic and mundane savagery of White supremacy in God's hands.

This makes me deeply ambivalent about what the Lord appears to be doing or allowing. I'm embarrassed by this, especially as an African American woman who does actually believe in justice, joy, peace, comfort, growth, and health for my people and most other beings on this planet.

To that end, in my younger years, I tattooed two God-related Adinkra symbols on my back. One means "child of God," which is evidence of my yearning. Another means "the omnipotence of God," which is what it is. What I know for sure is that some Black person in my life is always losing their mom or dad prematurely, getting laid off, getting cancer, burying their child, having a sudden heart attack, being terrorized by police, or trying to push through the trauma of homophobia or sexual violence. Piety does not seem to save them.

I am authentically moved by gospel music like the kind Walter Hawkins, Donny Hathaway, Aretha Franklin, Kelly Price, and Chance the Rapper's cousin Nicole are responsible for. I hear God happening in every brilliant bend and ad lib. I believe that God used Nina Simone to open up the possibility that we might be haughty and angry rather than supplicant in the face of racism. I hear this music and something physical happens to me that I can best describe as a pulsing in my chest and welling at the back of my throat. But when the music stops, I'm right back in my hard head.

Incidentally, I used to sing well enough to solo for my high school gospel choir. They let me onstage despite the fact that I was always marching in the wrong direction. In college, I was in a band, wrote songs every day, and did a few tracks for a girl group. I had a couple of managers and a voice coach who I adored and who died. During my early 2000s stint at *Essence* magazine, a few of us came together and killed "Oh Lord, How Excellent" and the *Sister Act* version of "Joyful, Joyful" at the Time Inc. holiday party.

But then I got sick and somebody (Satan?) marred my voice with an unintentional rasp and a flatness in my lower register. Just like that, one of my most dependable pleasures in life became a reminder of the worst moments in my life.

At this point, it would be helpful for me to be specific about what I mean when I say, "I got sick." What that means is that I am clinically depressed and that this illness has led to what medical professionals politely call "decompensation" and I call "losing my fucking mind for a minute."

I have decompensated twice in my life. The second and last time (because I am never going back there, trust) an auntie who is a Yoruba priestess came up from South Carolina to perform a ritual that would banish the sickness and danger from my soul. She identified my Orisha and told me to start wearing white. She also told me I should come stay in her village for a while, so I could finally get off meds for good. This is not going to happen.

She's not the only loved one who has imagined that a better connection with God would trump my chemical imbalance. One of my exes—a lapsed Muslim with a stunningly self-serving patchwork of practices—told me we could together replace my meds with a spiritual practice that honored the true nature of man and woman.

Another ex, whose religion could best be described as "quasi Five Percenter from Harlem," told me that he could replace my psychotherapist with himself, some sage, and some prayer.

This other dude you actually know: Chew Stick Fuckboi the Third. I did not tell him about my depression because he was too busy being Old Testament about sharing a bed with a woman who was menstruating and "protecting" the kids he had conceived via premarital sex from being dragged to hell by gay serpents.

I believe that everyone except Chew Stick truly meant well. I believe that every Black person blessed enough to know and practice rituals that feed their spirit want everyone else to get this good thing too. We do love each other very much, and that is an act of faith.

I also know that I am blessed by the amazing people who love me, the fact that I can make a decent living, and my suite of great health benefits. No one I am close to has been maimed or murdered. I know in my heart—and from their texts and live-action hinting around—that my good peoples believe in me. One of my girls even gave me a get-well card with "I believe in you!" written inside.

On my low days, I feel sorrow for what I suspect is my chemically determined inability to throw myself into spirit and faith and stay there. On my best days, I meditate on my loved ones and the miracle that is my life. I may be wracked by ambivalence and anger, but I never doubt that my folks have faith in me. If I am ever going to learn how to keep the faith, I will learn it by watching them and loving them back, fiercely.

~~~~~~~

Kenrya

I've always had an interesting relationship with God. As far back as I can remember, I've thought of Him as my homeboy. Brown, with a big 'fro, always listening, even when our conversations are happening in my head. I carry His heart with me (I carry it in my heart), and He gives me comfort, peace, and mixed signals when I'm shady, laughing a little, while also admonishing me to do unto others and all that. Our relationship is the epitome of the definition of faith that has always stuck with me: "Now faith is the substance of things hoped for, the evidence of things not seen" (Hebrews 11:1, *New King James Version*).

But as a child, I worried that wasn't enough. I didn't grow up in the church. We prayed over all our meals and sometimes at night, but I didn't regularly attend worship service until I was old enough to drive myself in our little maroon Dodge Plymouth. By that time, my father was going to his own church, but when I was younger, it seemed he was more interested in sucking up all the knowledge he could get than spending his Sundays on a pew. When Jehovah's Witnesses knocked on our door, not only did my daddy not turn off the television and ignore the door—he invited them in for Bible study and even took us to a meeting at the local Kingdom Hall. He didn't just buy bean pies from the men of the Nation of Islam who stood in traffic selling treats and copies of *The Final Call* to people stopped at the light on Lee and Harvard in Cleveland—he bought cassette tapes of Farrakhan speeches that he played on his hi-fi stereo system on weekends.

We weren't affiliated with a church, but I felt like I was enveloped by God's presence, like our willingness to open our hearts to many ways of worship brought us even closer to the Lord. It made me understand at an early age that spirituality and religion are not the same, that we all have to find our own ways to faith if that's what we desire. But by the time my teenage self joined a citywide gospel choir, I had developed a deep inferiority complex, 'cause teenagers carry around sooooo many fucks. I wasn't well versed in the old hymns of the church, I didn't yet know the "Doxology," and I worried that my lack of concentrated religious training wasn't pleasing to . . . the other kids in the choir.

My perceived otherness made me meek(er), even though back then my soprano was clear and sweet, more than capable of taking on the lead vocal in the latest Kirk Franklin song. It felt like I, the unchurched, hadn't earned the right to sing "Now Behold the Lamb" for the congregation at Antioch Baptist Church.

Some might say I was kinda right.

I had to audition to be invited to join the choir, which meant preparing a song that showcased my voice. My fourteen-year-old self was torn between two songs: Aaliyah's version of the Isley Brothers' "At Your Best" and "Stroke You Up," a song from the girl group Changing Faces that was penned by Robert Kelly and talks about ways to please a penis.

Yo.

I subjected my father to a trial run, where I stood before him and sang both songs so he could help me pick the right one to perform. How this negro kept a straight face, I will never know. "Well, you clearly have a lot of passion when you sing 'Stroke You Up,'" he said when I finished. "But 'At Your Best' is so beautiful."

Clearly, I needed Jesus.

And He has always been there. The reality is, I never imagined that there was an option *not* to keep the faith. Yes, I knew that there were atheists and agnostics out there who didn't subscribe to a higher power of some type. But it never occurred to me to opt out. Not as a young Black girl whose daddy never met an evangelist he didn't like, and certainly not as an adult who has an intimate relationship with both trauma and joy.

When I was twenty-five years old, a very dear friend died in a motorcycle accident. I was devastated. I could barely stay in my skin, sitting up at all hours of the night unable to close my eyes out of fear, working in a darkened office for months because there was no more light for me, holding my breath to see if I could just fade away and not have to confront the hole left in the world. But even in the middle of my grief, I vividly remember thinking, *This would be so much harder if I did not have faith.* If I did not believe that this isn't all that there is. If I did not have a track record of surviving my worst days because God propelled me through them.

Four years later, I took a pregnancy test just before getting in the car for a three-hour drive to a funeral. It was bittersweet, learning that I was carrying new life as we were about to say goodbye to my then-husband's aunt. But I marveled that day—and even on the many, many, many days that I was unbelievably sick during my pregnancy—that God was doing amazing things in my body. I don't know how to make a baby! I mean, I have the sex part down, but the whole dividing cells and creating a brain stem and fingernails and eyelids? Nah, homie, that's not me. And yet. It was happening, every minute of every day in my little retroverted uterus. And she came out of my vagina, y'all. Pale, not crying at first, because the umbilical cord was wrapped around her neck, then wailing until she was placed on my breasts. If that's not evidence that there is a God, I literally don't know what is.

Listen. I have never seen a day where White supremacy didn't impact where I live, the work I do, or the way my child views herself. But I have faith that that day exists. Faith that one day we will only know a world that resembles Wakanda (without all the hoarding of vibranium). Faith that the history books that focus on our time spent enslaved will add new chapters that detail how we successfully demolished the idea of Whiteness and the oppression it has wrought. Faith that a force not seen is ordering our steps toward freedom. Onward.

SIX
YOU CAN'T TELL ME NOTHIN'

The typical telling of why style is so essential to Black survival would begin with the violence of the Middle Passage. It would conjure up brown skin cracked and almost silver with ash, hair matted with dust and dander, clothes too tattered to protect violated bodies from the heat, cold, fleas, and burrs.

Of course, that story—one of strength to be sure—is true. But it is incomplete. Take the magic of our hair. Before the European narcissists kidnapped us and dragged us across the world, we used our cornrows, braids, thread wrapping, and ornaments to communicate to one another who we were. Ayana Byrd and Lori L. Tharps's *Hair Story*, the definitive social history of African American hair, lays it out:

> In the early 15th century, hair functioned as a carrier of messages in most West African societies. The citizens of these societies—including the Wolof, Mende, Mandingo, and Yoruba—were the people who filled the slave ships that sailed to the "New World." Within these cultures, hair was an integral part of a complex language system. Ever since African civilizations bloomed, hairstyles have been used to indicate a person's marital status, age, religion, ethnic identity, wealth, and rank within the community. In some cultures a person's surname could be ascertained simply by examining the hair because each clan had its own unique hairstyle. The hairstyle also served as an indicator of a person's geographic origins.

And of course, our style isn't limited to hair. We put our babies' freshly bathed and oiled bodies into quality garb so that this hostile world won't assume that they are not loved. Our big geometric hats, high heels, and skirt suits are part of how we honor the divine. Steve Harvey suits, Carmelo Anthony suits, and our favorite, Mahershala Ali suits, tell the world that we intend to act good and grown and very sexy. Our shoe game defies reason and sometimes budget, which isn't so great, but it feels great and pleasure is something we deserve.

We also stunt on haters with our cleverness and our pride in our intellect. How many times have you seen that article about Michael Brown, the Black, Houston-based senior who applied to twenty colleges and got free rides from all of them? Who is more wicked with Photoshop than our freelance meme-makers who skillfully mocked the Oakland White woman who called the police on two Black men barbecuing? For us, style is more than capitalist materialism and unhealthy competition. The creators in this chapter show us why.

~~~~~~~~

Michael Arceneaux on Shade as Resistance

Michael Arceneaux is a Houston-born writer for *Elle*, *New York*, the *Guardian*, *Ebony*, and *Complex* and the author of a comedic memoir about being unapologetically Black, gay, and sexual called *I Can't Date Jesus*. Akiba and Kenrya chatted with Arceneaux about the art of employing shade as resistance and why a little disrespect just might save us all.

If you ruled the world and everything in it, what would you change?

Student loans are the bane of my existence. I basically took out a payday loan to go to Howard. So if I ruled, I would start by making higher education free.

What else would you do?

Well, if I could bippity-boppity-boo one thing for everyone, it would be to make them less concerned about what other people think. People forced a lot of stuff on me early on. Now I'm more myself.

So you stopped caring?

Well, a lot of people would call it "no fucks given," but I find that it can be a false premise. We typically care what other people think, no matter what. It's just that we can't let what people think control us. We should just have this kind of openness, this embracing of doing whatever we want. I wish I could be as free as like a Cardi B or Joseline Hernandez. People try to trivialize what they do, but they remind me of people I grew up with. Even though they're broken in some places, they're rewarded for being who they are.

So to take that to the macro level, how can not caring about what other people think help Black people to resist?

Sometimes, when we talk—even if we're talking about ourselves and identity and race—we are being reactive to what White people think. If I ruled the world, I would free Black people from ever having to think about White people in a way that centers them.

How does this play out for you?

If I'm around White gay people and they ask about dating, they want me to talk about it within the context of "White men don't want me. It's sexual racism." Because I'm a Black gay man, they assume that I'm broken and miserable and that I'm walking around so burdened by their prejudices. But I don't give a fuck about White people like that. I'm very much aware of politics and what's going on, but I don't wake up every morning thinking about what White people like or what they're going to do to me.

How did you grow up?

Growing up, I was mostly around Black people and Latinos. I dealt with Latino racism to an extent, but it was just different from having to deal with White racists. So I've always had a Black center. I didn't grow up with money, but I knew that Black people could become doctors and lawyers. So even though I'm the first man in my family to go to college, I didn't think anything was impossible.

You grew up Catholic, right?

Yes. I got approached for the priesthood at twenty by a Black priest in a curly wig! The only things I associated with being gay were "the AIDS" and hell. Literally, that's all I knew. My book is like my education about how to be what I am now: a semiconfident, secure, Colored sissy.

One thing we appreciate about your writing is that you're haughty and petty as fuck.

Am I?

Yes, in the best possible way! Once, after 45 tweeted something late at night, you responded, "Go to bed, thot." You called the president of the United States a thot.

I don't know if I'm petty! I just be talking. I be saying my shit. But I do think how I deal with people like him is very disrespectful. I give him as much respect as he gave the first Black president or as he's given Black people throughout his whole life. Personally, it's cathartic, because I get out my aggression. And I also think it's cathartic for the Black people I'm writing for. I never say his name in my writing. That disrespect is a form of resistance for me, because I don't think he deserves any of our respect.

What made you call a powerful man a thot?

I know there's usually a sex assigned to words like "thot," but I'm a gender-neutral bitch basher. I call men "bitch" a lot. I almost got in a fight with my dad for calling him a bitch. So I treat "thot" the same way. Technically, if you go by the definition, there is no bigger thot than a man who walks around talking about how he grabs people's pussies.

~~~~~~~~

I fight White supremacy each day by living outside of the invisible boundaries of my racial identity.

—Stephen Benson II, police officer

~~~~~~~~

. . . And Look Good While Doing It!
Tai Allen

often fashion marries form with function
it armors the confidence for the coming fights

clean shirts   white sheets
fly suits   ugly blues
slick kicks   pigs' feets

the smart selves dress like history is an ongoing affair
coffee & pray their flesh will stay free of/far from law & weapons

costly threads   shell cases
dry cleaning   steel ceilings
new jordans   smaller checks
                        for schools & potholes
                        makes it bumpy-hard
                        to ease along roads
                        or avoid standing

under dirty-light(posts)
while the pipes
and the lines
are tracking
& chaining
the poor
to potters, plots
& prisons

every avenue & address change, comes with both casual & "good" clothes
the iron stays burning & steaming, some jobs include interviews that outwit
the bosses

african names   day-job voice
black hard shoes   foreign soles
two degrees   good pay means
                        just a wee bit
                        below the mediocre
                        line of the all-americans

getting ready for *work*
has to mean a mirror

                        that smiles
                        nods and approves
when you model turn

Tai Allen is a creative who makes things pretty. His first book of poems is
No Jewels.

~~~~~~~~~

I fight White supremacy by being fabulous.

—Michell Speight, nonprofit chief of staff

~~~~~~~~~

Writer and Editor Penny Wrenn on Making Space Where There Is None

I fight White supremacy by being big Black in my small White town. I fight though I appear not to fight. My weapon is radical self-acceptance, a personal hospitality that lays down the I-am-because-we-are welcome mat of Black reception wherever I enter. I show up—proudly, unselfconsciously, loudly, jauntily—to streets and sidewalks where I've no explicit permission or invitation to be. I turn up my Black Music to drown out the White Supremacy soundtrack of Americana and folk songs on loop. I am an uproarious pedestrian, singing Walter Hawkins's "Thank You" at the top of my lungs and head-nodding Black passersby while running errands. When I'm behind the wheel on windows-down-driving sunny days, my joyful resistance is a bumpin'-ass bangin'-ass Bose sound system reverberating the horns, keys, and bass of "Black Man" from *Songs in the Key of Life*.

In small towns, noise ordinances against loud music and the many other law-enforcing ways of so-called well-meaning White people are the nigger-calling, dog-unleashing, and face-spitting racism of our time. In small towns, the superiority complexes have a way of masquerading as White shame sans atonement, as a fake kind of humility, as piousness in the wake of "well, we tried" failures, as hands-up exasperation that believes it is we who haven't shown up. So with my Black self, not only do I show up, but I show off. Big time.

~~~~~~~~~

Liberation Playlist

DJ Monday Blue

"I resist White supremacy by rejecting the notion that I should be anything other than my whole, unadulterated self; a self of my choice and creation."
—DJ Monday Blue

- ▶ "Black Maybe," Syreeta
- ▶ "Woman of the Ghetto," Marlena Shaw
- ▶ "Otherside of the Game," Erykah Badu
- ▶ "Golden," Jill Scott
- ▶ "Blacks' Magic," Salt-N-Pepa
- ▶ "Pure (Jay's Original Vocal)," Blue Six, featuring Monique Bingham
- ▶ "System," Labelle

Tracy M. Adams, also known as DJ Monday Blue, is a licensed and registered physical therapist by day and a DJ by night. She believes that twirling on the dance floor is as therapeutic as planks.

~~~~~~~~~~

Beverly "Bevy" Smith's Formula for Flyness

Bevy Smith has a long record of subversive fabulosity. In the mid-'90s, when hip-hop was still a subculture, the Harlem native broke ground as *Vibe* magazine's fashion and beauty advertising director. High-end brands were not interested in marketing to audiences they perceived as ghetto. Smith helped change their minds.

She went on to serve as a fashion advertising director at *Rolling Stone*, bringing fashion and hip-hop stars together for *Dinners with Bevy*, co-host Bravo's *Fashion Queens*, host morning satellite radio show *Bevelations*, and co-host *Page Six TV*.

One thing that Smith's résumé may not tell you is that she is a dark-skinned, curvaceous, self-described "Blackity, Black" woman over fifty with short hair. By most measures, she is not supposed to be in the room. So Smith creates the room. In this as-told-to, she offers some of her ingredients.

On Fashion

"I'm from Harlem, and growing up you only had two options. Be fly or be a bum. Either you were at the lowest rung or you were appropriate for business. Business could mean that you were ready for the cookout, or you were ready for a conference room.

"Fashion was a natural interest, as was advertising. So between loving advertising and being innately fly, it was like heaven to get one of my first jobs at a fashion advertising agency."

On White People

"At the firm, I met these magical White people, who became my patrons. Although my parents were raised in the Jim Crow South, I never heard any negativity about White people in my house. Some people grew up with very woke parents. My parents were like, 'Work hard. Take care of your family.' End of fucking story.

"My mother grew up in Durham, North Carolina, in tobacco land and went to work at thirteen. My father grew up in Yemassee, South Carolina. He lost his mother and father very early on and was raised by his aunt. Plus his little sister died of polio. One time I asked my father why he didn't march in the Civil Rights Movement. He was like, 'I was too busy working.' Interestingly, his family never worked for White people.

"My parents were just not concerned about what some White person was doing. I never heard that I had to be two times better to get half as far. I didn't grow up thinking of them having something that I should want."

On Creating an Image

"I would be lying if I said I didn't care when certain people have snubbed me. But mostly I care about whether people see me as nuanced. Some people think I'm just firing on one cylinder. But I am actually very aware. I like a kee-kee and a cackle as much as anybody else. But you have to understand that this is an educated approach. I'm saying something witty, and wit takes intelligence.

"On *Page Six TV*, I'm set up as the queen of the scene, the person who's traveled the world and been a business executive. I didn't tell them that that's how I wanted to be seen; they discerned that fact. I'm never going to do a show that casts me as the single, big Black bitch who says things like, 'If only I could stop eating!' I'm not doing the self-deprecating thing. I think that's a dangerous trope that a lot of Black women over the age of forty who are curvy and dark-skinned fall into on television."

On Self-Determination

"This is so sappy, but I believe that everybody's got their something. You've got to look in the mirror and find it, find what draws other people to you. I do this thing called Life with Vision that's going to be the basis of a self-help book. I'm really trying to teach people to dig deep and figure out what the fuck they really want to do. Most of us are shrouding, hiding, running from what it is that we really want to do, for fear of rejection, failure, and fear, but we're wasting time."

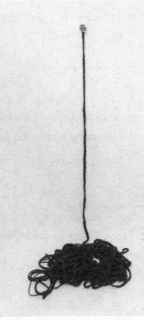

"Kaas 4C" by Diamond Stingily (2017)

Kanekalon hair, knockers, barrettes. 131.9 feet in length

"I want to reconstruct the idea of art for people who grew up in situations similar to my social and economic background. I don't believe art should be intimidating or only for the privileged; it's an outlet for everyone. As a writer and an artist, I want to show how an object can tell a story and share an experience. It makes the experience universal and hopefully through this form of vulnerability creates necessary conversations. I don't think art will save nations, but it *can* reflect current events and ideas and hypothesize the future." —Diamond Stingily

Diamond Stingily is an artist and poet from Chicago, based in Brooklyn, New York. Stingily has exhibited and read at numerous galleries, fairs, and museums, including the Foire Internationale d'Art Contemporain (FIAC)

at the Grand Palais, the New Museum in New York, and the Serpentine
Galleries in London.

~~~~~~~~

**I fight White supremacy by building and supporting
Black political infrastructure in the South.**

—LaTosha Brown, philanthropic strategist

~~~~~~~~

A Poem in Which No Black People Are Dead

Hanif Abdurraqib

here, the bouquet of bullets
instead find a patch of fresh dirt
and just like that,
it is spring again.
in this poem, I speak of the grandmother
but not of time's eager shadow
reaching for her legs.
instead, there is no ancestor
that cannot be touched
by a hand four generations younger.
in this poem, we weaponize joy.
gospel is sung during the week
without burying anyone,
because it is what the living demand.
no one dead looks like anyone's child here,
because there is no one dead here.
there is no child who is not called a child,

even when they have sinned against the earth.

all of our heroes are still living,

their statues bronze and tall on street corners.

jamal from the barbershop. ms. rose who put her foot

in some fried chicken once, and ain't never pulled it out.

here, no one asks for permission to celebrate their living

and so it is:

the night pulls back its black mask and gives way to more black.

the type that turns the speakers up loud and runs into the streets.

the type that don't know how to act,

but ain't here to impress nobody.

a whole city opens its cracked palms and holds the buzzing within.

in this poem, it sounds like a prayer.

not the hushed kind, but the one that arrives on the lips

after a lover trusts you with their undoing.

the kind that comes from a table

where the spades are up and the tea is sweet.

here, everyone black is a church that never burns.

everyone black is the fire themselves.

eternal light, blood still hot and never on the pavement.

if heaven is a place of no pain, let this be heaven.

here, the god of bulletproof rapture is washing a boy's feet in the river.

the boy looks up, summons every black bird from its nest.

commands them to cover the sky.

Hanif Abdurraqib is a poet, essayist, and cultural critic from Columbus, Ohio. His first collection of poems, *The Crown Ain't Worth Much*, was nominated for the Hurston-Wright Legacy Award. His first collection of essays, *They Can't Kill Us Until They Kill Us*, was released in 2017.

QUESTION, ANSWERED

Blackness is obviously lit, but to live as a Black person in America is to be bombarded with the bias and bullshit of other people. Here we consider: how many fucks do you give at this point?

Akiba

I have the rare problem of people believing that I don't give a single fuck when I am out here giving anywhere from 65.789 to 1,000.955 fucks at all times. People who like me describe this misperception with positive words like "direct" and "outspoken." Those who can't stand me err toward "shady" and even "evil."

The truth is, my feelings are easily hurt and I've been trained by life to respond to that pain with anger rather than vulnerability. I don't tend to yell at people (anymore). I now use weaponized sarcasm, which is more efficient, funnier, and lets you give a fuck without admitting it.

My sarcasm serves me well enough in most hostile environments. But it has, at times, foiled my attempts to resist racial microaggressions in a healthy way. In these sunken places, molehills become mountains, puddles become pools, a single cheese curl becomes a 26-ounce barrel of Chex mix.

For instance, I, like many a talented Black girl in publishing, was once underemployed as a freelance fact-checker at predominantly White outlets. Regardless of race or class, fact-checkers are the media version of undertakers. We are the ones who drape bangs over bruised foreheads and speak softly when everyone else is screaming and falling out.

At these workplaces, many of the people I was tasked with correcting behaved like the Molly Ringwald character in *The Breakfast Club*. They weren't exactly mean. They just confused their privilege for talent and thought they were a little better than people who were browner, larger, and less wealthy.

At one place, my coworkers not-so-secretly called the fact-checkers' section of the office "the ghetto." They would also respond to me correcting their errors with bizarre, stupid, or irrelevant utterances. "Have you ever counted your dreadlocks?" one once asked as I tried to get her to focus on percentages. "But you have a swayback!!!" another remarked after I told her that it is physically impossible for 99 percent of grown women to lie flat on the ground with "zero" space between the floor and their backs.

Most of my coworkers weren't conscious of what was happening. But I knew I was being cast as an extra in an early '80s movie where the home-boys spend their days stripping cars and menacing unlucky honkies with switchblades.

Even worse for me were the raised voices, snatched papers, and tears. While I would try to defuse these tantrums with an even tone and a gentle pat to the shoulder, my inner self would declare, "I am a Black girl who was hired to be right. You are a fucking dumbass. Do the math."

That combination of outward calm and inner rage inevitably resulted in, you guessed it, sarcasm. "I know I am soooo annoying," I once heard myself say. "I could totally be wrong. But I'm pretty sure the secretary of state isn't in charge of ordering the president's paper clips." (Okay. I never had to tell anyone something that obvious, but I came very, very close.)

In these moments, the value of barely masking my hostility with "jokes" was that the tantrum-thrower recognized that she was being clowned but couldn't call it out because I hadn't actually said anything wrong. The prob-lem was that I stayed very angry and my feelings were still hurt. Conversa-tions about lipstick and cheese were never really about lipstick and cheese. They were about what Miss Millie did to Sofia on Christmas.

Today I like to think that better employment helps me give fewer fucks about winning stupid power struggles and forgiving microaggressions. I do ac-tually say, "I am hurt," sometimes. But that petty, shady, sharp-tongued, sar-castic girl is always on the ready for a battle of wits. Plus, she tells better stories.

~~~~~~~~

Kenrya

None, maybe.

So here's the thing: I'm a food co-op–shopping, cloth-diapering, aluminum-free deodorant–wearing, birth doula–working hippie. I've led more workshops on the power of vision boarding and daily affirmations than I can count, and I never met a low-effort craft project I didn't like (I'm tired, y'all). So I greeted 2017 crammed into one of my daughter's tiny wooden fold-up chairs so I could sit at her teeny wooden table with poster board and Crayola's finest to create an intention board to guide me through the next twelve months. It's massive and colorful, and it has sections for all the big areas in my life—parenting, career, friends, fun. You get the picture. In the section that details how I want to upgrade my lifestyle, alongside "Be kind to myself" and "Walk by faith," I wrote "Give fewer fucks" (see "Exhibit A").

I made the mistake of telling my bestie, Erica, about my plan to hoard my fucks.

Her response: "Bitch, you don't have any more fucks to give."

She's not wrong. But that's a relatively recent development. I used to have an abundance of fucks. I cared *so* much. I worried about being perceived as aggressive when correcting folks who said my name wrong. I worried that Black men wouldn't find me attractive when I big-chopped and freed myself from Saturdays trapped in the salon waiting for a touch-up. I took great pains to be polite, even when my manners hadn't been earned. I was a miniature version of my daddy, extra concerned about keeping the peace and saying "Yes" even when I wanted to say "Hell, no," like my mama.

My life of caring too much put me in a bad place. I'm empathetic by nature, but when I found myself making a life with a man who was so threatened by my success that our marriage was only comfortable when I dimmed my light, I knew I'd taken this caring thing way too far.

But, as usual, God intervened, and I walked away. Away from the marriage, away from the constant weight of other people's expectations, away from consistently putting myself last. Let me tell you: the confidence that comes with being forced to learn hard lessons is phenomenal. Once I realized how great it felt to be my whole, unrelenting, brilliant self, fretting about what other people thought about me ceased to be an option.

And my recovered glow informs the way I move through the world as a Black woman. I center my work around dismantling White supremacy. I never do that whisper thing—you know what I'm talking about—when talking about race or White people in public. I teach my daughter to value her impressive intellect and her strong body and her natural sweetness and her loud voice and her fluffy hair, and I show her that shrinking and giving a fuck about the opinions of people who wish her harm is neither healthy nor natural.

So why the "maybe"? I figure we're losing the game when we assume we have it beat, so I'm ever-vigilant, lest a fuck creep into my pocket.

SEVEN
SHOW THEM WHO WE ARE

While much attention is paid to gaps and beefs between generations of activists, we know that respecting and learning from our elders is a key tenet of Black survival. Many of our activists, culture-makers, and writers of today have mentors who helped them make sense of history and taught them tactics. We see this cross-generational love in slogans such as "Assata taught me," slang such as "the OG," and our propensity for shouting out everybody who came before us in award speeches.

But more than that, we inherited what seems to be a biological propensity to demand more. More rights. More dignity. More humanity. More freedom. You know, the little things. So we fight, building on the work of those who came before to gain more secure footing for those who will come after. Via interviews with Harry and Gina Belafonte and Ta-Nehisi Coates, a note from former Black Panther Mumia Abu-Jamal, a strategy for resistance inspired by Muhammad Ali, and more, "Show Them Who We Are" explores how cross-generational activism and knowledge-sharing propels our fight.

～～～～～

Harry and Gina Belafonte on Art as a Change Agent and Legacy as a Road Map

To call Harry Belafonte an icon is to tell the truth. The Emmy, Grammy, and Tony Award–winning singer and actor crafted a legendary career that most can only dream about. But it is his commitment to racial justice that truly sets him apart as he leverages his platform—and his wallet—to be, as his friend Rev. Dr. Martin Luther King Jr. once called him, "a key ingredient to the global struggle for freedom and a powerful tactical weapon in the Civil Rights Movement here in America." From creating the spark that became "We Are the World," to pushing for the end of apartheid in South Africa, to working as a UNICEF Goodwill Ambassador, Harry Belafonte has devoted his life to making the world a more just place for Black people.

His work continues via Sankofa.org, the social justice nonprofit he founded with the mission to "elevate the voices of the disenfranchised and promote justice, peace, and equality." One of his three daughters, producer and actress Gina Belafonte, serves as codirector of the organization, where she works every day to extend her father's legacy and use art to break new ground in the fight for racial equity.

Here, Kenrya and Akiba settle in for a conversation with Gina and Mr. B, as the ninety-two-year-old is called, about the role that art plays in activism, the importance of building on the knowledge and work of our ancestors, and what gives them hope in troubled times.

Gina, could you please describe what you do in one sentence?

GB: I'm an artivist.

Can you tell us what that means to you?

GB: I'm an artist who uses my craft and my artistry to create, support, and develop social justice missions. As it relates to Sankofa.org, we're a social justice impact enterprise that's in the business of increasing the power of the arts as a core method to understand and challenge inequity. We work with an incredible community of storytellers, activists, creators, and influencers to amplify whatever is going on in our communities and create content to shift the mainstream narrative to educate, to motivate, and to activate in service of grassroots movements. Whether it's a song, a piece of art, a play, a film, a documentary, or a dance, we work to elevate our issues through the arts and institutionalize the capacity of my father's life and legacy.

Mr. B, what do you see as the difference between what being an activist meant when you were coming up versus now? Do you see the need for a shift in tactics between generations?

HB: Yeah, because I don't think people are distracted with getting the right to vote. That's taken off the table. But the things that we've acquired have left a large menu of things that still need to be done. Right now, we primarily need to hear from women, to follow what women are setting forth as the agenda for how to deal with the issues that face the human family. And not just about gender; women are mothers, women are workers, women are participants in almost all levels of human endeavor, and they face discrimination in all of those areas. Women have got to seize the initiative—as they are doing—to change the agenda.

Awesome. Gina, can you please tell us a bit about how you formed your activist self?

GB: Well, I was conceived and born in activism. It's been integrated in my life, it's part of my generational legacy. I was at marches, strategy meetings, organizing meetings, community rallies, so it's just a part of my DNA. Over time, as I was introduced to many different movements and saw the plight of suffering around the world, I garnered a sensitivity to the human condition. In particular, I was introduced to a young man by the name of Bo Taylor who titled himself as a gang interventionist. He was the facilitator of a life management skills course that dealt with anger management and early childhood conditioning. He worked this program in and out of correctional facilities, and I had the good fortune to meet him and take the course that he facilitated. My classmates and I graduated at the same time as a class of incarcerated brothers, so we chose to graduate together. Seeing the way Bo viewed and interacted with the men and women who were caught up in the system inspired me to work with him. He knew that it was important to elevate their voices and support them when they returned home. That was maybe twenty-five years ago, and I've been a prison abolitionist in service of dismantling the criminal justice system ever since.

Mr. B., we've seen a lot of articles about how you've worked with artists like Jesse Williams and Zendaya. We're really interested in why it's personally important to you to train the next generation of racial justice activists.

HB: It's important to me because I am a victim of those inequities. I mean, I am African American, I am Black, I'm in America, I'm in a society that is quite punitive to people of color, not just Blacks but Native Americans and people of Hispanic descent. There are a lot of inequities, and the specifics of our campaigns were really based on the laws of the state that were severely punitive and unjust and denied us our human rights. We successfully engaged aspects of those denials, but we did not achieve everything. I think this present generation has a responsibility to not only sustain the victories that we gained, but also to add to them.

You've talked a lot about gender, Mr. B, and that's actually something that makes us hopeful. We are wondering what makes you hopeful right now.

HB: Oh, what makes you think I'm hopeful?

Well, sometimes that's all we have.

HB: It's like asking a drowning man, "Can you swim?" I'm not too sure that I've had that much to be hopeful about. On the issues of race, I think our moral space is terribly contaminated. I think America has lost its moral compass, if it ever had one. It was conceived in violence, and it still perpetuates a great deal of violence on us. When you see what's happening in all of the cities where there has been racial tension, when you see all the places in which policemen have taken open season on Black men and the cruel application of the law to Black people, there's a lot to be done. Men have a role to play, but I think women have to become the leaders of how to handle the challenge.

Is there anything that makes you feel hopeful, Gina?

GB: Similarly to my dad, I find that we're in a very depressed space and moment. I think we're in a state of shock and in trauma, as a country. I think our trauma is multigenerational and it's just coming a little bit more to the fore. I think that in some ways, consciously or not, it's even by design that we're in this feeling of impotence. But at the same time, I feel there is a resurgence of a movement and a tempo and a reclamation wanting to make a shift. I think that we're seeing that in spurts, and I'm hopeful that within the next few years we will come together as a large, unified movement. My daughter and her generation make me hopeful that they will not play the same kind of ego games that past generations have fallen to.

So, Mr. B, over the years of being involved in movements, have there been personal or professional costs that you've paid?

HB: I don't know that I paid a price. I think there's a price that Black people pay before we meet the challenge of ending racism, and in meeting it, we minimize the cruelty of it. I faced the challenges with all the tools that were at my disposal, I successfully met them and moved on with my life and my career, dealing with all the obstacles that were put before me. In the final analysis, I have survived all the challenges, I have made some contribution to the progress that people of color have made against racism, and I've made some progress on the issues of peace in times of war and struggle. As a matter of fact, the consequence of my behavior has been most rewarding.

What does freedom for Black people look like to you?

GB: Well, I think there's multiple ways of answering that question because we have such a sordid history. I think freedom for Black people right now is for our country and our world to claim accountability around the egregious violations committed for centuries—since even before Christ—against people of color because of greed. I think that we are a nation that has systemically criminalized people of color in poverty, and I think freedom and liberation will look like those who are oppressors being able to call a thing a thing. They need to become accountable and find truly healthy and loving ways for us to come together for a greater healing and a greater good.

What do you want your legacy to be?

GB: I want my daughter to think I was a good mother. I would also like my legacy to be that I continued legacy, whether it was my own or that of those ancestors who came before us in struggle who tried to find a better way for us.

HB: Really, I have no desire for my legacy. I don't think that very long after I have passed away there will even be a memory that I existed. I have no idea who the great leaders were in the dawning of slavery, though surely there were a lot of people who should have been recognized and made indelible in our nation's history. But we haven't done that, in part because we're denied our space in reality as a people, as a people in struggle, as people who have rights. And that problem is constant because inequities in this nation are constant.

GB: One of the things that I frequently speak about is that we have to, as cultural organizers, affirm the importance of creativity. Creativity is the cornerstone of our liberation; the arts open hearts and minds in ways that straight-up speeches and textbooks cannot. While my father is not concerned so much about his legacy, I am, because I feel that his legacy is a road map and a tool for us to organize. To look at a life such as his is to not only see that one man can make a difference, but to appreciate the way he made a difference: by bringing many people together.

~~~~~~~~~~

I fight White supremacy by collecting and preserving Black history and telling our stories through exhibits.

—Susan L. Hall, museum archivist and curator

~~~~~~~~~~

Journalist, Author, and Former Black Panther Mumia Abu-Jamal Writes about the Long War of Black Resistance from the Cell Where He Is Serving a Life Sentence for the Alleged Murder of a Philadelphia Police Officer

How do you spell resistance? B-L-A-C-K.

From the first captive arrival of Africans upon these North American shores to the present, the very essence of being a Black person in America has meant being in a perpetual state of resistance. There were as many forms of resistance as the imagination provided, and acclaimed twentieth-century historian Herbert Aptheker argued that there were at least 250 slave revolts in the North American territory that we today call the United States. Aptheker's 1943 masterwork, *American Negro Slave Revolts*, broke new ground in American history by telling great tales of resistance that were regarded as in poor taste by respected guild historians.

And the resistance goes on, driven by the exigencies of lives lived under a base oppression. In speech, song, dance, dress, naming, religion, and even in cuisine, we continue to find the resonance of resistance, the frisson of Black identity that reveals the resilience of Africanity in Black life in America.

<p style="text-align:center">~~~~~~~~~</p>

A Path to Black Healing: Cultural Understanding, Mentorship, and the Building of Independent Black Institutions

Haki R. Madhubuti

Framing the Problem

In my short tenure on this earth—seventy-six years—I have experienced the seen and the unseen, the known and the unknown. My people and I have gone through the gates of other people's definitions, imaginations, incarcerations, provocations: enslavement, radical European acculturation, negro, nigga, coon, colored people, Black, YellowBlack, Afro-American, Africans in America, African American, and beyond.

If this is confusing, remember that these are the results of White people's ideas of the nation they built for themselves on the backs of Indigenous and African people and poor White people who have bought into the fiction of White supremacy.

This number includes the millions of African people stolen from their homes, transported thousands of miles in horrid conditions, separated from their families, auctioned and sold off, worked to death, raped, lynched, terrorized, killed for literacy, entrepreneurship, and organizing, redlined, and unfairly incarcerated. All of this is very basic, but not often truthfully taught or discussed nationally.

Within this context, the personal has always been political for Black people in America, whether we as individuals acknowledge it or not. Deep cultural ignorance has been among our primary enemies. If you do not know who you are with certainty, vision, and mission, anybody can and will name you.

Framing a Solution

My life changed measurably when I was nineteen and Africa-cultured mentors came into my life. In all, there were six people in the 1960s who took me in, often including me as an extension of their families. They were:

- ▶ Margaret and Charlie Burroughs, cofounders of the DuSable Museum of African American History
- ▶ Dudley Randall, founder of Broadside Press
- ▶ Hoyt W. Fuller, managing editor of *Negro Digest*, which became *Black World* magazine
- ▶ Barbara Ann Sizemore, first Black head of the Washington, DC, public school system
- ▶ Gwendolyn Brooks, master poet and the first Black person to win the Pulitzer Prize

And although he never mentored me directly, Malcolm X should be included because, by the early '60s, the philosophy of Blackness he articulated gave me a Black fighting voice and consciousness. Likewise, Martin Luther King Jr., by way of Marcus Garvey, Richard Wright, W. E. B. Du Bois, Paul Robeson, and Langston Hughes, will always be foundational in my maturation.

When you seriously measure the development of the success of nations, what universally grabs your attention is the existence of first-rate institutions beyond the family. These institutional structures are educational, business and industry, medical, think tanks (both public and private), and fraternal institutions, among others.

The critical vacuum nationwide that is seldom, if ever, contemplated is the limited number of independent Black institutions (IBIs) functioning positively at every level of Black survival and development. I define an IBI as (1) self-sufficient (primarily receiving monies, aid, and inspiration from its founders) and (2) Black, always with a capital "B" (defining a people's color, culture, consciousness, and location).

IBIs are geared toward solving the problems facing Black people. They supply the people they serve with a sense of identity and answer the questions: *Why do we exist? How did we get to this land? What is our liberation narrative?*

Critical to building successful IBIs is the adoption of a philosophy of African-centeredness that draws on values, bonding traditions, and enlightened attitudes from all of Africa. It is absolutely necessary that our people understand the current struggles and successes of the multiple nations in Africa, so that we don't duplicate the worst of any culture.

I, along with my wife, Dr. Carol D. Lee, and many others who helped to build several institutions in Chicago, have visited multiple African nations. We believe that to be African-centered means to create a philosophical operating worldview from our collective experiences as African people, one that is universal, and one that should be shared with our children. I believe that all mentoring and educational programs targeting Black youth will fall short of their mission if they don't employ curricula deeply rooted in the culture, history, politics, financial realities, and psychology of people of African ancestry.

I know firsthand that this approach works, because we made it happen through the schools I cofounded with a collective of young activists and educators starting in the 1970s. We began with two storefronts on the South Side of Chicago that expanded upon the location of Third World Press (which I founded in 1967) and the Institute of Positive Education (which I cofounded in 1969). We began servicing local young people after school and on the weekend. These were our first liberation schools and the foundation for work we continue to do to this day.

I believe that the traditional American educational experience has failed our people. We have been reacting to the destructive and deadly forces of White world supremacy for hundreds of years. But it is long past the time for reaction; we must be proactive in our own best interest. Our fight begins with ownership of self. People who are in control of their own cultural, financial, political, educational, landmass, and military imperatives are concerned with the healthy version of themselves and, most importantly, their children.

Haki R. Madhubuti is an award-winning poet, essayist, and educator and one of the architects of the Black Arts Movement. He is the founder and publisher of Third World Press and Third World Press Foundation and the author of more than thirty books of poetry and nonfiction, including 2017's *Not Our President: New Directions from the Pushed Out, the Others, and the Clear Majority in Trump's Stolen America.*

~~~~~~~~~~

Liberation Playlist

DJ Junior

"I use music as a tool for resistance in two ways. First, I find solitude in it. Its different genres, vibes, and textures are the soundtrack of my life. Second, I use music for inspiration. Sometimes it's powerful lyrics, other times it's pure musicianship. Either way, it pushes me as I resist, offering me salvation, fuel for my soul, and the will to continue the fight." —DJ Junior, also known as D. Bruce Campbell Jr., PhD

- ▸ "Down on Bended Knee," Helsinki Headnod Convention
- ▸ "Acknowledgement," John Coltrane
- ▸ "I Am the Black Gold of the Sun," Rotary Connection
- ▸ "Don't Pat Me on the Back and Call Me Brother," John W. Anderson Presents Kasandra
- ▸ "Say It Loud I'm Black and I'm Proud," James Brown
- ▸ "To Be Young, Gifted, and Black," Nina Simone
- ▸ "Ego Tripping (there may be a reason why)," Nikki Giovanni
- ▸ "Our Lives Are Shaped by What We Love," Odyssey
- ▸ "Fight the Power," Public Enemy
- ▸ "Alright," Kendrick Lamar
- ▸ "Africa," D'Angelo
- ▸ "Act Won (Things Fall Apart)," The Roots
- ▸ "The Day Women Took Over," Common, featuring BJ the Chicago Kid
- ▸ "Black," IG Culture
- ▸ "K.O.S. (Determination)," Black Star
- ▸ "Truth," Kamasi Washington
- ▸ "Philadelphia Child," Ursula Rucker
- ▸ "Liberation," Outkast
- ▸ "Beautiful Me," Donnie
- ▸ "UMI Says," Mos Def
- ▸ "Beautiful," Joy Jones

D. Bruce Campbell Jr., PhD, is an associate professor in the School of Education at Arcadia University. Dr. Campbell runs the independent record label Record Breakin' Music. He co-hosts *Eavesdrop Radio* in Philadelphia and DJs internationally. He lives outside Philadelphia with his wife and son.

~~~~~~~~~

Writer and Brand Strategist Kierna Mayo on How Her Connection to Our Ancestors Informs Her War Against White Supremacy

I fight White supremacy by consciously loving exactly what it instructs us to hate about ourselves. I admit that I keep in my mind a romantic notion of an essential Blackness—and I use it as armor. As a Black person in the world, as a woman, I feel consigned to fight with everything against the lie of White supremacy, and just plain ole surviving is half of that battle. So I live. My warrior visions (because we are at war) of us as a people metaphysically connected to our ancestors, moved by the drum, and naturally super-brilliant are informed by my actual Black experience. My resistance comes through those pillars. The bedrock of White supremacy is a simple idea taught to children all around the globe: White people are fully human and the rest of us are not. Well, I have resisted that lie since childhood in myriad ways—from rocking my beloved brown baby dolls to creating entire spaces for Black storytelling as an adult professional. Today, as a mother, above all in the fight against White supremacy, I bequeath that guiding spirit of "fuck your lies" to my young. To resist isn't optional in my mind, it is to declare our humanity, and it may be all we got.

<hr />

A Muhammad Ali–Inspired Strategy for Fighting White Supremacy

Shawn Dove

When imagining and executing a strategy for successfully fighting White supremacy, I first acknowledge that we are engaged in a centuries-long fight, and then I immediately think of the best Black fighter who ever lived: my first hero, Muhammad Ali. Fifty years ago, at the time of Rev. Dr. Martin Luther King Jr.'s assassination, the poetic pugilist was completing the first year of a three-year exile and ban from boxing because he refused to enlist in the United States military to fight in the Vietnam War. While I was first drawn to the charismatic glow of Ali because of his floating and stinging exploits in the boxing ring, I came to truly love him when I learned more about his assertions and acts of Black love, unity, and defiance.

Since 2011, the Campaign for Black Male Achievement (CBMA) has organized and facilitated an annual intergenerational gathering at the Muhammad Ali Center in Louisville, Kentucky, called Rumble Young Man, Rumble (RYMR), where leaders gather for renewal, healing, and the exchange of best practices to engage in their collective fight to improve the life outcomes of Black men and boys in America.

In our partnership with the Muhammad Ali Center, we incorporate the six core life principles of The Champ into the curriculum for RYMR gatherings across the country. Those principles—confidence, conviction, dedication, giving, respect, spirituality—provide Rumblers with a framework for leadership development. I believe they can also help us fight White supremacy.

Confidence. Ali won many of his fights before he even stepped into the ring, as he brazenly declared exactly which round his opponent would fall. Why is confidence so important? In his book *Brainwashed: Challenging the Myth of Black Inferiority*, advertising icon Thomas Burrell writes that since slavery, White supremacists have designed and executed the most successful marketing campaign in history by convincing Black people to buy into a product called Black Inferiority, which has been perfected through four centuries of propaganda, policies, and practices where "Blacks were programmatically stripped of their cultural identity and brainwashed into a mindset of Black inferiority." A strong cultural identity and belief in the humanity of Black people is the first telling blow to White supremacy. It counters the pervasive mind-set that we are deserving of less than others, the lie that our humanity is on a lower level than White people's.

Conviction. Fighting White supremacy requires "a firm belief that gives one the courage to stand behind that belief, despite pressure to do otherwise," as our curriculum outlines. We must acknowledge that we are the dreams of our ancestors and that our fight will require a long view and the ability to bounce back from one painful setback after another.

Many people say that the most iconic photograph of Muhammad Ali is the picture of him standing victoriously over a prone Sonny Liston in the first round of their 1965 rematch. However, for me, the most iconic picture is one of him falling to the canvas after taking a vicious left hook to the jaw from Joe Frazier in their first fight, in March 1971. This was Ali's third bout after returning to the ring. He could have easily stayed on the canvas after Frazier's powerful punch. After all, it was the last round of a grueling fifteen-round brawl. But his conviction to rise up is what we must embrace and embody in the fight against White supremacy, because we will continue to absorb debilitating blows that will make us want to quit. Only with conviction will we succeed.

Dedication. The battle we're in requires "the act of devoting all of one's energy, effort, and abilities to a certain task," as the Muhammad Ali Center boasts on its walls. Folks like to elevate the bright-light moments of victories, whether in the ring, on the front lines, or in front-page photo ops. But dedication is not about the big splashy moments; it's about the quiet ripples of preparation and hard work before and after you jump in.

Ali always wondered why the press never talked about his supreme commitment to roadwork and preparation before his bouts. He said, "I hated every minute of training, but I said, 'Don't quit, suffer now, and live the rest of your life as a champion.'" Winning the fight of our lives requires us to mirror this dedication.

Giving. In the RYMR leadership guide, Dr. Torie Weiston-Serdan, author of *Critical Mentoring: A Practical Guide*, says, "Muhammad Ali showed us that giving, even at the point of personal sacrifice, is an investment in our community's legacy." In magnifying this core principle, she reminds us that the fight will require personal sacrifice and resources—big resources to fight a well-resourced opponent in structural racism that keeps the feet of White supremacy firmly planted in the center of the ring. We have to transform the immense buying power of Black people in America into immense battling power. We must give to candidates for elected office who will leverage their legislative power to destroy racist policies; we must give to organizations that are fighting the battle on the front lines; we must give to people and institutions that nurture the next generation of leaders. The power of Black philanthropy must be multiplied for us to secure the fuel to keep fighting.

Respect. The Muhammad Ali core principle of respect demands "esteem for, or a sense of the worth or excellence of, oneself and others." In our battle against White supremacy, we will need to embrace an intersectional approach to winning that embraces the fights of Black women, Native Americans, the LGBTQ community, and other groups who are battling the oppressive forces of White supremacy.

In *Freedom Is a Constant Struggle*, Angela Y. Davis reminds us that "new organizations such as Black Lives Matter, Dream Defenders, Black Youth Project 100, Justice League NYC, and We Charge Genocide are a few of the new generation organizations that have developed new models of leadership and that acknowledge how important Black feminist insights are to the development of viable twenty-first century radical Black movements." Davis highlights the urgency of leaders, especially old-school leaders born in the midst of the Civil Rights Movement, to respect young leaders and the strategic ways they show up for the fight.

Spirituality. Finally, the fight against White supremacy will require an unrelenting faith in God and the sense of divine connectedness and timing that this faith provides us. Ali described spirituality as "a sense of awe, reverence, and inner peace inspired by a connection to all of creation and/or that which is greater than oneself." It will take spiritual fortitude—followed by focused, strategic action—to win the fight against White supremacy. Prayer, meditation, and self-care are essential spiritual practices of self-love.

Muhammad Ali provided us with a set of core principles. It's up to us to get in the ring and remember what The Champ said: "He who is not courageous enough to take risks will accomplish nothing in life."

Shawn Dove is founder and CEO of the Campaign for Black Male Achievement, a national membership network that seeks to ensure the growth, sustainability, and impact of leaders and organizations committed to improving the life outcomes of Black men and boys.

~~~~~~~~~~

**I fight White supremacy by remembering that any
opportunities available to me are the result of the
work and sacrifice of my ancestors and mentors.**

—Rechelle McJett-Beaty, auditor

~~~~~~~~~~

Ta-Nehisi Coates on the Importance of Mentorship and Making Sure Black People Know We Are Not Crazy

Baltimore native Ta-Nehisi Coates is one of the nation's most celebrated Black writers. In 2009, he published his first book, a hip-hop generation memoir titled *The Beautiful Struggle: A Father, Two Sons, and an Unlikely Road to Manhood*, about growing up in the Black nationalist household of the book publisher Paul Coates. Ta-Nehisi Coates's 2015 letter to *his* son, *Between the World and Me*, garnered praise from Toni Morrison, a National Book Award, and a MacArthur Fellowship. After the surprising election of 45, Coates released an essay collection titled *We Were Eight Years in Power: An American Tragedy*.

At the time of this interview with Akiba, he was finishing up his next book and emerging from a period of general wariness. Here they discuss what makes a good mentor and why so many veteran Black feminist writers are nice to him.

**Let's talk about who has mentored you and how
they did it in tangible and intangible ways.**

Early on, my biggest mentor was [the late] David Carr [of *Washington
City Paper*]. He was capable of giving incredibly blunt opinions and assess-
ments. But at the same time, he fought for me. Because he was so direct,
when he said good things and displayed confidence in me, I really believed
him. That was crucial.

In my life right now, I've been blessed by a number of Black women who
have really stepped up. And I'm not saying that in a really corny or sentimental
way. I mean it's literally true. I've had the luxury of spending time with Sonia
Sanchez. I've had Nell Painter really, really look out for me. I don't know if
this is mentorship, but I know really if not for Toni Morrison, my life would
not be as it is right now. Jamaica Kincaid has been supportive. I've never met
her; we have this email relationship where she checks in at least once a year.
I really treasure that because she started doing it at a time when I wasn't sure
what was going to happen. She was talking about *The Beautiful Struggle* and
how she was going to give it to her son. It was really early. But I don't know
why all these Black women are willing to mentor me. I haven't had that relationship with the brothers. I have plenty of male friends, Black male friends.
But in terms of elders, the relationships have been a little different.

**Do you sense that it hasn't been the same for
men because of feelings of competition?**

I don't know. I'm gonna throw something out here, and I don't know if
this is true, Akiba. I really, really don't. But with so much of the stuff that's
come out with #MeToo, I wonder if in some of the brothers' minds, part
of being a writer with some fame is having access to women. I don't have
a problem with you printing that, but I just want to be clear that I'm still
working that out in my head. Because of how society's set up, that women
who become more powerful [don't] suddenly have more access to men in the
same way that men have access to women.

Can you break down what you think a mentor should be within the context of White supremacy and Black folks?

It's funny. I've talked to [the *New York Times* reporter and MacArthur Fellow] Nikole Hannah-Jones quite a bit about this because she's a lot better at it than I am. I'm actually just getting this figured out. I literally have three meals scheduled next week with younger writers just to talk to them. Up until relatively recently, I wasn't sure if I was going to be able to support myself writing, so I didn't even really feel like I had much to offer anybody. And then when I did find that I could support myself, I went through this paranoid period. I didn't trust anybody. It's like, I'm careful about who I talk to. And now I'm coming out of that and I'm trying to get back to it and just pay back some of the stuff that was given to me.

How did you start?

I'm trying to listen and to urge people. I think writing can be brutal and can make you want to quit, but it's important not to quit. I just try to serve for people as David Carr served for me as a person who is both offering unadulterated honesty, but at the same time love and support.

The part of your question about White supremacy is interesting. None of the people I'm seeing next week are White. I don't have anything specific against taking on younger writers who are White. But for obvious reasons, I'm attracted to Black writers and other writers of color.

So you said that you've been talking to Nikole about mentorship a lot. What specifically have you learned from her about it?

She is just so trusting in people. Nikole can have twenty young writers of color, young Black writers over at her house, and she'll just talk to them. I guess I've learned openness from her. And she's not any different from me in terms of having a period of time when she struggled. We've talked about how she was thinking of going into PR and saying, "Fuck this, I'm done with this journalism."

So it's not like I've suffered some amount of trauma on the way up that she didn't suffer. But I will say that when *Between the World and Me* came out, the sheer amount of attention it got made it unclear why some people were talking to me. I didn't know what their angle was. It was damn near . . . like I thought I was back on the street looking at everybody like, "What's up with you?" She was one of the people who I would talk to, who very slowly began to convince me to open it up a little bit and not be so damn paranoid. You know?

I do know about paranoia! So how do you fight White supremacy?

Well, how I fight it is through my writing. One of the things I always say is that there are the actual socioeconomic facts of racism and White supremacy, and then there is the attempt to make it look like nothing's wrong, as though there is no White supremacy. So my fight is actually on the second front—to outline it, to make it clear, to make sure that Black folks do not feel like they're crazy. That's my job.

～～～～～～

QUESTION, ANSWERED

It's clear that many activists draw inspiration from generations past. Here we explore the question: who inspires you?

Kenrya

Do you know how I spent my most productive, satisfying twenty minutes of today? Sitting in my truck, illegally parked on the side of a busy street in Washington, DC, with my hot-ass MacBook on my lap and my iPhone in my hand waiting for the clock to tick over to 9:00 a.m. EST so I could enter my Beyhive presale code and come up on tickets to see Beyoncé in concert for the fourth time. So it's understandable that the following playlist of the songs that I blast when I need to be inspired to exercise, tell somebody what they *not* gon' do, or turn a microaggression into a real live conversation about why White folks need to collect their people is heavy on the Bey. Fight yo' mama (but don't tell her I sent you—*I* respect my elders).*

Kenrya's Bad Bitch Playlist

▸ Beyoncé, "Grown Woman"
  Because sometimes you need a reminder of who you are.
▸ Lizzo, "Truth Hurts"
  "I don't play tag, bitch, I been it." A word.
▸ Beyoncé, "Ego"
  Key lyric: "Usually I'm humble / Right now I don't choose."
▸ Estelle, "Stronger Than You"
  Estelle sings this song while voicing Garnet, a character on my favorite cartoon, *Steven Universe*. Garnet is a "fusion," a being made up of two women who love each other so much that they can't bear to be apart, and every single time I hear her sing "I am made of love and it's stronger than you," I feel literal chills and the overwhelming desire to fuck shit up.
▸ Beyoncé, "Flawless Remix" (featuring Nicki Minaj)
  Because I do, I do wake up like this.
▸ Bone Crusher, "Never Scared (The Takeover Remix)"
  You can think I'm afraid if you want to, but I'm from Cleveland, my G.
▸ Beyoncé, "Run the World (Girls)"
  Bruh.
▸ Anything by Saa

---

* I wrote this before the legendary showing-out that was Beychella. If you watched that Black-ass performance and still want to fight yo' mama, you are either a hater of the highest order or willfully ignorant of the hardworking, sang her tail off, kill choreography without breaking a sweat, fuck y'all, I'm finna bring Howard Homecoming to this desert full of White people glory that is Bey. Either way, we can't be friends.

My kid has been singing since she started talking, and my phone is full of surreptitiously recorded audio of her belting out her favorite songs and her original creations. Whether it's her take on "Alexander Hamilton" or a lounge-ready freestyle (seriously, lately she has been turning the old hymns of the church and Disney classics into jazz standards while she showers), her singing propels me.*

~~~~~~~~~~

Akiba

Ida
Your danger was your friends.
Tom Moss
Calvin McDowell
Will Stewart, lynched for
Having more dry goods than the walking dead.

Ida.
Don't ask about that rope. That fire. Those pointer-finger bones. That smell.
Don't ask in the hundreds.
Don't print what will get your printing press bombed.
Or do.

Incorrigible Ida.

You bit a no-class hand pulling you off the train despite your premium receipt.
You sued.

---

* Yes, I know this chapter is about generational activism, and Bey and I are literally the same age. But you can't tell me that Saa and I aren't fortifying our hearts and minds against the ravages of White supremacy when we walk across the room like Naomi Campbell.

You co-made the NAACP but left for lack of action plans
You ran for state senate, started a Black kindergarten, bent the ears of two presidents

Your name rings bells.
Observers, chroniclers, reporters, narrators, secret squirrels, platform-makers, data-miners, creators, polemicists, historians, tellers, whisperers, role-model seekers, big-timers, and writers say your name.

What they truly want to know is how you made your trauma inflammable.
How you collected the evidence without becoming the evidence
How you died a nonviolent death

Ida the Incorrigible, Ida the Brave

EIGHT
LOVE ME OR LEAVE ME ALONE

First of all, love is not all you need. It might have been enough for four White dudes from Liverpool, but for Black people living and dying amid the wreckage of White supremacy, love is not life-sustaining.

L-O-V-E can't stop the bullet of a police officer who believes a Black boy playing on the swings outside a recreation center is a mortal threat. There aren't enough heart-eyed emoji in the world to make a racist Twitter troll recognize the humanity that lies beneath skin painted the color of the night sky. And if you've found a way to use compassion to protect our queer fam, come holler at us.

But, honey, love feels gooooooood. Whether it's self-love, romantic love, tenderness for those who share our DNA, care for the people who make up our communities, or a fierce adoration for our race, love has a way of buoying us, providing just enough lift to keep our heads above the roiling sea as we swim toward better days.

Struggle without love burns you out. It makes you mean. It kills your vibe. But when you add loving to the mix, alongside organizing and educating and creating, you birth an enduring form of resistance that is radical, expansive, and transformative at its core. The people highlighted in this chapter—including an ethnographer, a beauty expert, and an R&B singer—know that the answer to the question "Who do you love?" should always be "Us."

And a Hashtag Will Set Them Free

Dr. Yaba Blay, as told to Kenrya Rankin

The "click-clack" of braids and beads. The shuffle of little feet moving through steps in unison. The Inauguration Day side eye that spoke for us all. #ProfessionalBlackGirl moments are all around us, and Dr. Yaba Blay means to point them out via her video series and social media campaign, which celebrate the everyday magic of Black girls and women. As a professor, researcher, and ethnographer, she uses personal and social narratives to disrupt fundamental assumptions about cultures and identities. As a cultural worker and producer, she uses images to inform consciousness, incite dialogue, and inspire others to action. Here she gives us a window into the genesis of Professional Black Girl and why it's so important to live into our joy.

––––––––––

"Professional Black Girl began as a hashtag in 2015. I started using it on social media when I saw pictures and videos of little Black girls doing something that I thought was extra Black. Extra Black girl. The things that I knew in my spirit that nobody had to teach them, they were just doing. I used the hashtag as a way to note like, okay, whatever she's doing, she's doing it to professional levels.

"The following year I moved to North Carolina. Every time one of my girlfriends came to visit, we wound up taking field trips to one of the biggest beauty supply stores I've ever been to in my life. We'd be in there for hours. I mean they have clothes in there, they have shoes, they have hair products, they have hair, a big old jewelry section. We'd try on wigs and reminisce on products, opening bottles of Pink Oil Moisturizer and being like, 'Oh my God, remember that smell?'

"I had this idea that I wanted to do a video series with nuanced conversations about hair, with the beauty supply store as the foundation of the conversation. In my mind, I was going to end each episode with a quick segment called 'Professional Black Girl.' I started recording my friends, but when I watched the footage, it looked like its own thing to me. And so it came to be a web series.

"I had so much fun producing it. We really reverted back to the innocence and joy that comes with girlhood. While I initially started using the hashtag to specifically point to girls, my experience playing in the beauty supply store with my friends made me realize that the project could be used intentionally to capture the lightheartedness and simple joy of being a Black girl *and* help girls see themselves as connected to Black women. I think the language of 'girl' allows us to do that because, ultimately, when I think of my identity and what makes me who I am, I'm still a Black girl at heart.

"Much of my work focuses on identity, so I have lots of conversations with us folks about the ways that we think about ourselves. Teaching at an HBCU, I see some very well-intentioned Black administrators and faculty members who think that we're training the next generation of successful Black 'professionals.' But I'm watching us train our students away from themselves. Students have told me of instances where someone told them that they need to straighten their hair, or told them that they need to lose weight. They correct the ways they speak and how they dress. I get it, but I'm also troubled by it.

"Just think about the impact. What does it feel like, what does it mean to be looking at your reflection, somebody who looks like you, who's in a position that you aspire to be in, telling you that who you are and how you are isn't good enough? We need to create opportunities for our youth—and for ourselves—to be okay with being ourselves. Look, I think our ability to code-switch is beautiful. I don't have any evidence, but I wonder if it is a product of the experience of enslavement and colonization, this ability to act a particular way, talk a particular way, be a particular way in certain folks' presence, and then go home and be free. I think it's a skill and a talent.

"And I get it if we are teaching our youth how to do that well. But I don't think that's what we're doing. Instead, we're teaching them not to be themselves, and judging them when they are. So I want to live as an example. There's a freedom in being able to be whoever the hell I think I am, despite, or possibly even because of, what anybody thinks or expects of me.

"Yaba is my investment. That's who I'm invested in, for my happiness, my joy, my ability to be myself. I think that—an investment in themselves— is something we should be encouraging and supporting in our youth. Because they're going to have to deal with so much and fight so many people in this world. The last person they should be fighting with is themselves. And I think it's important that we see examples, happy examples, real examples of folks being able to navigate all these spaces fluidly and still maintain themselves. And that's what I aim to do with Professional Black Girl.

"That said, I've had a couple conversations with folks who have questions about some of the content I post on the Professional Black Girl Instagram account. They say things like, 'Why are you elevating reality TV folks?' And my response is, 'This is not a place for you to think.' Come have the joy, the laugh, then go about your business. If we can't do that, then we're doing it wrong. For me, it's always been important to reach as many people as possible. That's the point of Professional Black Girl: every one of us has access to it, and every last one of us reflects it.

"I always say that White supremacy is one hell of a drug. It did a number on us. The ways in which we think about ourselves, the ways in which we reflect upon ourselves, are no different, in many ways, than the ways that *they* think about us and the ways that *they* reflect on us. We're doing exactly what they want us to do, to the point where you don't even need White people for White supremacy anymore. But these ways that we criticize ourselves through their lens just aren't real. So this type of imagery and representation are crucial. We have to see ourselves differently, because if we rely on the mainstream to show us ourselves, we will remain under the foothold of White supremacy. Other people are going to think what they want to think about your Blackness no matter what you present to the world, so you might as well be free.

"This idea of Black joy as a part of our liberation strategy is an honor to our ancestors. Again, thinking about the period of enslavement and colonization, none of us have any idea what that could have possibly been like, right? But whatever it was they experienced, whatever it was they endured, they still laughed. They still had families. They still danced. They still sang songs. If they could do that, then—even though we feel like we are in hell's belly right now—we can still make time for joy.

"In this moment, I need it and I deserve it. And the response to Professional Black Girl tells me that other people need it and deserve it too."

~~~~~~~~

I fight White supremacy by being authentic in a field that is dominated by White males. White supremacy believes that only those who act and look like them are smart, but I make sure my difference reflects who I am in my dress, my personality, and my approach to problem-solving.

—Kevin Porter, engineer

~~~~~~~~

Touching White Supremacy, Touching Beyond It (Strategy: Intimacy)

adrienne maree brown

"The role of the artist is exactly the same as the role of the lover. If I love you, I have to make you conscious of the things you can't see." —James Baldwin

I am the child of a Black father and a White mother. In spite of violent racist conditioning, they saw home in each other across a college library in the mid-'70s in South Carolina. They married three months later and, like most couples, began creating a world, choosing what to keep from their blood families and what to release. They kept a light, communal practice of Christianity and an idea that family is a central focus of life.

They left almost everything else.

I was raised in an intimate home. By that I mean, love was explicit and intentional. My parents knew each other, teased each other. They loved each other, and they loved us. They were affectionate and aligned with each other. We rarely saw them fight. They told us not to go to bed angry. Anger was contained in the framework of punishment; once the punishment was complete, the anger dissipated and we would continue with life, dinner, homework.

Sex with someone of another race, intimacy with the other, isn't necessarily an act against supremacy—part of the deep resentment against light-skinned Blacks in this country is because we are a walking reminder that so many people with the same racial makeup as me come from a lineage of rape.

But to truly love someone of another race, particularly in a dynamic where one partner is White or has White-skinned privileges, can be a direct act against White supremacy. To love someone and not need to take anything from them or add anything to yourself, to be equals—that is how my parents love. I would not call them radical in their politics, but they're definitely radical in love.

To raise children in an environment where race does not make someone more or less of anything, to raise children as equal to anyone they meet—my parents built us a foundation from which it is very difficult to leap into a framework of White supremacy. I think this was my parents' intention; they took us out of the country on purpose, certain that we would return to a nation evolved. They wanted to give us a beginning of life different from the stratified racial beginnings they had experienced.

But my parents couldn't see all the ways White supremacy had shaped them, and I don't remember them even talking about race until much later, when it was explicitly being weaponized against us. When people asked us what we were, we were free to come up with our own answers. My go-to answer became, "What do you want me to be?" Precocious. But I realized in elementary school that what people wanted was to feel comfortable, and if I played with that, it gave me some power. Later, I layered in the understanding that those who would ask me what I was, where I was from, wanted to know where to place me in the construct of superiority and inferiority in their minds.

Children always learn the things adults can't speak.

I was in the seventh grade when I understood that the way my parents loved, across the racial binary so central to the United States, was exceptional. Up until then, my sisters and I were raised on military bases, mostly in Germany, where a lot of couples and many of our friends were multiracial, Black and German, Black and Japanese, Black and Italian.

It was a shock to move to Georgia, to go to a school that was a mix of kids from the base and kids from the town of Hinesville, a school and a community that was much more segregated than any place I'd ever been. I learned the hard way that my flippant answers on race were never going to make racists comfortable, or playfully uncomfortable. It was too free of me, evidence of an agency they would not allow. To them I was not White, so I was Black, and I was inferior. I was parts of a person, and the Black parts were undesired. There was a new language of assumptions and insults to learn, so comprehensive that it pushed the German words of my childhood out of my mind.

It was a shock to be asked to pull myself into colored parts after a life of experiential, if wishful, wholeness. I say wishful here to speak of what my parents were up to. They truly believed that humans were slowly leaving racism and White supremacy behind.

Racism waited for our return from Germany, waited with a violent education, where it confronted us in school, on buses, and in Waffle Houses and bubbled up in my extended family.

As I became more aware of racism, of Blackness and White supremacy, I began to hear and be offended by things spoken casually by strangers, by loved ones. I began to understand that racism had been in my life before,

I just hadn't had the context to understand what was happening, what was being said to me when someone complimented the texture of my hair, my light skin.

It didn't register to me because I knew White people, and I knew they weren't superior to anyone. Up close, it is impossible to believe in White supremacy. Close to a *real* White person, there is humanity, the smell of skin and the pinch of bones, the flatulence and eye crust, the dumb questions and botched relationships, the beating heart and the beauty of animation, that mysterious energy of life that does not discriminate. There is miracle too. Magic. We all come from that mystery in the mud of stardust, and we will all return to it with the shared scar of death.

I am friends with White people, beyond the unconditional love of my mother. My White friends have in common that they are nonbelievers in White supremacy. We can be friends, intimate and vulnerable, because they know better and try to do better.

Any system of supremacy is a system of distance: a commitment to stay far enough away from each other that a mythology can be generated and maintained, a mythology of being supreme, while others, due to some minor difference in skin (or genitalia, class, desire, ability, birth place, familial religion, etc.), are inferior. To assert superiority over another human being means repressing or hiding the full reality of one's own humanness, the flaws and the chaos.

As a life choice, White supremacy is a tragedy. To sacrifice being of a wildly diverse species for the sake of a false supremacy is to step away from the possibility of being truly known. It is isolation as socialization: it is violent to teach children to hold themselves apart from others.

We have been swimming in the waters of supremacy for most of human existence, as if rivers could flow away from the sea, splitting themselves, cleaving the multitudes into different territories.

Perhaps God struck us different in this way to keep us from reaching heaven, from realizing we are in heaven, on heaven. Togetherness can feel divine.

Perhaps, as Octavia Butler taught us, the essential flaw of our species is intelligence combined with hierarchy, that we use our genius for the work of separation and supremacy.

White supremacy is a virus that distorts every lens of the mind, making it impossible to see the vulnerable, mundane, same same same body. Intimacy is about honesty with our flaws—White supremacy has to pretend that White people have none.

Authentic intimacy with the other is one of the ways we can remember we are all bodies and break the curse of perfection embedded in the myth of superiority.

I also had to learn to be intimate with myself, to look at my skin and my eyes, the shape of my body. To love my ass even though it wasn't small and flat like the ideal of the White girls around me. And then to love my ass even though it wasn't round at the top like the ideal of the Black girls in my class. To learn that most people don't have the ideal version of an ass or any other part—we have reality, and reality is beautiful because it pulses with life and desire and movement. I've learned to love my skin when it was nearly translucent in the Northern winters, and when it was red brown in the summer. To love my hair where it frizzes into a curly halo when I want it to lay flat, and to love the parts that have straightened as I've aged. To love my insatiable longing for a Black Power Afro. To learn that my body doesn't trend and doesn't self-segregate. White people have a million kinds of bodies, as do Black people. I had to learn that nothing in my body was explicitly White or Black or superior or inferior. And that I didn't have to assert Blackness as superior to balance the trauma of White supremacy. I just had to love myself whole. I am miracle, that's all.

It feels radical to care for myself, to engage in the political warfare Audre Lorde called me to. It also feels radical to experience pleasure in my Black body, and with any body that is not White. And it feels radical to see White people experience pleasure that isn't about dominance.

I feel liberated by my desire for myself. I feel liberated in my desire for those who look like me, and those Blacker than me. I feel liberated when I feel intimacy with White people that doesn't require either of us shrinking. All of this allows me to be my whole self. Each experience of wholeness makes it less possible to participate in segregation, within or without.

Intimacy allows the transformation we so desperately need, beyond Whiteness as superiority.

adrienne maree brown is the author of *Emergent Strategy: Shaping Change, Changing Worlds* and coeditor of *Octavia's Brood: Science Fiction from Social Justice Movements*. She is the "Pleasure Dome" columnist at *Bitch* magazine and co-host of the *How to Survive the End of the World* podcast. She facilitates and mediates for social justice movements, with a focus on Black liberation. She lives, writes, and loves in Detroit, Michigan.

~~~~~~~~~

Dr. Joy Harden Bradford Wants You to Be Vulnerable

Dr. Joy Harden Bradford is an Atlanta-based licensed psychologist, but her work reaches women all over the world via her podcast, *Therapy for Black Girls*. In the following interview, she talks to Kenrya about breaking down the stigma surrounding mental health, why she almost exclusively works with Black women, and the importance of seeking out spaces built with Blackness in mind.

Why are you a psychologist?

I think most mental health professionals have a story about being the person who friends turn to, and the same is true for me. It feels like a calling to help people through difficult times, and to offer a listening ear and a place to share difficult things.

Why do you choose to work pretty much exclusively with Black women?

That's what I feel is important. I think less than 5 percent of all mental health professionals are of color, and if you drill that down to Black women, it's even smaller. My experience has been that Black women usually want a Black woman therapist. It feels like it's really important to me to be available to do that work for us.

What led you to start Therapy for Black Girls?

I was watching *Black Girls Rock!* in 2014, and I felt so inspired. There was an energy that you could feel through the TV screen. I thought, *How could I do something like this for mental health? What might give people that same kind of vibe?* I immediately jumped online to see if the domain was available, and *Therapy for Black Girls* was born. It started as just blog posts, and then I added the podcast in April 2016.

Why is this work important?

I think often there are things going on with us as women that we don't even recognize as a mental health issue. It's really important for me to give people everyday language for some of the stuff that we may be experiencing. You know, mental health is definitely about anxiety and depression and all of those things, but it's also about setting boundaries, knowing whether a friendship is healthy, and figuring out how to stop people-pleasing. All of those things are important to your mental health, so I want to help us have these discussions.

How does tackling our mental health tie into expanding our self-love?

If we're not taking care of ourselves, that's an ultimate act of not loving ourselves. Sometimes that's because we don't have the language, and we don't know *how* to love ourselves. But also, the idea of the Black superwoman is not new. That is something that has been placed on us, to always be the one who has to hold it together, and it's just not feasible. Why are we not allowed to be vulnerable and have moments of weakness and need other people just like everybody else?

How does your work help Black women endure the ravages of White supremacy?

I think sometimes people don't realize the impact of racism and just constantly living in a system where you never know what the news is going to be about the president, what new scandal is going to break, what ridiculous law he will try to put forth. It really takes a toll. I try to help listeners understand that their feelings are real and offer strategies for managing the accompanying anxiety and depression.

Are there mental health benefits to being in spaces that are built just for us?

Oh, absolutely. That doesn't mean it doesn't have some challenges—we're not all alike, we're human, we have different personalities—but I think those challenges are far less than the ones that come with being in spaces where you're constantly having to ask yourself: *Do these people think I belong here? Am I making sense? Do they understand where I'm coming from?* That's a large part of where the imposter syndrome comes in for us. We don't have to do as much second-guessing of ourselves in spaces that are created just for us.

Are there any costs to building this movement around Black people?

My clientele would be bigger if I didn't target my services for Black women, and I probably miss out on opportunities. But that doesn't matter, because I've been able to create something that's really important to me. I've heard some White therapists say that they don't think it's "fair" that I prefer to see Black clients. My rebuttal is, "All other therapists can be for everybody else. It's okay for us to say that some stuff is just for us." If this allows more Black women to take their mental health more seriously, then I'm fine with whatever kinds of criticism and feedback come my way from other people.

~~~~~~

Dancer

Patricia Spears Jones

The man with the black feather tattoo pares this space
Between fantasy and the memory of a man's carved
Torso, designed for stroking and celebration

Today the sun's brightness is like that lover's kiss,
Wonderful in the present and greater in memory

A memory that brings me back to that black feather's
Flutter. Stars dazzle in some other part of this world
Where the sun has set and the moon illuminates
Swans diving into voluminous waters.

Patricia Spears Jones is Arkansas-born and -raised and a resident of New York City. She is the author of the award-winning poetry collections *Painkiller*, *Femme du Monde*, and *The Weather That Kills* and five chapbooks, including *Living in the Love Economy*. Her fourth collection, *A Lucent Fire: New and Selected Poems*, features her 2016 Pushcart Prize–winning poem "Etta James at the Audubon Ballroom." "Dancer" was first published by Poets.org for Poem-a-Day on October 27, 2015.

~~~~~~

You Got the Juice Now, Man

Aja Graydon

Aja Graydon and her husband, Fatin Dantzler, are Kindred the Family Soul. The two singer-songwriters met in the late '90s on the Philadelphia neo-soul scene and married within a year. They went on to have six children, release six critically acclaimed albums, and perform for thousands all over the world. Aja and Fatin write about a range of real-life topics, including the recession, making their kids do housework, White supremacy, and materialism. But what they are best known for is their love. Here is Aja's take on being an example of an everyday pair of Black folks doing all they can to stay together.

———————

Dancing well requires many things—rhythm, coordination, musicality, and memory.

Marriage is a dance.

There's that initial spark of inspiration and those moments of pure joy—then the real work begins. That means learning routines, perfecting them with discipline, and accepting that a change in the style of the music can land you at square one. That's why I practice multiple styles of engaging with my beloved and my children. This is what makes Kindred the Family Soul the model Black couple—if marrying young and broke and having six kids while trying to maintain a career in the music business is the goal.

Because we write so many songs about our love, we perform as a couple, and people have seen our kids on the reality show we created, *Six Is It*, our fans expect us to exemplify the perfectly intact, God-fearing family. They want perfection because it gives them hope, and hope is essential to Black survival.

To be honest, I'm ambivalent about this being our role in the struggle. On the one hand, I know that a drama-free image can hamper us as artists. On the other hand, who doesn't want to be seen as the epitome of Black love? But we aren't the Huxtables set to music. In the beginning of our relationship, we saw ourselves as a rebellious pair of young lovers. Now, waking up together, year after twenty years, humbles us.

People forget that we have written extensively about our imperfections and our learning curves. And our years of working together, touring the world, and connecting with other couples have opened my eyes to why it is so uniquely challenging for Black people to love each other.

For us, marriage sometimes mirrors the more critical work our community requires. It's great to say, "I love being Black," but we have to do the more intense work of loving ourselves and whoopin' White supremacy's ass. This takes levels of trust, intimacy, and self-awareness that are difficult to achieve because of our collective trauma. If you expect your beloved to never hurt you deeply, that is naive. It's what happens after you've been hurt that determines the outcome. As a people, our victory over trauma makes our love for one another extraordinary.

No pressure, though.

From the outside looking in, there is no way to tell who has the juice and who doesn't. There's no way to say what will last or what won't, so bravery is the bottom line. Bravery isn't as fun as the other qualities associated with love. A couple of times we've almost failed, but we've lasted due to the bravery that we inherited from our enslaved ancestors. They lived in the very worst conditions and still loved each other.

Like most acts of bravery, ours have been preceded by circumstances that forced us into conference with our coping skills. We've had to learn to ignore the echo of divorce statistics and of our parents' failed marriages. We've taught ourselves to relax and trust our instincts. We don't fear losing our relationship because we understand who we are and what we're capable of. And that, I think, is the true gift of our Black love. We know we are connected by purpose and destiny. And we are lucky as f#@k.

~~~~~~~~~

I fight White supremacy by telling our untold stories.

—Janelle M. Harris, media producer

~~~~~~~~~

On the Exhausting Notion of Guarding Our Beauty

Ayana Byrd

It started with a boy.

I liked him. One day in the school lunchroom, I was talking to his best friend, a White boy. He wanted to tell me a secret about my crush. If it were a movie, it would have been the moment I leaned in closer to him, though I remember I willed myself to look like whatever he had to say was no big deal. But it was, because I really liked his best friend, who was Black and who had just broken up with White, blond Laura. I made my expression as neutral as I could. *Tell me.*

"So . . ." he said, dragging it out. "Chris said he would like you, if."

If. He paused again.

"If your body was on someone else's face."

As one of the only seventh-graders with breasts, liking my body was not an act of original thought. But I understood the coded language his friend used: Chris liked White girls, and my Black face was not attractive to him. And he actually told a White boy this. I felt ugly and racially sold out, and I needed to stand in a locked bathroom stall to have whatever moment I was about to have alone.

Before I made it to the restroom, Chris walked up to me in the hallway, oblivious to what had just happened. For the first time in my life, I had an out-of-body experience. I heard a voice—my voice—in my head. It spoke so clearly: "Don't hit him." *Of course not*, I thought. I had never hit anyone. But then I watched my right hand move in a wide arc until it connected with Chris's left cheek, and I slapped what my grandmother would have called "the mess" out of him.

Another example.

"You sho' is ugly."

In the midst of the physical and sexual and emotional violence that is inflicted on Celie in *The Color Purple*, she meets her husband-abuser's mistress. This cackling declaration of Celie's unattractiveness is the first thing

Shug Avery says in both the book and film versions. The sentence has become iconic in Black popular culture, five syllables that bring on an immediate cringing shame. Celie instantly believes this pronouncement; her entire life has taught her to believe in her own ugliness. But by the end of the story, she is a homeowner, an entrepreneur, a woman who has experienced sexual pleasure, and one who smiles and laughs freely. She is beautiful.

Both of these two stories—the fictional and the achingly real—include acts of resistance. In one, literal physical resistance, the violent consequences for someone who desired White beauty saying my Black face should be swapped out.

And in the other, survival and transformation were acts of resistance. "I think it pisses God off if you walk by the color purple in a field somewhere and don't notice it," Alice Walker writes in the novel, explaining that the title is a call to arms, a reminder that everything is a creation of God and we should love it accordingly. Celie is this color purple, ignored and neglected her entire life. But when she recognizes the God in herself, she also finds her beauty.

I thought of both of these experiences as I struggled to write this essay about White supremacy, Black resistance, and beauty. The struggle was because of what felt like competing beliefs that couldn't be reconciled.

First, there is my belief that our culture's beauty ideals are drenched in the poison of White supremacy, idealizing straight hair, White skin, and European features. Popular culture, mass media, curricula, and hiring practices enforce the privilege that comes with White beauty. And, as Black women, we are constantly in a position where we must push back if we are to be seen properly. We declare in print, on social media, in teaching our children, and in our daily lives that our hair, our lips, our noses, our brown-skinned Blackness is beautiful and we are not less than.

This is the resistance.

And this is my other belief: feeling beautiful is not an act of resistance. If we are the color purple, feeling beautiful is running through the field. Open arms, wide hearts, in the sun. Feeling beautiful is carefree; resisting is work.

Resistance also implies that there is another, a thing, idea, person, or notion, to push back against. And when the acts of resistance are to assert Black beauty in a White supremacist world, the other is Whiteness, centered and ever-present. White women look like this—but we are this and that is also beautiful. Light skin is considered the ideal—but our brown skin is also beautiful. Experiencing our beauty as an "also" or a "but" is reductive.

It is also not true to how most Black women live. We constantly experience our beauty in a way that does not reference Whiteness. When we are feeling beautiful, it is a solo act, just us and our reflection. To bring it back to popular culture, when Black women watched the 2018 film *Black Panther* and the bald, braided, kinky-haired brown bodies on the screen, we cheered the beauty and it had nothing to do with White people. The dazzle of Wakanda was all ours.

Still, what I first saw as the struggle between these two beliefs is actually a necessary progression. To get to the place of feeling beautiful, we must first resist. That is because the path to owning our beauty is pocked with the craters and dangers of White supremacy. The politics of beauty ensnares even the most decidedly unpolitical. Every woman is told she is meant to be beautiful, and she is told what that looks like. And capitalism pretends that it is within our purchasing power to get there, through skin lighteners, hair straighteners, gym memberships, and plastic surgery. And White supremacy wants to forever remind Black women that we will never actually get there, we will never be White, we will never be invited all the way into the gilded hallways where the beautiful live and thrive.

For Black women, our resistance is to lean all the way into the mirror, so close that we can almost touch the image we see reflected there. And to stare and believe, "I love everything I see." And then to share with another Black woman how she can also experience that.

How do we get to this? How do we see and know beauty in the mirror and in each other's faces and bodies? What does this path to beauty look like? It looks like books, documentaries, and talks that dismantle the hegemony of these European ideals. It looks like studying the unsung history of our hair, style, and beauty culture. It looks like the growing number of Black women entrepreneurs like Jamyla Bennu, Jane Carter, and Anu Prestonia who have used their love of Black hair and skin to begin beauty businesses, diverting some of the billions of dollars we spend away from multinational corporations and back into Black communities. It looks like the phrase "Black is beautiful," first used by abolitionist John Swett Rock in 1858, that became the name of a consciousness movement in the 1960s.

This is the resistance. It is a fight that never ends. There will always be another racist declaring that we are not beautiful, that we look like baboons or gorillas—even when we are First Lady Michelle Obama. There are always cultural appropriators called Bo Derek, Kim Kardashian, and all those other White women we see every day playing dress-up in our beauty and calling it something else.

This constant vigilance, this guarding of our beauty, can be exhausting. And so, when I need to regroup, I turn to women like academic Yaba Blay and photographer Delphine Fawundu who have dedicated their work to tackling the space where beauty, Blackness, and White supremacy meet. I watch the Black girls in my life when they are playing and spinning and loving their beautiful selves. I find websites and Instagram accounts that are saturated in images of Black skin and textured hair. I use them like water, to stay hydrated in a world that wants us to be ugly and dry.

And I remember that telling us that we are ugly intends to cut to the bone and hobble us in a way from which we are to never fully recover. "You sho' is ugly" is not just Celie's denunciation. It is meant to be all of ours. But it is four other words, "you sure are beautiful," that act as our collective call to arms.

Resistance is necessary to position us more firmly in a space where we can see and love Black women's beauty. But once we are in this space, the resistance fades away to let in the euphoria of what we behold. This is the payoff, and the prize looks like the brilliance of our brown bodies.

Ayana Byrd is the coauthor of *Hair Story: Untangling the Roots of Black Hair in America* and coeditor of the anthology *Naked: Black Women Bare All about Their Skin, Hair, Hips, Lips, and Other Parts.* Her writing on beauty culture has also appeared in *O: The Oprah Magazine*, the *New York Times*, *Glamour*, and *Elle*.

~~~~~~~~

The Revolutionary's Hymn for Love during a Time of Political Unrest

Mahogany L. Browne

Bless the sun
Bright in its rising
How it kissed your face this morning
How your breath caught itself in your throat
Today, no one has left the earth violent, yet
No one has lost a war, yet
Only breath & here & the sun

Amen
Bless the boats
Each river that birthed a love despite the dirge
Each world that birthed a galaxy
Where it orbits like a colonizer's prayer
Still
no weapon shall prosper
no grandmother's juju
will wither in a knapsack
Only the breath of a body docking
to the land of its lover
& the sun
she is here too

—on fire
Amen
Bless the fingers that stretch away from the body
How it finds another body near the light
How the light makes everything familiar and safe
How safe becomes a new house
Here, the fingers drip heavy with shimmer
like a promise of a renewed nation

You & the sun & your love spread
against the skin of one another
The heat of survival pulling you close
Bless a prosperous love
& the hands unafraid of
The weight
The revolution
& the fight
your kind of kiss can bring
Bless the unafraid warrior
The beaten citizen
The steadfast agitator
The unyielding instigator
Bless this unconquerable lover
Let this song shred itself to bits in your mouth
Look how it stays
Amen
Amen
Amen

Praise your tongue
The way it holds every name like a spell
Praise the hunger

The way it led your ancestors
through Harlem
St. Louis
Oakland
& Detroit

Amen
Amen
Amen
Praise the way your wrists know steel
The way your heart murmurs its ache
The way your neck cracks in memory
& your knees quake but never crouch
Amen Amen Amen

Think of your house
Designed by the architecture of drums
Etched in the blood of an uprising
Once a dream that split you into an equator of vibration

Now, praise
The body that lived
to know a longing like this
The body that stays awake keeping wake
for the comrades, gone
The body that never romanticizes the shotgun
but the glory of the liberated

With the sunrise & this anthem
Thrumming insistent
a pulsing psalm
on your tongue

Mahogany L. Browne is a California-born, Brooklyn-based writer, educator, activist, mentor, and curator.

~~~~~~~~~

QUESTION, ANSWERED

As we examine the importance of love in all its forms in the fight to dismantle White supremacy, we consider the question: who do you love?

Kenrya

Myself, finally. And can I tell you? That feels like a revolutionary act.

To be a White child born in America is to burst onto the scene filled with love. It expands their lungs when they take their first breaths, flows into their guts when they suckle, straightens their backs as they begin to understand the space they occupy in the collective imagination. And because they are born into a loving world, one filled with *philia*, or goodwill, loving themselves requires little effort, and certainly no coercion from their parents, no hurried pep talks about how their tightly curled hair is gorgeous and unique before they walk into a school where the locks are mostly straight, no tear-filled reassurances when they leave dance class upset because someone laughed at their skirt that carries the intricate patterns and vibrant colors of Nigeria, no serious talks about how, yes, some police officers *have* shot dead little people who look just like them when they were playing on a swing set just like this one.

Bullies may try to steal it for themselves, men might work overtime to extract it from their female and femme peers, and the ravages of very real personal trauma might push it to the back of their minds, but the moment White people enter a space with someone whose identities fetch a lower market rate, they are subconsciously reminded of who they are and what they have been blessed with: an innate sense that because the world loves them, having love for themselves, *philautia*, is a foregone conclusion, a feeling they couldn't escape if they wanted to.

Maybe there was a time, before I could understand the world around me, when I felt that love. Back before I learned that much of the nation I was born into was invested in a system that placed me at the bottom of the racial hierarchy. But I know that it wasn't long before self-love had to become more than a feeling. If I was to thrive, it had to become an actual practice. But learning to do it took many moons.

I'm not talking about self-care, though it has its place. I know that my health depends on scheduling time in my day to sit and eat a meal without simultaneously typing an email, on pouring lavender essential oil into the tub from time to time so I can soak while I make the most of my Netflix subscription. But, for me, seeing past the damage that the world has inflicted on my self-esteem—via media that tell me that without white skin, blond hair, and blue eyes, I am worthless; men who would act out the dredges of patriarchy on my body and mind; a bloodline deeply scarred by colorism that discouraged me from wearing bright colors because I was "too dark"—requires actual work. Not the work of remembering who I was before I was told that I was unlovable. Not the work of imagining a time in the future where I feel the full weight of *agape*, Godly universal love, in my spirit. But the work of manifesting a timeline where I can adore my whole self *right now*.

Where I can grant myself permission to be still and breathe in the warmth of my own company and know in my bones that it's enough. Where I don't have to code-switch because if I deliver the ain'ts and gon's that reside on my tongue with the twang that seeped through the generations, some White-aspiring person will think I'm uneducated and undeserving of their respect. Where I expect people to both remember and pronounce my Black-ass name correctly because it is mine. Where I demand more from a society that would begrudge me scraps and deem me uppity for still being hungry. Where I remember that if I extinguish my light to comfort others, it will only leave us all sitting in the dark.

And so I am embodying that love. Not just claiming it, but making it so, overflowing with it and pouring it into the barren cups that surround me.

Because the only thing that can break a worn-out cycle is to invest in a new one. Ase.

～～～～～～

Akiba

"Be Real Black for Me" has long been one of the most significant songs in my world. The 1972 duet by Donny Hathaway and Roberta Flack does a thing that none other does: it makes "Black" shorthand for being sweet, reliable, vulnerable, honest, communicative, loyal, kind, and truly committed to someone in a romantic relationship. "Be Real Black for Me" is Tea Cake and Janie without the abuse. It's Ossie Davis and Ruby Dee without the fame. It's my parents, who met via my mom picking up a handsome hitcher from the city of Philadelphia bound for Cheyney State University where they were both doing the super Black things of the time.

Lyrics I love from "Be Real Black for Me": You don't have to search and roam / 'Cause I got your love at home / Be real Black for me.

This concept of Blackness-as-home has formed my own romantic fantasies and the occasional debacle. Once, for a talent show in downtown New York City, I had a friend make an original backing track of the song for me that I could use again and again. I figured since "Be Real Black for Me" had been sampled by M.O.P. for "World Famous" and Scarface for "My Block," the song would connect. I walked out onstage to hundreds of Japanese faces, some framed by fake dreads. The song did not connect.

But more important than leading to a bad show was that this Blackness-as-love concept made cultural touchstones—like natural hair, shared musical taste, a decent grasp of history and politics, African garb, yummy-smelling oils, and a healthy, bushy beard—the evidence that a relationship was sound and would last beyond the fun parts. That the blinding Whiteness of the love that rules rom-coms is not the only way to a shared life.

So I was always falling in "love" with that dude with the waist-length locs and big beard who called me some form of Kiba Biba and made beats. In fairness to me, he fell for me too. But in place of real connection were intense moments, quirks, and physical engagements that I took as sharing.

Extra props went to "conscious" dudes who were secure enough not to use quasi-Black nationalism as a cover for their homophobia or sexism.

Once, one such gentleman, whom I was on and off with in an undefined relationship for ten years, came home and announced that a gay man had walked up to him that day as he sat outside for lunch and started talking to him.

"Word?" I said, scared of what was going to fall out of his lips. "Then what happened?"

"Nothing really," he replied. "He seemed lonely. We talked about a painting he was carrying. He was an artist. Then he kept it pushing."

Mmmm.

That guy was so very sweet and absolutely noncommittal. He had keys to the house and fed the cat when I was away despite the fact that feline thug life once attacked his feet at the bottom of the bed. But real life intervened. He didn't finish college due to some abuse of his credit that he did not inflict. He had never left home and didn't talk about his family. He did security at an art school where he should have been a student and then a professor. He cared that he didn't finish college but didn't do anything about it. I couldn't decide if I cared about his lack of ambition or if I was just worried that my own get-up-and-go would make him resent me.

The answer came after a very long break. I can't remember how we reentered each other's lives, but he had since enrolled in school and was more satisfied than I had ever seen him. We went to see an '80s R&B maven tear up a tourist trap downtown. It was one of our best times, which led to a disjointed discussion about love in which I blurted out, "Of course I love you. What are you even talking about?"

"I never knew that!" he lied. "You never showed that. That time we fought about money . . . "

Rather than hate him for acting confused on purpose, I locked him out of my house, my phone, my head, my heart. Every surface is absent him.

There have been several more hims, before and after:

I loved him. He fucked a White prostitute and others in his travels.

This one threw a duffle bag full of pots at my head, punched a wall and broke his hand, and told my mental health business to all of his messy friends.

That one said he loved me too, when she was not around. But, "revolution!"

I got ready to love him, but after many years of flirtation, he had twins with a woman he never mentioned as more than a friend.

I still love one, but I believe that something died in him when he was little, that someone touched him in the wrong way. He has never come out and said it, instead leaving crumbs in jeans pockets, dropping hints like loose change. "That jawn is a sociopath," said my married-with-kids sister Asali. But I can love him because the idea of his touch now seems inanimate. We laugh like kids. I say, "Please take care of yourself," and mean it.

Most recently, I wasn't in love with, but was relieved by a him. I was finally claimed and claiming! He knew about my anger, my bad luck, my bursts of unavailability, my corniest notions of what a lasting relationship should be. We talked all day on text. (Emojis as adults are fun. Don't front.) We talked about a future and our mistakes. Private jokes were key, as was our shared idea of what Blackness meant. He was a protector, someone who would get into a fight on the street with a man laying hands on a woman. He was a traditionalist who got a kick out of my Black feminism. "Be Real Black for Me" it was, until he asked me for some small, strange sum of money. I asked him something that my gut knew would end it: "What's it for?" He bounced with an attempted lecture that was very far below both of us.

But it's okay. Not a ten-year entanglement or a forever wound. Progress.

Donny Hathaway plunged to his death in 1979. My parents have been married for forty-eight years. These two facts are as unrelated as "Be Real Black for Me" is to a reality beyond exceptional songcraft and a very groovy first dance for folks with surprising taste. Yet the song stays on my playlist for nostalgia's sake. I still enjoy fantasizing that a beard is a viable symbol of longevity and that sweetness will move throughout our bodies, reviving every dead or dying piece of psychic tissue until we become something real and whole together. Yes, I still do this knowing full well that the best that could happen is me being real Black for myself.

NINE
I MAKE MONEY MOVES

There's no other way to put this: on a scale from "pitiful" to "killing it," the state of Black wealth is firmly at "pitiful." As it turns out, decades upon decades of slavery, Jim Crow, redlining, land theft, mass incarceration, predatory lending, education discrimination, gentrification, deindustrialization, and zero reparations really *have* done a number on how much we have to live on and pass down to our kids. A 2016 study from the Institute for Policy Studies and the Corporation for Economic Development found that it would take 228 years for the average Black family to amass the same level of wealth the average White family holds today. Even when we are born wealthy, this nation is designed to bring us down: A 2018 study[*] from researchers at the US Census Bureau, Stanford University, and Harvard University showed that Black boys raised in the nation's wealthiest families are more likely than their White counterparts to live in poverty when they reach adulthood; the study points to racism as the reason.

And yet we keep pushing, using our considerable skills to crack open the door to collective prosperity with a heart. Black women are the fastest-growing group of entrepreneurs in the United States. We're out here building our own tables, creating platforms where our art can thrive, using money to directly attack a system that uses poverty as an excuse to lock us away, and

---

[*] Raj Chetty, Nathaniel Hendren, Maggie R. Jones, and Sonya R. Porter, "Race and Economic Opportunity in the United States: An Intergenerational Perspective," Equality of Opportunity Project, March 2018, http://www.equality-of-opportunity.org/assets/documents/race_paper.pdf (accessed June 6, 2018).

marshaling our resources to demolish a supposed representative democracy that works only for those who are able to grease the wheels with cash.

From the streaming service CEO, to the couple fund-raising for progressive Black political candidates, to the folks using technology to bail Black people out of jail, "I Make Money Moves" holds up the fam who are working hard to build Black income, wealth, and culture, for all our sakes.

DeShuna Spencer on Eradicating Black Unemployment One Stream at a Time

DeShuna Spencer is the founder and CEO of kweliTV, a video streaming service that curates independent films, documentaries, web series, and children's programming from the entire African Diaspora. A master brand evangelist, she has secured six figures' worth of funding via pitch and grant competitions alone, winning over judges from the National Black Chamber of Commerce and the Harvard Africa Business Club alike. In this interview, DeShuna, a native of Memphis, Tennessee, talks to Kenrya about the joys and pains of fund-raising while unapologetically Black, why truth reigns supreme in storytelling, and how streaming will set us free.

Tell me kweliTV's origin story.

The idea came to me as I was watching television in 2012. Back then I had cable, and I was flipping, flipping, flipping, and couldn't find anything that I wanted to see. So I cut cable and got Netflix, hoping that I would see more diverse content there. And while they had *some*, it was the same romantic comedies and throwback movies. I love the Black movies from the '90s, but how many times can you watch *Juice*?

Meanwhile, I follow all these blogs, and they write about great independent films that screen at festivals, but I couldn't find them. I realized that once these Black films finish the festival circuit, they have nowhere to go if they don't have a big name behind them. I was crazy enough to say, "I'm going to create a place for them to go!"

How did you get started?

I entered a pitch competition, where they didn't pick me because they weren't sure about the future of streaming! But in 2014, I won $20,000 in the Unity Journalists for Diversity New U competition. We used that money to build our beta version of the service, which allowed us to do further testing to see if people actually cared about what we were doing and would pay to subscribe. Then it took two years to get out of beta. That's a book within itself, the challenges of bootstrapping the company. I had no idea that Black women only get 0.2 percent of all venture capital investments until I was looking and saying, "Where's the money?" and people were saying, "Good luck with that." Technically, we're still a startup company, we're not fully funded. I'm doing this off blessings, holding it together with tears, bubble gum, and glue.

Why is kweliTV important?

It's about owning our stories. It's one thing to say, "Yeah, you know, we're getting our foot in the door from mainstream spaces like HBO and Netflix." But there's also something to be said for something that we own personally, where *we* control our narrative and don't have to dilute our voices, dilute our culture, for a mainstream, colloquial audience. kweliTV is unapologetically Black. I think that us being authentic is relevant for no matter *who* watches the content.

Another thing is the global aspect of it. When I tell people we're focused on the Black global community, or the African Diaspora, most people tend to just think African Americans. They tend to forget that we're basically everywhere—the Caribbean, Europe, Latin America. My goal is to show our stories from all over the world in a way that's not monopolistic or stereotypical. I see kweliTV as an avenue to share the Black experience no matter where you are.

What does "kweli" mean?

Kweli means "truth" in Swahili. And our mission is to curate content that is a true representation of the Black experience. It doesn't always have to be positive, it doesn't have to be feel-good—just true. There are realities in our community that we may not necessarily like, but it's okay to tell those stories here.

How does exposing that truth help us resist White supremacy's pull?

By dispelling some of the myths we see in mainstream media. I remember when Trump ran for office, he was like, "What do you have to lose? You get shot when you walk outside. . . . " He was basically saying that we're all poor, we're all dumb, we're all going to be killed. He assigned that narrative to all Black people in one swoop. And he's not the only one. There was a study that came out about media and implicit bias, and it showed that Black people are swallowing the negative imagery we're being fed. Will kweliTV solve White supremacy? Not totally, no. But there comes a point where we just cannot be afraid of being who we truly are. For those who are actually open to learning about Black culture without blinders and filters about what they *think* it is, we can definitely challenge stereotypes and help them get there so we can see our full selves.

What has been your biggest unexpected challenge in running kweliTV?

When people ask about my exit strategy. When you have investors, they want to make a return within five years. Having an exit strategy essentially means selling your company to a Netflix or some other company that's not Black-owned. And if we want to continue to be a Black-owned company, then we may not be able to take advantage of all the possible investment opportunities. I get emails from people saying, "Don't become BET," which means, "Don't sell out." But how do you reconcile that desire with the fact that one day you're going to have to sell it? That's something I'm still trying to figure out.

That's real; I never thought about it that way.
Meanwhile, you've been raising money by crushing
pitch competitions. What's your secret?

I think it's passion. You want people to know that it's something you would still do even if you made absolutely no money. Because if someone is going to give you money, you still have to be just as passionate at 2:00 a.m. as when you were up onstage asking for money. Another thing is that I know my numbers. If you're fumbling during questioning, then even if you're passionate, you're not going to win. Also, I always pray before I pitch to make sure that people are positively impacted by what I'm about to say.

If you could snap your fingers, how would you make us free?

If kweliTV is in the place where I want it to be in, let's say, the next fourteen years, I would try to eradicate Black unemployment. That would be my mission. I have this really lofty idea where, if you're a Black person and you're unemployed, I want to offer you a job paying a living wage, or resources to start a business and hire other Black people. The reality is that no matter how hard we work, no matter how many degrees we get, there will still be people who will deny us jobs and access because we're Black. I'm not a separatist, but if we can hire each other, if we can help Black people create our own companies, then we can be self-sufficient and paid what we're really worth. That's my biggest dream.

～～～～～～

I resist White supremacy by using data science to dismantle the myths that sustain its power and creating digital pathways for more people to participate in advancing systemic solutions.

—Samuel Sinyangwe, data scientist and policy analyst

～～～～～～

Three Questions for Appolition's Dr. Kortney Ryan Ziegler and Tiffany Mikell

In 2017, Dr. Kortney Ryan Ziegler (creative director) and Tiffany Mikell (managing director) created Appolition, an app that allows users to automatically round up purchases and donate their change to bail relief for Black people who are stuck behind bars simply because they can't afford to pay their way out. Inspired by the National Bail Out—a campaign that works to reform the cash bail system and free people charged with misdemeanors—they created the cleverly named Appolition in just four months and were soon raising thousands in bail relief daily. "Why not play on that word by using technology that's going to prevent, in some ways, the enslavement of Black folks in the United States?" Ziegler says.

Ziegler and Mikell chatted with Kenrya about the purpose and promise of using their role as technologists to bolster the lived experiences of Black people everywhere.

Why is Appolition an important project for you to pour your energy into?

KZ: Honestly, it's something higher. It's part of our journey and our fate. We've both been in technology for a long time, and we are also very radical and believe in the civil liberties and rights and humanities of Black folks. Being able to do something that can galvanize people on a global level is just— it's part of our thinking, design, and fate.

TM: All of our work together over the last three and a half years started from a place of, "How do we use technology, design, and user experience, to make the world a better place for Black people?"

How does the app help dismantle the system of White supremacy?

TM: The beauty of Appolition is that all of the donations come from individuals. There are some bail relief programs that are completely funded by larger entities like foundations, and they're oftentimes run by non-Black people who are not really connected to the issue. Here, we're doing it on our own.

KZ: Right. Black Americans have tremendous spending power, so how can we leverage being consumers? We are rerouting that money and using it to help victims of the prison industrial complex.

TM: I think that because of White supremacy, a lot of times, when we talk about the buying power of Black people, it's from a place of shaming. We're shaming Black people for not being able to do certain things collectively in spite of the buying power that we have. But because we understand how White supremacy works, we understand the challenges that we face. It's been really cool to see how we can leverage that buying power to actually free people while others work to secure policy changes. We're showing that there are multiple ways to address the problem, and we can all bring our skills to the table and make a major impact.

What does freedom look like to you?

TM: I'm constantly asking myself, *How can I bring my experience as a Black woman who grew up in Chicago to this role?* I know there are a lot of Black people who feel like, in their professional roles, they have to leave all of who they are at the door. I think it's a shame. A big part of my life's work is creating organizations and safe spaces for brilliant Black people to come and bring their full selves and create the things that they feel like have to exist in the world, making sure that we embrace the Black community's brilliant, nonconforming creators. That's what freedom looks like to me.

KZ: It's important to be who I am as a Black person in the world. My ideal of freedom for Black people is the ability to exist. Whatever that may mean, in whatever space and whatever context.

~~~~~~

Attempts at Self-Care for a Corporate Black Girl

"MacKenzie Jones"

Hair Story I: A Presentation

I was natural in college and decided that in order to get a finance job, I needed to wear my hair a certain way. Now, I have coarse hair. There's no slicking it back with just water and gel. So I thought it would be easier to perm it.

A few years in, after breaking up with a boyfriend who did not like natural hair, I cut off my straight hair. My mom was like, "Uh, MacKenzie, what do you plan to do with that?" I promptly went to an African braid shop and got Senegalese twists.

At work, I knew it would be a big to-do. So I grabbed my coffee and my ham-egg-and-cheese sandwich (don't judge me) and got to work extra early so I could avoid walking past a bunch of White coworkers on the floor and in the hallway who would ask me about my hair.

It still happened, though. I went to a meeting that morning where I was, as usual, the only Black person, the only woman, and the youngest person in the room. I was giving a presentation when the most senior person in the room asked, "How long did it take to do that?" I knew he meant my hair, but I wanted him to say it directly. "How long did it take to prepare my presentation?" I asked, playing dumb. And he was like, "No, your hair."

This opened up the floodgates. Because the boss asked me about my hair, the topic was fair game.

One guy goes, "When I was in Jamaica, I was thinking about getting some braids," and laughed. After a while, my direct supervisor interrupted and said, "MacKenzie, you changed your hair. It looks nice. Can we move on?" Only then could I go on with the presentation.

Hair Story II: Preferences

Once I had to pull aside one of my peers after I got braids for an upcoming vacation because she said, "I really do prefer your hair that way."

I said, "Well, it really doesn't matter how you prefer it," and went back to talking about work.

But then she goes, "Oh, did we wake up on the wrong side of the bed?"

I laughed it off, but addressed it later that day. Her response? "I hope you didn't think what I said was off-putting. I was just giving you a compliment." The next time I changed my hair she mumbled that it was nice and kept it moving. That was a victory. My hair should never be a discussion at work. White people here change their hair all the time—they color it, cut it, straighten it, get extensions. Disrupting a meeting or work discussion is about people gawking at you and feeling ownership of you.

Smiling

I have heard so many comments about how my tone of voice and my face are aggressive. It's like, "MacKenzie, you're not smiling enough," and I'm like, *I'm trying to calculate a fucking standard deviation ratio and you want me to smile?* I've had to put a lot of time into figuring out what to say in these situations. I've landed on: "I appreciate the feedback. I'd like to take a moment to think about it, and then schedule a follow-up, because I want us to have a fruitful conversation." They never follow up.

Other People of Color

I've seen coworkers of color born in America say that recent immigrants are too hard to understand. *And then they imitate them.* I want to ask them, "What's wrong with you?" Instead, I say, "Actually, I understand him. You just need to listen a little closer."

Stereotypes

For most of my childhood, I would say my family was poor. Around high school, my mother went back to school, so we became lower-middle-class. I think this plays a role in how I see things. I want so badly to not be a stereotype of a Black woman that I don't ask for the help that I need. A lot of success in my field is about connections and the story of your life. So what do you do when you're in an environment where you're trying to defy the stereotype, but you *were* the stereotype?

Wu-Tang Who?

Sometimes when White coworkers try to connect with me, they want to discuss rap. I just play dumb. I remember one time I acted like I didn't know who the Wu-Tang Clan was.

Plans

I tell my mentees, "Corporate America is cool, but you've got to have a plan for what's next." I wish I'd had a plan for not staying in it too long. But it is what it is, is it not?

"MacKenzie Jones" is the pseudonym of a thirty-something marketing executive at a major financial firm in New York City.

~~~~~~~~

Bakari Kitwana on What Activism Is Worth

Bakari Kitwana is a writer, editor, and activist. Early in his career at Chicago's Third World Press, he edited titles like Frances Cress Welsing's *The Isis Papers*. He went on to become a political editor at *The Source*, and his 2002 book, *The Hip-Hop Generation*, led to the formation of the National Hip-Hop Political Convention, which attracted some four thousand mostly Black and Brown young adults in 2004. Kitwana went on to found Rap Sessions, a youth-centered discussion tour led by a panel of artists, scholars, activists, and journalists as varied as Rhymefest, Tamika Mallory, Sybrina Fulton, Marc Lamont Hill, Joan Morgan, Rashad Robinson, and Michael Eric Dyson. In this Q+A, Akiba talks to Bakari about the value we place on activism.

A major role that you play in Black organizing is that of a connector. You're always plugging someone into

*funding and speaking engagements, talking up someone's
work, or helping people who aren't locked into elite
institutions figure out how to format and promote
what they're doing. Is this a natural tendency?*

I think it's natural to a degree. But I also think that it's rooted in activism. Part of fighting White supremacy is fighting capitalism. Connecting people is an anti-individualistic approach. And on a spiritual level, nobody can stand in the way of what is for you; helping other people isn't interfering with you getting to where you have to go. I help people because people have always helped me. None of us have gotten anywhere on our own, even if we tell ourselves that mythology.

*As my boss in the late '90s at The Source, you were the first
person to say—out loud and with no shame—that
people should be paid livable wages for activist work.
Back then, we didn't have Beyoncé saying, "F you,
pay me." We had to "do it for the culture."*

You know, one of the big rifts in our history, particularly in the late '60s and the early '70s, was between Marxists and cultural nationalists. Cultural nationalism is often demonized among radicals, but one of the things they had right was that we have to instill a sense of values into our people if we're going to win. In a capitalist economy, one of those values has to be about economics. If we value the output of political knowledge, we have to engrain that into the culture of our people.

A lot of how I think about this is influenced by how I was nurtured as an activist and thinker. At Third World Press, I sat in conversations with Nathan Hare, Gil Scott-Heron, Amiri Baraka, and Gwendolyn Brooks. These folks were real people who were serious about the future of Black people. They wanted to get paid and have their art and political ideas valued, but they struck a balance. Gwendolyn Brooks used to say to me, "Some stuff we're just going to do for the people. But then we got to get out here and make money so that we can still do those things for the people."

***Talk about how you involve local organizers in Rap
Sessions, given that speaking gigs are episodic.***

We rarely go to a place where we haven't been in ongoing conversation
with people who are organizing on the ground. This is an idea I gleaned
from Amiri Baraka. One of the things he said we needed to fight White
supremacy and capitalism was to create spaces around the country. His em-
phasis was on cities where there's a large Black population. So if we've got
an artist, poet, or author who's speaking to our truth, we can take them to
at least ten cities around the country, and they can be in conversation with
Black people. Even though we've evolved out of that time, the value of that
is still important.

~~~~~~~~

Liberation Playlist

Jay Smooth

"I resist White supremacy by loving my people, thinking about systems,
and telling the truth." —Jay Smooth

- "Backlash Blues," Nina Simone
- "What Can I Do for You," Labelle
- "Wear Clean Draws," The Coup
- "In Time," The Jungle Brothers
- "In Time," Sly and the Family Stone
- "Original Faubus Fables," Charles Mingus
- "1,000 Deaths," D'Angelo and The Vanguard
- "Soldier," Erykah Badu
- "When Will We B Paid," Prince
- "ShapeShifters," Invincible
- "Bring the Noise," Public Enemy
- "Keep on Pushing," The Impressions

Jay Smooth is the host of New York City's longest-running hip-hop radio show, WBAI's *Underground Railroad*, and the acclaimed cultural commentator on the *Ill Doctrine* video blog, where his dissections of race and politics have become teaching tools in schools around the country.

~~~~~~~~

Clocked in Still Starving (annotated)

Tongo Eisen-Martin

My money being
The nonviolent part of rage*
A kind of courtesy worship
Or caste-system blues†

Bullet casings in the comb
I learned their language immediately‡
I watched an animal explode into hundreds of flags

---

* I think that the United States itself is the invention of Whiteness and that Whiteness has two expressions. The most primary expression is organized violence. This line is about Whiteness as a deputization that exists to keep enslaved Africans in check.

† I'm speaking to class versus race here. There's the class analysis that says that the principal contradiction in society is rich versus poor, ruling class versus the oppressed. And you have schools of radical thought that say it's not class, it's Black versus White. I think it's more of a complicated hybrid of the two, where both realities are at play with, reinforce, and sometimes contradict each other.

‡ This line is not to say that all we need is armed resistance, but to say that any solution or any resistance to White supremacy that doesn't come to terms with the fact that it is completely tied to an organization of violence—a monopoly of violence—is not going to get us to the Promised Land. Money can express some things, but money will not save us. And then the extension of it is this: If you cannot get resistance out of a dollar, then what is that dollar really doing? That dollar to me is really evidence of our surrender. What you're really saying is, "We give up. We don't really want any problems. And you can continue to brutalize whoever you want to brutalize here and abroad, kill whatever you want to kill, and enforce and really enforce an insane mode of production."

Judging by my wounds
The government has counted me in*

Face to face
With a police officer's family history
My anecdote is only just beginning†

Originally from San Francisco, Tongo Eisen-Martin is a movement worker and educator who has organized against mass incarceration and extra-judicial killing of Black people throughout the United States. His latest curriculum, *We Charge Genocide Again*, is used as an educational and organizing tool. His book of poems *Someone's Dead Already* earned him the California Book Award. His most recent collection of poetry is *Heaven Is All Goodbyes*, which won the 2018 American Book Award and the 2018 California Book Award for Poetry.

~~~~~~~~~

Stefanie Brown James and Quentin James Want You to Put Your Money Where Your Votes Are

Quentin James (executive director) and Stefanie Brown James (senior advisor) launched The Collective in August 2016 with the goal of build-ing Black political power. The four-pronged organization—it includes a

---

* This just means that to resist White supremacy is to accept that there will be state or state-sanctioned violence against you.

† What are some of the units or atoms or molecules of a monopoly of violence? One of them is giving the White vigilante, the White police officer, absolute rein and power to do whatever they want. I mean, it was law in some places that when insurrection appeared to be afoot, White peo-ple had to patrol African people. It was like, literally, "You are drafted." You could kill anybody as long as the person who so-called owned the African felt compensated fairly enough or thought you did them a favor by killing a possible seed of rebellion. That's the way a vigilante, the way that a soldier of Whiteness, is programmed—to not see a human being and to only be trying to enforce one thing: their absolute power.

political action committee (PAC) for collecting grassroots-level donations, a super-PAC for soliciting the big bucks, a 501(c)(4) social welfare arm that allows them to directly fund campaigns, and a nonprofit education fund—is working overtime to increase the number of progressive Black elected officials at the local, state, and federal levels. Both are veterans of major political campaigns: Stefanie ran the national Black vote program for Barack Obama, while Quentin did the same for Hillary Clinton. Kenrya talked to the wife-and-husband team about why simply voting for your favorite candidate isn't good enough.

How did The Collective come to be?

QJ: In the summer of 2016, we saw an explosion of a lot of different issues, including Trump's campaign—which was obviously extremely racist—in combination with more Black people being killed by cops and the subsequent cases that were not being decided in favor of justice. A lot of people rightfully directed their energy toward protesting. But at the same time, there wasn't an analysis around power and the individuals who hold it, whether they be elected sheriffs or prosecutors or mayors who hire police chiefs. We wanted to turn the focus of that outrage to people actually putting their money into the political system.

I think Black people have been told the biggest lie in American political history, which is that if we just vote everything will be okay. And what we saw in 2012, with Stefanie's leadership on the Obama campaign, is that Black people voted at a historic high. But between 2012 and 2016, we saw tremendous inequitable administration of the law when it came to criminal justice reform. So obviously it's not just about our votes. It's also about our money, and the fact that if you ask any Black politician in this country right now, "Are the majority of your donors Black people in your community?" the answer will be "no" 99 percent of the time.

We don't have a stake in the game when it comes to our money, and these things keep happening even though our community is voting. People of color make up 40 percent of this country's population, but we have this huge

underrepresentation. It can't just be the same thing over and over: register
Black voters, get Black voters out to the polls. We need Black prosecutors and
state's attorneys.

How do you reconcile asking folks to contribute financially with the economic situation of Black people in this country?

QJ: The reality is, our situation is that Black buying power is at $1.3 trillion
per year, and we spend our money on what we value. The people we elect
control the biggest pot of money in the world—the United States budget.
And it comes from our tax dollars. They decide if we spend our money on
wars or schools, prisons or jobs. So that is power that *we* can yield with a little
investment. I'm not asking people to take a pay cut or give us 10 percent of
their salary. But what we could do with just a portion of that $1.3 trillion
would be amazing.

How do you decide which candidates to support?

QJ: First, candidates come to us and go, "Hey, I'm interested in your en-
dorsement." Then we give them a candidate questionnaire. We ask them
everything from where they stand on criminal justice, civil rights, health
care, education, the economy—it's pretty detailed. Once they pass that
questionnaire—and we define passing as scoring 90 percent or above—then
we assess their viability. Can they win the race? Then we take a vote; any do-
nor who has given us $1 to $5,000 gets an equal say on who we endorse via
a simple majority.

SBJ: Candidates have to truly fit what we're looking for, as it relates to focusing on progressive candidates who can make substantial changes through
their position.

What does "progressive" mean to you?

QJ: I think people want a candidate to be perfect, to be 100 percent of where
they want them to be on all the issues. So we said 90 percent, right? It's a lot

of questions, but there are some pretty simple, progressive questions that we think people should be able to answer. "Where do you stand on a woman's right to choose? Do you believe that climate change is real? Are you willing to stand up to corporate interests? Do you want to raise the minimum wage? Do you believe we should outlaw 'stand your ground' laws?" We think if you get nine out of ten questions right, you're with us, you're progressive.

How does The Collective help Black people resist White supremacy?

QJ: I think one of the first ways is that we promote ownership of our leaders. If we support them, not just with our votes but with our money, they are very much beholden to their constituents. And people often think "constituents" only means voters, but it also means donors. So if the developers, if the corporate interests, are supporting all the Black candidates' campaigns, they're also going to have an ear. It is White supremacist to use money as a weapon, and until we realize that our money can be used to *resist* White supremacy, we're going to be in trouble.

SBJ: Having the option of an entity like The Collective gives people the opportunity to be engaged in something that can make substantial changes on the ground. Lack of access and the inability to channel your beliefs into an institution that can create change stop progress. The Collective gives people a tangible way to support Black candidates and in turn fight White supremacy, which is working to continue to keep us subservient and beholden. Our donors know this organization is theirs; they can see the victories and the change we are bringing about collectively.

QJ: I would just add that the fact that White people are overrepresented in our political system is a form of White supremacy. So by trying to equal things out and get more Black people represented, we are literally resisting White supremacy through the democratic process.

~~~~~~~~

**I fight White supremacy by supporting authors,
journalists, writers, podcasters, entrepreneurs,
and community leaders of color.**

—Tina Perez, project manager

~~~~~~~

QUESTION, ANSWERED

It's no surprise that money is a fraught topic—it touches every part of our lives, for better and for worse. Here we tackle the question: what's your relationship with money?

Kenrya

"How about you spend less time modeling self-sacrifice, and more time modeling self-care?"

My therapist is dragging me again.

We're talking about my relationship with money. I just confessed that while I essentially work a part-time job to send my daughter to a private school because the local joints are, shall we say, lacking, I have been lovingly, longingly looking at the Sonicare electric toothbrush that I abandoned in my Amazon cart six months ago because I feel guilty spending $40 on myself when I could use it for her violin lessons or this coding game I know she would love. Meanwhile, I bought her a more expensive version of the toothbrush, plus two packs of replacement heads. Hence the dragging, already in progress.

———————

Pattern. *A reliable sample of traits, acts, tendencies, or other observable characteristics of a person, group, or institution.*[*]

———————

———————

[*] "Pattern," *Merriam-Webster,* https://www.merriam-webster.com/dictionary/pattern (accessed April 22, 2018).

I've never felt richer than I did on book delivery day as a kid. The homie Google tells me that it's all online now, but way back in elementary school, I'd get hype when the teacher walked across the front of the classroom, handing the kid at the head of each row a batch of four-page, full-color newsletters that detailed all the books we could order from Scholastic that month. I'd take mine from the hand of the person in front of me, grab a pencil, and circle everything that looked mildly interesting, then spend the evening curating the list, striking the things that seemed boring on second read, and making sure I was properly advancing my collection of "The Baby-Sitters Club" titles.

Then I'd tell my daddy it was book time, and he would hand me a signed blank check. I'd total my books, make out the check, and hand it to my teacher with the order form the next day. Two weeks later, I'd feel flush. Most folks would get a book here or there, but I'd always have an entire box of treasure to carry on the bus and dive into when I got home. The way that I felt on book delivery days—loved and seen and cared for and lucky—still sticks with me. My daddy might not have been able to buy me every toy I begged for, but he spared no expense when it came to my favorite companions.

We didn't have a dining room in my childhood home. Why? 'Cause the previous owners of our three-bedroom ranch-style house thought it would be dope to have a stage instead.

It stood about five inches higher than the floor in the rest of the house and was covered with the same deep brown carpet as the living room, which it faced. One wall sported a window that looked out on the street, while the other was covered in mirrors, floor to ceiling, in the shape of square tiles, with smaller diamond-shaped mirrors that accented the corners where they met. In the center of it all was an airbrushed picture of a mama koala bear with a baby on its back. My little sister and I always said that was us, me carrying her on my back while we feasted on bamboo. Our marsupial selves were a captive audience as we sang into an old school microphone, hand-danced with Daddy, and practiced twirling routines on that weird little stage.

The day that I let myself in from school and found my father—home hours earlier than usual—sitting on the edge of the stage, glasses on the floor beside him, long legs blocking the path to the rest of the house, I immediately knew that something was wrong.

He had worked at a computer company for as long as I'd been alive, but on that day he was laid off. And as he was raising us alone, our sole income was gone.

We had always struggled to keep up in our suburban neighborhood. As Daddy once explained when I asked why I couldn't do something or other, one income just didn't go as far as the dual joints my suburban friends enjoyed. They went on vacations and college tours and were presented at cotillions on the weekends. *I* spent Saturday and Sunday at Granddaddy's house, playing drive-by with my cousins.

(Bare feet black with dirt from jumping over the extra-long phone cord that passed as a rope, my cousins, my little sister, and I would scope the street, looking left and then looking right past the long row of parallel parked vehicles, waiting for a car to come barreling toward us. When we'd see one in the distance, we'd abandon the hot asphalt, dash past the scraggly tree lawn and the strip of sidewalk, and hide behind the row of short bushes that rimmed my granddaddy's yard, as if they could stop the bullets we imagined the drivers were spraying at us.)

But we ate well, and our gas was usually on, if not our lights. My father stretched himself to root us in a neighborhood with excellent public schools because he knew that while there is no such thing as a great equalizer, education is the closest thing we have.

To make that happen, he sacrificed himself, carving off small pieces of his well-being and offering them up to my sister and me, his creditors, and the many people—from blood relatives to a family that was experiencing homelessness—who slept on our couches for months at a time. He'd skip lunch to make sure we had enough to buy those cardboard-ass pizza squares in the cafeteria. He'd wear the same pair of high tops until they were mushy and gray, barely recognizable as shoes. He'd wait to get haircuts until *he* was barely recognizable.

The pieces just got larger after he was "downsized"; he eventually landed as a subcontractor servicing one of his former clients, dropping from a steady salary to hourly pay that squeezed us tighter. But he persisted, constantly working and somehow finding a way to pay for most of the things we needed, if not always the things we wanted.

These days, as I offer up my can't-see hours to finance my daughter's education and social calendar, I understand the method behind his madness. But having insight into his motivation doesn't mean that it isn't mad.

———————

Pattern. *An original or model considered for or deserving of imitation.**

———————

In my willingness to do *anything* for my Saa-Saa—she of the soft brown skin, bright eyes, quick mind, and awful jokes—I thought I was making her feel loved and cared for, like I felt on book delivery days. And maybe I am, in the short term. But subjecting her to my marathon work sessions, my exhausted and distracted mind, and my old school–brushed teeth is really just teaching her the same lesson that I got from my father: You should find pleasure in taking care of the people around you and feel guilty about taking care of yourself.

Over the years this belief led me to a bank account that was depleted from spending to meet the wants and needs of others, lopsided relationships where I was more caretaker and secretary than equal partner, and a therapist who forced me to read a book about codependency.

And it doesn't stop at being a martyr in my personal relationships. Black women in the United States are paid 67.7 cents for every dollar paid to White men.† I've been taught both at home and in these White supremacist streets

———————

* "Pattern," *Dictionary.com*, http://www.dictionary.com/browse/pattern (accessed April 22, 2018).

† Ariane Hegewisch and Emma Williams-Baron, "The Gender Wage Gap: 2017 Earnings Differences by Race and Ethnicity," Institute for Women's Policy Research, https://iwpr.org/publications/gender-wage-gap-2017-race-ethnicity/ (accessed April 22, 2018).

(which are really the same thing, thanks to the toxic sea of racism and sexism we're swimming in, thanks) that it's not cool to demand what I'm worth. I'm expected to accept what I'm offered, or what will enable me to just get by, and use a fear of scarcity as my excuse for not wringing the joy out of each moment.

I do not want that for my child.

———————

Pattern. *Consistent and recurring characteristic or trait that helps in the identification of a phenomenon or problem and serves as an indicator or model for predicting its future behavior.**

———————

It's time for something new, for both of our sakes. I'm taking my therapist's advice and fashioning a new pattern that involves making space for myself financially, even as the world tells me that is selfish and shortsighted.

Recently, Saa and I tied our tennis shoes and headed out for a walk to the neighborhood studio where she takes a drop-in West African dance class with a Senegalese instructor. The breeze was a bit biting, but the sun was bright, and I tipped my face toward it as we strolled.

Each time my mind alerted me that I was supposed to be writing this essay or that I had a spring wardrobe of big kid clothes sitting in my Target app cart waiting for me to make the money to buy them, I deflected the thoughts, sending them hurtling into the distance as I reminded myself that joy, like what I felt strolling in the sun with Saa, is more precious than guilt—lighter too.

When we made it home hours later, I ordered Thai food because I was too exhausted to cook. Full and satisfied, I put away my phone so I wouldn't be distracted, then camped out on the floor with the little one for rounds of

———————

* "Pattern," *Business Dictionary,* http://www.businessdictionary.com/definition/pattern.html (accessed April 22, 2018).

Uno and whatever the Ikea version of Jenga is called. Then I dozed while she lay on me and sketched a fabulous tiered dress that she dubbed "Sherbet." Just before putting her to bed, I found my phone, popped open the Amazon app, and bought that fucking toothbrush. Here's to living in our abundance.

<center>~~~~~~~~~~</center>

Akiba

I've always admired people who are proactive and intentional with money. I like the idea of having a savings account at like age five, buying a home, buying rental properties, having enough cash to work with a financial planner, having a college fund for your kids, saving six months' worth of operating funds in case you get laid off, using coupons, eating the lunch you made at home, having perfect credit, paying every single bill on time, and *turning off all of the gottdamn lights because are you going to pay this electric bill?*

For the most part I've been lucky. I am a single, childless writer and editor in expensive-ass New York City, but I know that if crisis comes calling, I can move back home to Philly to the two-parent, paid-in-full house where I was raised.

Both of my parents are college-educated and retired from full-time jobs with savings. From day one they made it clear that my sister and I were going away to college on scholarship. ("Mom, do we have a college fund?" "Yeah. Your brains.")

After an early foray into entrepreneurship—selling shiny rocks, making comics, peddling Kwanzaa cookies as one half of the "Ujamaa Bakers"—I started working at fourteen. It was a summer job at CoreStates Bank, filing canceled checks next to adults who had the Gucci, Louis Vuitton, and MCM bags I envied.

Compared to my Black peers with single moms, we did pretty well. Politically speaking, we were not supposed to even care about that. All of our clothes came from Jomar's, House of Bargains, Artie's, and Marshalls. One time, during the designer jean craze of the '80s, my mom snagged me a pair of Pierre Cardins at an outlet. I went around the house chanting, "Pierre

Car-DIN!" in what I believed was a French accent. My mother scratched out the labels.

Lesson learned.

But things changed when, after several school strikes and denied applications to our local magnet school, my parents shipped my sister and me off to a predominantly White, all-girls prep school in the Philadelphia suburbs. We were Black superstar geniuses benefiting from the affirmative action that our ancestors sacrificed for and that we certainly deserved. The people at that school were White and rich. They had "au pairs" and summer homes. They had multiple bathrooms and swimming pools. Their jackets had those crumpled-up zipper tags that one gets during a ski trip. Everybody lived in the suburbs and some would ask dumb questions like, "Do you see pools of blood on your street?"

One night my mom hit the Lotto and called what seemed like all of her girlfriends screaming, "I WON FIFTY DOLLARS IN THE LOTTERYYY!" I bragged about this at school the next day. But when I disclosed that it was a $50 come-up, I got peculiar looks and silence. These third-graders carried $20 bills in their LeSportsacs.

These early experiences created a class-consciousness that I will charitably call "multilayered."

We went to private school, summer camp, music and art class, gymnastics, ballet, African dance, screen-printing, and a bunch of other activities. Occasionally our only living grandparent, Mamie Nichols, would take the whole family out to Seafood Shanty, where we'd ball out on shrimp cocktail and Shirley Temples. Our clothes were not hot, but we wore uniforms anyway. My sister and I were able to circumvent most of the 'hood entry points into conspicuous consumption due to my parents' politics and the fact that the rich White girls at school couldn't make a distinction between us and any other Blacks.

At White girl school, Asali and I were "poor." When we first got there, me in the third and my sister in the fourth grade, White girls we had never met invited us to their homes for dinner. I still wonder if they thought we were Feed the Children recipients.

Then there was a bizarre, Negro-on-Black incident in which some of the parents whose kids went to ours and other area prep schools invited Asali and me to join Jack and Jill, then revoked the invitation because we "lived in the city."

By far the most confusing and damaging class-related trauma I faced came at the hands of one of the few Black girls in my class. She lived in the city like me, and we bonded over freestyle battles and the nightly countdown on Power 99. This girl's dad owned a market, but there was not much on the shelves and everything was dusty. She was "light-brown-skinned" with "good" hair, which, by non-crunchy, non–Black nationalist standards, was supposed to mean that she was better than me. One time this frenemy and her mother popped up at our home uninvited. They just didn't believe that our dark-skinned asses could have a house when they lived in an apartment.

And there were a few violent incidents between us. After trying unsuccessfully to humiliate me in front of the White girls with poorly drawn diagrams of the African art at our house, she lunged at me. Ultimately, I came very close to throwing her out a window. Another time, during a rare out-of-uniform day, she ripped my flannel, big-shirt-over-leggings situation wide open to expose my puny nibblets wrapped in a white bra. Shoving and slapping ensued.

But this girl's attempt to be better based on internalized White supremacy (that was not her fault, I should note) backfired in the Blackest of ways. At slumber parties we were pity-invited to, she would bring like eighty pairs of pajamas. These White girls didn't even shower in the morning. "She's an obnoxious show-off," one such girl told me as she brushed her long hair in one of the four bathrooms in the house.

What I learned from this amalgam of experiences is that being rich and White meant being proudly oblivious to what you had, laughing at lower-income people of color who tried to look rich like you, calling Italians and other ethnic White folks "mall-chicks," and screaming, "My dad works at the stock exchange!" in a pinch.

Whiplash!

Here lies the suspect benevolence of rich White girls I didn't know; some mean-spirited classism from suburban Black adults; a frenemy whose good hair didn't do anything for her family's bottom line; and a deep shame about knowing any of this.

What kind of child of Black nationalists gains intimate knowledge of class politics across race, immigration status, and ethnicity from a *suburban prep school*? To me, not a proper one. I took simplifying matters very seriously. I bought the biggest gold earrings I could afford, lots of Reeboks, and multiple Liz Claiborne bags with my job money. I entertained a certified nutjawn drug peddler from Richard Allen Projects in hopes that he would catch me up on what I'd missed. I wore seven different permed hairstyles at one time while my family looked on with concern and then annoyance. I gave boys on the el the wrong name but the right number, because I was scared to be too bougie with, "No." I dreamed of being another iteration of the Malcolm X that Public Enemy and everybody else exalted.

Then my baba from down the way busted me with the realest things ever said to my confused self. Some things like, "You are not Malcolm X. The Klan didn't kill me, and your mother is alive. You were never separated from your sister. You were never hungry. You're not a pimp, a number runner, or going to jail. You're not getting a process that you have to wash out in the toilet. You're not a minister in the Nation of Islam. You're not getting murdered for the people. Be yourself, please."

This lesson settled in at Howard University, home of Black folks who had actual generational wealth. Some were ridiculous, and many were cool, even as lifetime members of the Links or Jack and Jill. I met AKAs, Deltas, Alphas, Kappas, and study-abroad students. I met artists from all over the country. I met historians and engineering students. Some had nice cars and went to cotillions but did not act a damn fool about it.

In adulthood, I have come to understand that if you are not poor, you have choices for yourself and your family, have uncontaminated drinking water, have nephews living charmed lives, have uncontested citizenship rights, are cisgender and straight, have a college education, have not been incarcerated for being poor and possessing two joints, have not been financially or physically abused by a sadistic man, have never had police or a vigilante kill or maim you or a loved one, have a family that is still alive for the most part and can afford to take care of you when you get very sick, have a sister with a PhD and an MFA, have a place that pays you to write, edit, and think, have the freedom to say "White supremacy" with few overt consequences so far—your story is a funny-at-times tale of Black working- to middle-class girl angst.

I make enough to eat out rather than cook (poorly). After many, many years of freelancing, I have benefits, taxed income, and paid vacation days. I get to pretend that I don't care if a suitor has enough money for us to be on equal footing when I'm too working-class for that to be true.

I still occasionally look around my rent-stabilized apartment and wonder what I might peddle in case this whole thing goes off the rails. But I know, thanks to my family, education, and early job experience, how to hustle up legal cash. When I'm able to retire at eighty-six, I'm going to take my nephews to a Seafood Shanty–type establishment every once in a while. And if anyone ever again asks me about my relationship with money and how that is connected to resisting White supremacy, I will be able to say without an ounce of glibness: "It's complicated."

TEN
SOMEDAY WE'LL ALL BE FREE

The point of this whole thing isn't just to fight White supremacy; it's to destroy it and create something that is liberatory for *all*. But we can't accomplish this without having a vision of what our own liberation looks like. That's why we all need to document our freedom dreams. Our picture of a place without police brutality, mass incarceration, grinding poverty, mass unemployment, untreated mental illness, early death, substandard education, gun violence, hate violence against Black trans women, homophobia, and sexism, must come from folks across the spectrum. In this chapter, we hear from futurists, survivalists, trans rights activists, and more about what they do each day to free themselves and how we can sprint toward a just future. Together.

Start with Quanshay

Imani Perry

I can tell you how we fight. I can't tell you how we win. That's probably obvious. If I knew, if *we* knew, the whole thing would be different. The long nightmare would be over, and we would be in the middle of the next epoch of our collective being. Maybe that would be like Wakanda, or the Republic of New Afrika, or Atlantis, or a great big neo-Atlanta. Who knows? We're here, though. And we can fight. We do fight. And knowing how to fight, I think, is identifying the necessary. It is about hitting the right note with our state of being even when the piano is out of tune. Even when we want to throw the damn thing out the window and let it crash into a million splinters on the concrete.

The world knows, but it denies, that Black people love being Black. Of course, I don't mean every single Black person loves being Black. We can think of some very prominent exceptions to that rule who have surnames like Dash, Thomas, and Carson. But it's true. Loving being Black is a commonplace state for Black folks, even in this White supremacist country in a White supremacist world. Sit in a room with Black folks for a day, or even just a few hours, or for fifteen minutes on a street corner, and the fact is undeniable. We love the heft of our laughter. We love the swing of our voices and the timing of our bodies, the subtlety of our eyebrow gestures and glances, the thickness of our own embraces. We love our mastery of combinations and permutations—the mathematics of our entertainment—with cards, dice, stories, and dance. We love the way we praise the higher power, however we call her. We love the knot of our genealogical ways of being that allow us to slip in and out of each other's neighborhoods and nations and find a way in wherever we go because we know the language even if we don't know the language. My friend Nate once said to me, "It's a myth that we can't go back to Africa. Start telling jokes with the kids in the village and you're *back* in a minute." He's right. We don't have a Standard English term for this, but we know that robust good feeling of being inside of being with other Black people.

Despite this truth, we are forced to listen to a steady parade of well-paid commentary about how we don't love being Black. It goes like this: "I wanted to be White. I hated myself. I changed my voice. I wasn't like the other Black kids." On and on and on. "There!" I imagine some collective White supremacist personality (or publisher) saying. "I fixed it. We have told them they are inferior and they believe it. Told you!" Ridiculous. Okay, I admit that some of us believe this pernicious lie. But most of us know in our guts that it isn't true. We are definitely not inferior. We are in fact remarkable and breathtakingly beautiful. And what a marvelous resilience that is. Really.

As far as I am concerned, knowing it is good to be Black even when it is terrible to be Black is at the core of how we fight. Start from there and Bob

Marley's "emancipate yourself from mental slavery" and the Funkadelics' "free your mind and your ass will follow"—those one-sentence sermons—have a chance to come true.

Black names, from African to African American vintage, are a good example. We like the sounds of a hard *k* and a *kwa* and a *sh*. We like *-ay* at the end. And for some reason we like to borrow the flourishes of French at the same time as we keep the rounded sounds of Bantu languages. Our names are a common source of mockery, sometimes even from our own. Well, it is true: We like to make up names from an old grammar of sounds that came before Columbus. And just think about what it means to celebrate sounds of our own, to claim them as the banners of our identities. It is a defiant deed in a White supremacist society.

No matter what they say, we aren't naming our daughters "Susie."

So whenever someone makes fun of Black "made-up names," I remind them that Milton made up the name Susannah. And I ask, "Do you mean to say that only White men are allowed to make things up?" They usually get uncomfortable. But I am very serious. The Black imagination is essential for the road to freedom.

When I was seven years old, I told my teacher that the map of Africa in our classroom was wrong. It said Rhodesia, but the Black people had reclaimed that country as Zimbabwe. I had been taught that renaming was decolonial. To her credit, my teacher, Risa (it was a progressive school; we called them by their first names), took a piece of tape and wrote Zimbabwe over where Rhodesia had been. Like many other African-named children of the 1970s, I was raised to reject the colonized mind. Steve Biko's lessons in Black consciousness had been put into practice as the enterprise of parenting.

I like to think I have carried that on. I tell my children when they learn in school to call European expansionism "The Age of Exploration" to remember that it was the age of unjust conquest. I like to think that when my younger son is tasked with doing a language project and he chooses African American Vernacular English, and when my older son says the foreign language that he is most interested in learning is Jamaican Patois, that this is part of the work of emancipation—this is the work of freedom-fighting.

The point, I hope, is clear. But in case it isn't, I will be more explicit: the boldness of our laughter comes from the same fabric as insisting upon other ways of knowing, ways that weren't built on the altar of our degradation and subjugation. It is of the same fabric as having vocabularies and designations of our own design. To tell our story truthfully is to turn the official story on its head again and again, based on the core principle of loving who we are.

To get from there to here, however, from the rough act of self-love to a deliberate way of being, is community work. We have models for it. We have books and a history of schools and organizations. There is a lot to draw upon. The problem, however, is so often when we embark upon that work we start from a place of denigration of what *is*. We repeat the core formulations of White supremacism with "the problem is that Black people . . ." as a precursor to "where do we go from here?"

But what if, instead, we begin with "the beauty is that Black people . . ."? What if we begin the story of our greatness and our possibilities with where we are and what we love about ourselves right now? What if we see in the grammar of our dances a thousand permutations on grace under pressure. What if we see a refusal to be held captive in the timbre and echo of our voices, which carry even when we are held in cages, or behind invisible electrified fences of ghettoization, or under leaden glass ceilings. I believe that is how we must fight.

Start right here.

Imani Perry is the Hughes-Rogers Professor of African American Studies at Princeton University, where she is also affiliated with the Program in Law and Public Affairs, the University Center for Human Values, and jazz studies. She is the author of several books, including *May We Forever Stand: A History of the Black National Anthem*. She lives in the Philadelphia area with her two sons.

I fight White supremacy by understanding its nuances.
Most racism and oppression isn't overt; but by pointing
out racism at its subtle level to my sons, I equip them
to avoid and beat covert White supremacy.

—A. Jermaine Mobley, songwriter and composer

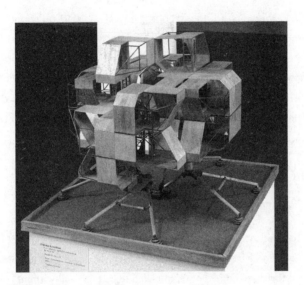

"Variable Facility" by Olalekan Jeyifous (2008)

What were you thinking when you planned and created this work?

I was thinking about creating a modular, mobile, and elevated housing construct driven by an experimental yet organic design and sited within a repressive political economy.

How does this work resist White supremacy?

A good deal of my artwork that derives from my background in architecture is about resisting or confronting White supremacy in some form or other. In this case, it's the very act of imagining spaces for Black people in the future. In the present, urban development often fails to adequately consider the needs of marginalized communities. This piece is an act of resistance against erasure and a history of discriminatory housing practices.

Olalekan Jeyifous is a Nigerian-born, Brooklyn-based artist and designer. He earned a bachelor's degree in architecture from Cornell University, where he focused on experimenting with the application of various types of computer software in the creation of art, design, and architecture. Since then, he has served as a senior designer at dbox, exhibited his artwork in venues throughout the world, and created visuals for a variety of clients.

〜〜〜〜〜〜〜

What Freedom Feels Like

Maori Karmael Holmes

What I'm interested in for Black people in the United States is that we would be free to have a mundane life. To wake up, to go to the store, to shop, to see our lovers, to come home, to watch television—all without considering the White gaze. And not watching somebody grab their purse in the elevator, or dealing with microaggressions at work, or skipping the major you love because a racist counselor said, "You can't."

I don't think freedom would look the same for everybody; I'm actually more curious about what it would *feel* like. It would hinge on being able to make decisions that aren't based on a legacy of trauma or impoverishment. We would no longer have to choose how we take up space—or don't take up space—as a response to this world, even down to the clothes we wear. For example, when I see free White people, particularly the wealthy people I've met, I notice how they're free to wear the same clothes every day. They don't dress up if they don't feel like it; they dress up if they want to. Either way, they're making these decisions purely based on their own interest. To me, that's what freedom would feel like.

Maori Karmael Holmes is the founder of the BlackStar Film Festival.

~~~~~~~~~~

The Eight-Point Plan of Euphorically Utopic World-Making
Elissa Blount Moorhead

My father took me to see Miles Davis a few times growing up. What struck me most was his now-infamous tendency to play music with his back to the audience. Some say it was not a deliberate act of defiance, but rather a deep focus on his work and his stagemates. Maybe he would've said, "My back was not to the audience; I was facing my band." Regardless of his reason, to my young eyes it was a gesture that resonated as a manifesto for so many aspects of life. It called out to me: "Don't look over your shoulder. Let the world come find you—you don't have to go to it. When they do find you, be totally into and enjoying your own bag."

In other words, I haven't really given Whiteness my back. I am facing Blackness.

I've had a few bags throughout my life—career, crews, cities—but the bag for which I have always had an unwavering love is Blackness. I never tire of pondering who we are and what we do. I suspect it has to do with what I am retroactively calling the "Eight-Point Plan of Euphorically Utopic World-Making."

This is the plan that my counterculture parents created. Their insistence on world-making shaped our current existence and our understanding of it—specifically, their experiments in child-rearing. I was taught to decentralize any notion of the White gaze, which means I had a fighting chance at agency, self-worth, and cultural entitlement in a country dead set against us having any of it.

I grew up in Washington, DC, during the time of liberation movements, communes, pan-Africanism, *shules*, arts movements, Islam, Vodou, and Black political and cultural nationalism. Black folks, including my parents, were searching for alternative ways to live together and raise a new consciousness. They were clear that being raised in an intentional community of Black artists, thinkers, activists, and pioneers was going to give us the grounding we needed to not just avoid the White gaze and misguided ideas of White "supremacy" but to utterly ignore its existence. Don't get me wrong. There were inconsistencies. They were jumping off cliffs and building wings on the way down. Most parents are really figuring it all out in real time.

Even though the world at that time was trying to convince them racial integration was salvation, they knew that was not enough. A half-century before "Black Lives Matter" was a mantra, they bet on Black and, in my opinion, won.

Some of these memories started to congeal when I had my first child. I began to recall these stories under loose categories that protected me (as much as possible) from White "supremacy" during my formative years.

1. Squad

When I was young, I never understood why people of color were called "minorities" when we comprised the majority of the world. Of course, later I came to understand this Western fiction was a tactic to advance the idea of Whiteness. It was a numbers game and a proximity mind trick. Whiteness was a catchy recruiting tool that allowed anyone throughout history wishing to distance themselves from Blackness to promote my inferiority.

But DC in the 1970s and '80s looked more like the rest of the globe. This was nearly an all-Black city—residents, leadership, services, and commerce. It's home to Howard University, nicknamed "the Mecca," which is what drew my parents there. Growing up in DC made it easy for me to take this fact of our majority status for granted.

Once, after college, a Black friend from London came to visit for the first time. I was amused by the first places he wanted to visit. "Where can we get bean pies?" he asked. "Let's go to Howard and where are the go-gos?" After a day of fairly mundane hanging in the city, he said, "My God, *everyone* is beautiful! The traffic cop, the bank teller, just regular people, are fine."

His being awestruck made me realize that I had a sense of entitlement that rested, not in the fact that I had Black teachers, leaders, and visual validation, but in my ability to be nonplussed about it. If someone said the phrase "French bakery," my mind's eye went to Avignon Frère, where Francophone Africans would hang out. When I imagined a pediatrician, she would be kind-faced, brown Dr. Clark on Sherman Avenue.

Numbers mattered when I was formulating identity. Because I had numbers, I didn't have to count. There was a deep-down "they can't kill us all" kind of safety, to assume the whole world looked and lived like me.

2. Isolation

Doing away with America's "separate and unequal" brand of segregation was the Civil Rights Movement's raison d'être. However, since *Brown v. Board of Education* was decided, some Black people have spoken in hushed tones about the negative effects of desegregation. If you listen closely, you will hear longing for many attributes of segregation. You'll hear yearnings for the space to elevate spirit via Black sociality and euphoria. That seems essential to me.

So my assumption is that the Black psyche has been impaired or at least affected by the White gaze. Even in all-Black spaces, the specter of the White gaze fuels our perpetual impulse toward doing what is deemed respectable. I came to believe that we could interrupt this impulse with room to try things on and fail without it being attributed to Blackness or lack thereof.

I remember being mildly chided in high school as "punk rock." At the same time, I was voted "Most Creative." Today I realize that people calling me "punk rock" was a way of saying that I was into some weird stuff that wasn't really that Black but did not make me an outcast.

With Whiteness out of the frame, this was, "Lisa who likes weird shit," but I was not "acting White." I had no real-life pressure to avoid "Whiteness" because it wasn't present in my life. In other words, in isolation my behavior and preferences were not raced and categorized in the face of "Whiteness." I don't want to confuse this with a post-Black ideology. This is more about transcendence and disregard of White people's view of us. It's Black privilege.

3. Multiplicity

Many scholars have written about what it means to remain at the "epicenter" of Blackness. Freedom from a one-dimensional view of Blackness allows for rigorous discourse and more expansive notions of what Blackness does and can mean.

Living in a diverse Black community allowed me a window into our diasporic bounty. Living in a Black community in America means the sinners and the saints all look like you and are potentially connected by history, circumstance, and culture. We see ourselves for intrinsic traits, not a romanticized Blackness.

4. Haughtiness

Segregation or isolation would not have been enough. Expressions of "Black is beautiful" were almost compensatory for what America was dishing out. I'm guessing this is what we needed to level things after church burnings and hoses. But alongside this prideful proclamation was also benevolence—the cousin of haughtiness.

Benevolence is usually reserved for the group of people holding power. But in my near-utopic example, power was a shifted perception. Benevolence allowed for a lack of ire that is not typically associated with a Black Power stance. I remember my mother and grandmother talking about the dysfunctional behavior of our people that we'd hear about on the news. They would say, "Poor thing. He doesn't know any better. He was taught that." There may not have been genuine feelings of sympathy, but the performance of superiority resonated with me.

Whiteness, to me, was the condescending pity and its belief that it was above it all. So my grandmother would not answer if a White person called her by her first name or used the wrong tone. Her haughtiness worked as an

antidote to White "supremacy." Disregard as resistance had another side effect: the erasure of the excuse that racism is a "sickness" rather than a learned
culture. This was the ultimate high-siddity smackdown.

5. Global Context

When I was young, a five-year-old girl in my building spoke five languages that I knew of, including Amharic and English. When you got on the
elevator, she could size you up based on gestures or clothing or style and speak
to you in the correct language. I think about how she had so many keys to various kinds of Black thought and culture so early. In our apartment building,
there were French/Kreyol speakers from Haiti and West Africa and Spanish
speakers from the Dominican Republic and Central America. Not to mention
Brazilians, South Africans, and West Indians from at least eight islands. It
was a Black United Nations. Before I even traveled out of the United States,
I knew I belonged and was not a minority. I knew that Pelé played a game
more popular than baseball and that slavery did not take everything away.

6. Chill

When I first went to college at American University, I remember meeting students who claimed to have always been the only Black person in their
schools or communities. This sounded heartbreaking.

Folks who are performing Blackness or proving (or disproving) their
connection to it all the time carry an unfair burden. Quiet confidence comes
from mastery of work and ideas, but also of self.

Last year I dropped off my niece at the hairdresser before her orientation
at the Mecca. The hairdresser said, "Congrats! What high school did you
graduate from? She said "Friends" (a private Quaker School). The hairdresser
said, "What made you choose Howard?" Without taking a breath my niece
said, "Friends."

7. Fun

Once when I was eight or nine, a girl from my second DC school—a
middle-class to wealthy Black school—came to my apartment. Seeing all the

pictures of Black heroes and African art, she said, "Do your parents lecture you about Black stuff all the time? Do they hate White people?"

Funny enough, they didn't do either. We just lived. There were always people at our apartment late, smoking weed, listening to records, arguing, and laughing. I loved the residue of it all. We lived in museums and at cultural events. We didn't know we were technically poor.

My wealthier friends I went to school with had similar fun—basement dances, roller skating, slumber parties where we'd pore over *Right On* and fight over who was going to marry Michael Jackson or Foster Sylvers. So Blackness always seemed lit to me.

Often, in an attempt to make sure our kids don't forget who they are, we make things prescriptive and, as one of my friends says, we take the fun out of profundity. We think ceremony and lessons are the only way to get them to know our history. But we are making our history now by loving, laughing, and being ourselves in front of them. Making sure I continue my version of my parents' fellowshipping is soul-feeding for me, and I hope it will make my kids want to hold on to their uncut joy free of any outside gaze. Full. Out. Lit.

8. Evidence and Expectation

Maybe I never bought the "White man runs the world" story because my near-utopian reality showed me too much to the contrary for too long. For me, there was no evidence of anyone but Dr. Clark and Marion Barry running the world. Really well, I might add. I knew that President Jimmy Carter was White, but his daughter went to public school in DC too, one that was not as good as mine. At my school, we sang "Lift Every Voice and Sing" every morning, so I thought all schools did.

No matter how hard you worked, teachers would say you weren't working to your potential. That bar was raised hourly. I remember thinking, *Well, maybe this* is *my full potential, lady. Leave me alone.* But I soon learned there was no ceiling. Teachers would then say, "This is your best? Please, child, I know your parents." Which is code for "You come from good stock," which is code for "We all we got," which is code for "You must win because you are mine." Even when naïveté wore off as an adult and I understood the economic realities, injustice, and racism we faced, I still couldn't buy it. No White man is running my world. Evidence was everywhere.

It was rare, too special, a coincidence of time and place that we will never get back.

My kids' schools are far from Shepherd or Harriet Tubman Elementary where I went, so I supplement with summer Freedom School—any element of this eight-point plan will have to do for now. I am trying to replicate what I can, when I can. It has to be strong enough to endure racist governments and all-White classrooms. It has to be seen and felt, not implied. There has to be evidence.

Elissa Blount Moorhead, artist and curator, has created film, public art, exhibitions, and cultural programs for the last twenty-five years. She is a principal partner at the film studio TNEG and the author of *P Is for Pussy*, an illustrated "children's" book.

~~~~~~~~~

We Can't Get Free by Osmosis: A Q+A with Robin D. G. Kelley

Robin D. G. Kelley is the Distinguished Professor and Gary B. Nash Endowed Chair in US History at the University of California, Los Angeles. Outside of academia, the writer, educator, cultural critic, and activist is renowned for using his dizzyingly multidisciplinary talent to talk about Black culture and politics with clarity and verve. His study of Black working-class social movements—including the books *Race Rebels: Culture, Politics, and the Black Working Class* and *Freedom Dreams: The Black Radical Imagination*—is what compelled us to talk to him for this project. Read on as he emails with Akiba.

These words on your website about your 1996 book, Race Rebels, stood out: "I concluded that there is nothing inherently radical or oppositional about daily acts of resistance and

survival; the relationship of these acts to power always depends on the context." Can you talk more about this conclusion?

The key words in that quote are "inherently" and "context." I don't want to give the impression that these everyday acts of resistance or survival are not valuable. On the contrary, the whole point of the book is to insist that we cannot understand working-class politics without paying attention to the realm of these everyday, quotidian kinds of struggles.

But to assume that these are conscious acts of rebellion or that they lead inexorably to revolution, the idea that they are proto-revolutionary and whatnot, is simply wrong. It both underestimates and overestimates our communities. What I mean is that we don't always recognize what a diverse and complicated people we are and how any number of tired terms like "rebel" or "reformist" or "integrationist" or "separatist" obscure more than they reveal. Even under White supremacy, we are not obsessed with this system or White folks or being oppressed. We are sometimes struggling with mundane problems, seeking joy, falling in and out of love, raising children, or more concerned with dignity than, say, protest. We do stupid things, exhibit vanity and selfishness and many other things that some might dismiss as signs of lacking consciousness. But how we come to know the world is usually through a dialectic of experience, knowledge, and reflection on both. This leads me to the second key word: "context."

A style, a gesture, music, even literacy may be looked upon by authorities as subversive and dangerous in one context, and a marketable commodity in another context. And the threat it may pose for White supremacy may not be evident to those who engage in these acts. In some instances, Black working people acted in ways that were never meant to "resist" anything, but the context—the policing of Black working-class behavior, the monitoring of Black life, the way the state perceived their acts as threats—rendered their actions resistance whether intended or not.

Furthermore, everyday resistance strategies can become double-edged swords. Vicious attacks on Black passengers by bus drivers could convince others of the futility of fighting back. Impeccable job performance as a strategy to challenge racial inequality at the workplace ultimately benefits the employer. Employing one's own labor for more pleasurable pursuits hardly alters social relations. And yet, like all double-edged swords, these same acts can temporarily disrupt the business of White supremacy by throwing a wrench into its operations, by instilling communities with a sense of dignity denied them by the racial regime, and by enabling folks to reverse the process of exploitation by taking back some of the surplus extracted from them. These things happen every day. The question is, how do we make meaning of these daily acts and skirmishes? And can they become the basis for disrupting the system we're trying to dismantle?

What do Black folks get out of valuing and even romanticizing everyday struggle? Did it ever make sense?

There is certainly no consensus among Black folks on the value of everyday struggle. Some of my biggest critics have been Black intellectuals who see no value in studying everyday resistance, arguing instead that they are diversions from "real" social movements. On the other hand, I'm surrounded by many students, colleagues, and activists who want to hold up these acts as evidence of Black people's "agency" or "humanity"—a claim I find incredibly dubious and that was powerfully critiqued recently by Walter Johnson in his October 26, 2016, *Boston Review* essay, "To Remake the World: Slavery, Racial Capitalism, and Justice."

I find it dubious because we don't have to prove that we have agency or have held on to our humanity. If we are human, then that should have never been a question. Moreover, agency does not mean resistance or rebellion—just the capacity to act, for better or for worse. Drug dealers and slave drivers have agency and humanity, especially in light of all the destruction and havoc around the world caused by and in the name of humanity. Of course, there is something edifying about celebrating our resilience and all that business, but that stuff never appealed to me.

I took up the study of everyday struggle to better understand and buttress the social movements with which I was involved. I learned that the most effective social movements develop organically and create agendas around people's actual needs and grievances, not according to Marxist or liberal logics. I understood the study of these kinds of everyday forms of resistance, survival, renewal, as diagnostic, intended as a measure of power relations and a way to gauge the grievances of working people who might not have other avenues through which to voice their concerns. The state's reactions to everyday struggles also tell us something about the workings of power, and that is precisely the kind of knowledge we need to create better strategies to contest White supremacy.

Do you see yourself as fighting White supremacy? If so, how do you do it?

Yes. For the last thirty-five years, I have tried to fight White supremacy through my writing and speaking, in the various organizations I have supported over the years, from the Black Radical Congress and the Labor/Community Strategy Center to the Movement for Black Lives and beyond. But we need to be clear that removing all racial barriers, vigilantly upholding antidiscrimination law, incorporating us into the system, and replacing White authority with Black and Brown faces is not the same as dismantling White supremacy. We should know by now that the state and the dominant class have no problems granting Black people and other aggrieved "minorities" recognition and incorporating them into the existing state apparatus. We've watched this happen over the course of the last four decades, at least, resulting in Black CEOs like Franklin Raines contributing mightily to the financial crisis of 2008; a Black president, a Black secretary of state, and Black national security advisers who advance the US war aims in Africa, Asia, the Middle East, and virtually everywhere on the planet; the right to same-sex marriage based on the same principles of marriage as a property relation; and the right of people of color, women, and queer people to kill and torture around the world.

And at least in my worldview, dismantling White supremacy is not enough; liberation requires a lot more. As the Combahee River Collective Statement, now four decades old, made crystal clear, we cannot wage an assault on White supremacy without fighting to end patriarchy and capitalism—its fetishism of commodities, its law of private property, its gendered logics, bourgeois individualism, its culture, its state apparatus. I know it is in vogue now to call racism "anti-Blackness" and to embrace a politics that forecloses the possibility of cross-racial and international solidarity, but I'm committed to resisting all forms of oppression, not just anti-Black racism. I really identify with those women of the Congress of Afrikan People in the late 1970s whose slogan—which they took from Lenin's essay "Soviet Power and the Status of Women" (1919)—called for "the *abolition of every possibility* of oppression and exploitation."

I Fight White Supremacy by Being Apocalypse-Ready

Mia Birdsong

When I was pregnant with my first child, my husband and I moved from the Bay Area to the Round House—a beautiful, funky home on forty acres off a dirt road in California's Central Valley. It's the house where my husband was born, and living there meant our cost of living was low enough for us to both stay home with our new kid. Surrounded by little more than oak trees and cow pastures, I discovered that I am a city girl. But I also discovered the satisfaction of living a less convenient life, one that requires and inspires learning some basic self-sufficiency skills.

There is this thing that happens to some of us when we become parents: we become paranoid as fuck. We worry about freak accidents injuring or killing our kid, we worry about our own mortality. We start planning for the worst. This is, of course, compounded when you are Black. While I never had any indication that there were violent White supremacists anywhere near us, being so far away from civilization freaked me out. Out in the country, no one can hear you scream.

Shortly after our daughter was born, my husband, a musician, started touring frequently. Every night he was gone, I would lie awake until I had thought through what I'd do if the White supremacists came for us. I'd probably hear them come up the driveway. They'd get in the house easily, because there were no locks on the doors, but the dogs slept downstairs and would keep them occupied long enough for me to strap my baby into the sling and climb over the second-floor balcony. I would have to escape through the woods, because the White supremacists would be blocking the driveway with their trucks.

But country living and parenting didn't just feed my fear. It also fed my sense of freedom. I gardened in earnest for the first time, growing inedible zucchini the size of my arm and hundreds of tomatoes that never ripened. Those early mistakes taught me as much as my successes. I learned that paying attention reveals what my garden needs and when it needs it. I learned that sometimes a little hardship creates studier plants, and that sometimes you need to cut back to encourage growth.

During the two years we lived there, I apprenticed with my mother-in-love, a brilliant midwife. Accompanying her to prenatal visits and births was mind-blowing. I had read midwifery books, but observing and supporting a master showed me the depths of knowledge and artistry it takes to guide, but not disrupt, a process that has a wide range of normal and deeply connects us to our animal selves. Most importantly, it reminded me that we are built for life. My brief apprenticeship did not make me a midwife, but in an emergency, during the apocalypse, I could catch a baby.

During our country-living years, most days I spent hours walking the land with my infant strapped to me, talking to her about the trees and birds. The landscape was foreign to me, which made me both uncomfortable and curious. I learned the names of the creatures and plants. Live oak, fly catcher, ceanothus, California newt. In the morning, from our bedroom window, I watched deer graze in the orchard. At dusk, I heard coyotes carry on and saw bats catch insects. I became aware of the rhythms of the natural world and realized that it was something I was a part of, not separate from. And if I was part of it—if it was my habitat too—then I could survive in it.

In the summer, klamath weed, a pretty yellow-flowered plant, bloomed in abundance. My mother-in-love told me it was also known as St. John's Wort, a plant I knew from the bouts of seasonal depression I experienced in college. It had kept me from spiraling into the abyss during long Ohio winters, and here it grew like a literal weed that I could harvest. I'd started studying herbalism several years before, but this encounter shifted my relationship to plants. I could make medicine. I remember thinking that if the apocalypse came, I could help out with all the anxiety, panic, and depression that would accompany it.

Since moving back to Oakland, my husband and I regularly talk about who we'd circle up with, what we'd take with us, and how we'd get out if society fell apart. I recently took up archery with my second child, in part because it's fun, but also because during the apocalypse, when all the bullets are gone, we still have to defend ourselves and eat.

I have maintained the curiosity that inspires me to know how to do things that support collective self-sufficiency. In our little backyard, I grow food and medicinal herbs. I took up beekeeping after a swarm of the honey producers landed in our yard on my birthday a few years ago. I care for a flock of six chickens.

Home invasion preparation and escape planning came from a place of fear. Gardening, beekeeping, midwifery, and my nascent archery practice are all practical skills that I can tap when the crisis is over and we need to rebuild. But they also keep me fully living now. When I'm pulling frames full of honey out of a hive or loosing an arrow, I must be totally present. Planting seedlings and sitting with a laboring pregnant person invites a kind of in-touchness that deepens my ability to be alert and aware of the rhythms of my surroundings. That's good in an emergency and for long-term staying alive—now and post-apocalypse.

Knowing that I have skills to bring to our survival when shit goes down gives me a sense of security when my news feed is full of Black death and so many of us are struggling to make ends meet and stay healthy.

I went into fall of 2015 feeling heavy. So many Black women in my orbit had recently died, were dying, or had been diagnosed with a chronic illness. Living at the intersection of patriarchy and White supremacy is traumatic.

Into that grieving walked Nwamaka Agbo, a restorative economics practitioner, at a retreat the Movement Strategy Center held in Oakland. During a break, she and I walked around Lake Merritt and we talked about the ways we saw the double-edged sword of Black women's strengths, ingenuity, brilliance, and excellence result not just in achievement and survival, but illness, disease, trauma, and death. All the exceptionalism, doing it ourselves if we want it done and making a way out of no way, came at a cost.

We also recognized that we, and the amazing Black women we knew, were helping White supremacy and patriarchy out by not caring for ourselves enough, by not dealing with our historical and lived trauma, by not examining deeply enough the ways in which we internalize racism and sexism.

We shouldn't have to do all that work. But in this too, no one is coming to save us. We knew we wanted to create a solution that would help heal us, and we wanted to start from a place of joy, with our eyes on freedom, because while it is key, healing is not the end goal—liberation is. It took us almost a year to start (because it is challenging for Black women to prioritize ourselves), but that conversation birthed Black Women's Freedom Circle. On a sunny day in August, twenty-plus Black women met at my house for three hours to nourish our bodies and spirits, to connect with and witness each other.

We each identified a time or practice that made us feel free. We discussed what that feeling was and how we could expand it beyond the moment we'd identified. We agreed that the exploration of freedom was imperative not only to our own personal well-being but to our collective emancipation.

Like most people, I imagine the apocalypse as a disaster (nuclear war, earthquake, environmental catastrophe, government collapse, zombies). My mind is full of all the dystopian possibilities I've absorbed from science fiction TV, movies, and books. And in a world that hates Black women, where the state is not designed to care for or protect us, I feel some imperative to be able to care for and protect myself and my loved ones. But I also understand the apocalypse as an opportunity for renewal. A world shaken off its foundation can be built differently, better. But we have to hold a vision of what future we really want so as not to re-create the messes we have now. As Lucille Clifton made clear, "We cannot create what we can't imagine." Freedom from oppression is not a linear path we travel toward the future. It is something that has to exist inside each of us—a moment that we can repeat, a spark we can fan into fire.

Black Women's Freedom Circle has been gathering regularly since we started. We have talked about anger, grief, safety, family, intimacy, and purpose. We laugh and weep and hold expansive space for all our feelings and experiences. We do witchy shit and research internet security. We circle up to make real the world we want to live in.

This too is being apocalypse-ready.

Mia Birdsong is a pathfinder, community curator, and storyteller who engages the leadership and wisdom of people experiencing injustice to chart new visions of American life via her New America public dialogue series, which centers Black women as agents of change.

–––––〜〜〜〜〜–––––

Blak Kingz

A song by Jasiri X

I had a dream I met Lebron James
We were speaking on Black empowerment
Sending money to a Black bank call it power trip
If it ain't Harriet on my twenty that shit's counterfeit
Black faces in my denim lining
Tailor-made stitching like we 'bout to win the Heisman
Call my brother Sun 'cause I love it when he's shining
The pressure made me precious my flesh is a living diamond

We buying back the hood and consolidating wallets
A principle of Kwanzaa cooperative economics
Raid Wall Street and put the stock up in my pockets
My checkbook is like the Bible, its full of Black prophets
Satan in my rear view
The devil whispering but I don't hear dude
Earbuds for the bullshit I gotta steer through
Freeze everything and run away that's what fear do
It's hard to stay asleep when your dreams are so near you

I gotta dream
All white furs for the team
I gotta dream
Diamond chains, watches and the rings
I gotta dream
Counting my money with a machine
I gotta dream
Bow down to a Blak King

I had a dream I was talking to Chance
Seen him in the street and then offered my hand
Not for the 'gram or all of the fans
'Cause even though we write verses God authors the plans
The most merciful
Please make my life purposeful
Make me an example to those who still worship you
Make me like water for those who may have deserted you
And please forgive all my curses too
And all the times I wasn't present in that church's pew
Reverend I got work to do
Heaven and an earth to move
Judge me with your surface view

Haters throwing dirt on you
I don't take it personal
My coat is reversible
Bursting through the birth canal
Lord, I was an earnest child
But I promised if you gave me light that I would burn it down
You admonished if you gave me sight to never turn around
Word is bound
'Cause every real king gotta earn the crown

I gotta dream
All white furs for the team
I gotta dream
Diamond chains, watches and the rings
I gotta dream
Counting my money with a machine
I gotta dream
Bow down to a Blak King

'Cause they don't wanna see Blak joy
Do your dance Blak girl do your thing Blak boy
'Cause they don't wanna see Blak joy
Do your thing Blak girl do your dance Blak boy

Jasiri X is the first independent hip-hop artist to be awarded an honorary doctorate, which he received from Chicago Theological Seminary in 2016. Still, he remains rooted in the Pittsburgh-based organization he founded, 1Hood Media, which teaches youth of color how to analyze and create media for themselves. Jasiri received the Nathan Cummings Foundation Fellowship to start the 1Hood Artivist Academy, and he is a recipient of the USA Cummings Fellowship in Music and the Robert Rauschenberg Foundation Artist as Activist Fellowship.

~~~~~~~~~~

I fight White supremacy by hiring directors and producers of color in an industry where they might not otherwise get the opportunity.

—Gideon Moncrieffe, live event and
media production executive

~~~~~~~~~~

On Restoring Our Humanity in a World That Wishes Us Dead

Wazi Maret

My spirituality, sense of self, and ability to remain soft are my greatest weapons here in a world that has tried to kill me.

Fighting White supremacy isn't always by way of an action; I believe it can also be an embodiment. In my case, it has required a complete rebirth of and a reorientation to everything I was taught about life, including the harmful messages I was fed from birth. Messages like: White is right. Blue is for boys. Skirts are for girls. God loves us all unconditionally, but with conditions. We are only worth as much as we can produce. These messages taught me more about fear and the urge to control those who are different than they taught me about love, acceptance, and appreciation.

White supremacy has an explicit history of using race as the basis to inflict violence on Black people and rob us of our humanity. But it took me a long time to realize just how insidious it is, how malleable. It thrives on disconnection—from nature, from each other, and from ourselves. It thrives on exploitation of the land, culture, ideas, and labor. It uses fear to separate us via racism, classism, transphobia, homophobia, sexism, ableism, and xenophobia.

I believe, then, that fighting White supremacy requires getting more curious, saying yes to all that I have been taught to fear, reconnecting to my body and presence, and developing everyday practices that will contribute to my personal well-being and healing. It requires saying yes to myself every single day.

I have been harmed by many things in this world because of the identities and experiences I've inherited. I am a Black man, I come from a working-class and mixed-race family, I am queer, I am transgender, I am incredibly soft, sometimes I find myself somewhere in between genders, and many days I am afraid to walk through the world visibly. I also know that I have a little more freedom and safety to exist only because Black trans women made it possible by saying yes to themselves unapologetically.

White supremacy has created a world conditioned to fear and hate Black trans people, to shun us when we express ourselves outside rigid gender roles, to dispose of us when we cause discomfort in others, to contain us when we have become too free, to punish us when we resist. It draws strength from the trauma it creates, which has haunted our communities for generations. If I am to resist all of this, then, my mandate is to pledge a deep commitment to healing myself as a Black queer trans man and investing in the healing and empowerment of other Black trans people.

I fight White supremacy through an outpouring of love for Black people. I fight by reclaiming my body and affirming my gender identity, my gender expression, and all of my authentic selves no matter how different it was before. I fight by reclaiming my breath, by taking time to slow down and notice, feel, and understand the sensations I encounter and all the things my body does to support me in staying alive.

I resist through meditating, reading books, reclaiming my mind, remembering that what I was taught as a child is not the whole story. Because White supremacy encourages us to remain ahistorical, I resist by reconnecting to my ancestors and lifting up the narratives of those whose stories were intentionally omitted. I resist through creating—art, music, fashion—because I know that capitalism and White supremacy stifle creativity and encourage conformity, efficiency, and production for the sole sake of building wealth for a few.

I resist by establishing boundaries and maintaining them with dignity, by knowing that I have agency over my body, my life, and how I choose to live. I honor vulnerability and femininity because White supremacy has taught us to police and dishonor women and femmes. I trust Black women, especially Black trans women. I talk to my friends and family about White supremacy and how we can all do something about it. I build relationships with other men and seek to foster healing from toxic masculinity and patriarchy, and I encourage us to hold ourselves—and each other—more accountable.

Ultimately, I believe that fighting White supremacy means restoring my own sense of humanity and connecting to the humanity in others. This requires a great deal of healing and empathy for each other's unique struggles. If I can take small steps toward healing myself—if we *all* can—then we can heal ourselves collectively. To echo my comrades from Black Lives Matter Atlanta and Southerners On New Ground, who said it best: "The mandate for Black people in this time is to avenge the suffering of our ancestors, to earn the respect of future generations, and be willing to be transformed in the service of the work."

Wazi Maret is an award-winning, radical fund-raiser, strategist, connector, and creative based in Oakland. He has worked to support and sustain social justice organizations such as the Transgender Gender-Variant Intersex Justice Project, Transgender Law Center, Black Lives Matter, and BYP100, and he comes equipped with years of training and facilitation experience in the areas of racial, trans, and gender justice.

For Alicia Garza, the Future Is Dignified

As one of the cofounders of Black Lives Matter, Alicia Garza's name is synonymous with harnessing the power of social media to organize and advocate on behalf of Black people in real life. But she was fighting for us

long before the masses discovered her Twitter handle, and she is committed
to creating a world that will sustain us long after the concept of hashtags has
faded from our collective memory. As the principal at Black Futures Lab, the
Oakland native is constructing freedom dreams writ large, and she knows it
will take *all* of us to get there. Here she talks strategy with Kenrya.

In one sentence, what do you do?

I'm an organizer, I'm a strategist, and I'm a freedom dreamer.

Dope. Can you please tell me how you came to be an organizer?

I grew up in the Bay Area, born to a single mom who, at the time, had
a different plan for what her life was going to look like. When I came onto
the scene, she had to quickly figure out how to pivot. Part of what that meant
was that she put on her big girl panties and be like, "Okay. I have to make
some different choices around what it means to bring a baby girl into the
world."

Coming up, my lifestyle was really influenced by the way my mother
hustled. She worked three jobs, and she did that to take care of me. She was
raising me, initially, with her twin brother, who moved out to California to
support her. She worked during the day, he worked at night, and somewhere
in between there, when everyone else was taken care of, she pursued her own
dreams. When people ask me, "How did you get into this work?" the answer
is that I'm definitely my mother's child.

Part of how she has shaped me is that she is someone who is not an
activist—she's not even really that political, to be honest—but she raised me
with a sense of right and wrong, that there's a responsibility that I have to
leave the world better than I found it.

I got involved in activism at a young age. My first foray was around
reproductive justice, getting condoms and contraception into school nurses'
offices. It was a big conversation happening in my school district, and the
broader political context was that it was during Bush number one. This was
when the right wing really started taking power in this country. There was a

big fight over abstinence-only education versus comprehensive sex health education and access to contraception, and that sat inside of a context of what the administration was promoting at the time as "family values," which you and I both know was really a way to move a White, male, Christian agenda.

As a single mom, my mother talked to me a lot about sex. There was no stork, you know what I'm saying? She was like, "Look, check this out. Sex makes babies and babies are expensive, okay?" She really wanted me to understand the dynamics that come with being able to make decisions on your own behalf with information that helps you do that in a holistic way.

My entry point was around advocacy and service, and it wasn't until college that I started learning and understanding organizing. Since that awakening, I got trained here in Oakland in the art and science of organizing, and I started knocking on doors in East and West Oakland around issues of economic justice and racial justice. I worked at the University of California Student Association for a little while, helping students of color run and win campaigns on campus for equity and all that good shit.

I spent ten years in a grassroots organization in San Francisco fighting for Black people. The year I left that organization was the year that we started Black Lives Matter.

So we know your origin story. Now tell me about the beginning of Black Futures Lab.

The origin story of the Black Futures Lab starts in 2016. Being one of the cocreators of Black Lives Matter, that was probably one of the hardest years for me personally and politically. It was almost like you could see the storm coming: BLM starts in 2013. Ferguson happens in 2014, and there's this catalytic series of uprisings that signals a rupture in Black communities, in Black movements, and in Black freedom dreams. This period has really exposed both how Black people are always moving toward a different level of humanity and how there are big gaps and tensions that have really shaped what we think is possible for us.

And 2016 was predictable in some ways. It was the first major election after the first Black president in the history of this country was elected, and so obviously there was going to be a backlash. Then there was the weird positioning from the Democratic Party. It was scary to think about how there would be an extension of the kind of pandering that normally gets done to Black people during election cycles, but that instead it would be shaped around this movement moment and used in incredibly problematic ways.

We were in an untenable position. You have movement and protest happening. You have people pushing an agenda, and then you have an election cycle where there's really a choice around what you take on as your platform and your vision for the future of the country. What became really clear was that there was no vision from any candidate for what could be possible for Black America. There was a vision for the middle class, corporations, and White nationalists, but there was not a vision for how we move the needle around Black wellness, dignity, and citizenship conceived of in a broad way.

At the same time, we were in a position where candidates wanted to be in proximity *to* us, but weren't committed to building power *with* us. The electoral system itself is not designed for that, but that doesn't mean we shouldn't push for that. What I realized was that there was no way to have that happen unless Black people build political power that is independent and progressive and clear about the tensions and challenges of the electoral system, and also committed to wielding whatever tools are necessary to build the power we deserve.

That is really where the Black Futures Lab comes from. I always use the metaphor of being on a roller coaster that is absolutely batshit crazy and you're regretting you got on the thing in the first place. You're like, "I'm never going to make it." At some point in that process you have to imagine what could happen if you *did* make it. For me, in holding on tight to that roller coaster, I did a lot of dreaming. If this wasn't so wack, what would we be doing? What could we do in better circumstances to make this process work for us as much as it can? What else needs to be built to both challenge the system as it is *and* figure out how to leverage some of the utility of these systems?

The Black Futures Lab comes from that. It's a freedom dream geared toward transforming Black communities in the constituencies that build independent Black political power in cities and states. It is aware of our current political context, but it is not hamstrung by it. It recognizes that the problems our communities face are complex and that we need to experiment, innovate, and build political power. We can't cede control over what should be democratic systems to people who don't want democracy.

We can't just look at it and say, "Well, those people don't want democracy, so I'm not fucking with it." We actually have to say, "It's ours and we're going to fight for it." We have a number of different things that we're doing, but all of them are geared toward reimagining what Black governance looks like, reimagining what democracy for Black communities looks like, and having a clear vision of what it means for Black communities to have power.

What does that transformation, that reimagining, look like to you?

We have a pretty clear sense of what power looks like. It's the ability to make decisions for your own life and the lives of people you care about. It's the ability to shape the narrative of who you are, what you deserve. Power is about being able to implement rewards and consequences based on your agenda. And power is also very much about being able to lead everyone, whether or not they're in line with your agenda.

I think having that understanding of power then means that we have a different understanding of what we need to do to get it. The big thing that is critical for us at the Lab is that we understand that we need to get more proficient in how and when we build alliances and also understand that those coalitions need to include people who don't agree with us on every issue and people who might generally share our vision for what's possible, but have different approaches on how to get there.

If we think about all the people who need to be united to achieve what we deserve, there has to be an incredible diversity within that if we are really talking about building a new democracy. I mean, democracy doesn't mean everybody's on the same page, it means that everybody gets to participate in those decisions. And then leadership and organizing are about building a movement that is moving toward your agenda. That's what it looks like and feels like to us.

How does the Black Census Project move the needle toward that transformative vision of Black power?

We kicked off the launch of Black Futures Lab with that project because we think Black communities are incredibly misunderstood on the left and in the center. Our hypothesis inside the Lab is that the demographics of Black communities are changing very rapidly, but our strategies to engage those changes haven't caught up. What does it mean that Black people in the United States are increasingly migrant? What does it mean that Black people in the United States are increasingly openly lesbian, gay, bisexual, transgender, and gender-nonconforming? What does it mean to really listen to what Black people in rural areas are experiencing?

The Black Census Project is a way to reshape our strategies around engaging and activating Black people by saying, "Actually, Black people are not a monolith. Black people in the United States are all kinds of things, and that shapes our perception of what's happening to us, for us, and about us, and it also shapes our vision for what we want to see." Our prediction is that in talking to two hundred thousand Black people across the country from very diverse places, we'll not only expose that Black people are not a monolith, but we'll also be able to identify opportunities for deeper organizing and learn what is necessary for Black dignity and wellness.

Our goal is to use that data to change the way the institutions engage our communities and send up a flare that we intend to contend for power. And we hope that this project also helps to build the capacity of our movement;

most of us don't talk to two hundred thousand Black people. Hopefully, this data will also sharpen the ways we engage our own communities and help identify new possibilities for collaboration and coordination, which is also necessary for the movement that we need to build.

How does your work with Black Futures Lab help Black people dismantle the system of White supremacy?

We see ourselves as a capacity builder for Black communities. We are not a mass organization that people become members of. That is important work, but it's a different kind of work. We are building our people's capacity to govern and lead. And governance and leadership are about solving problems for Black folks, proposing what a different world should look like, and putting Black people in charge of changing systems, structures, and institutions to meet that agenda.

What does freedom for all Black people look like to you?

For me, freedom looks like being able to have dignity. For me, that word and that vision are really important. We could provide a whole litany of the policies we need to change, but for me all that adds up to is: Can Black people live full and dignified lives? Can we live in a way that is cooperative and not predatory? Can we bring our full selves everywhere that we are? I believe very deeply that not only is it possible, but it's necessary for this planet to survive. It's my goalpost.

What do you want your legacy to be?

If I'm lucky, my legacy will be that I contributed to energizing and activating a whole shit ton of people to fight like hell for our dignity and we won some shit that was pretty important.

~~~~~~~~~~

QUESTION, ANSWERED

Here we share our own dreams by answering the question: what does freedom look like to you?

Kenrya

There is a playground that sits beside my daughter's school. It's nothing special, just a play structure, surrounded by wood chips that are the bane of my existence on Saturdays, when I'm forced to pluck them out of her socks before I can toss them into the washing machine. But one of my favorite things is to watch Saa overwhelm the structure. She stomps to the top, flips her entire body over the rod that crowns the tallest slide, does some parkour-type shit off the fireman's pole on the far side, climbs up the other side upside down like some kind of fucking ninja, jumps off the ledge when it's time to choreograph a step with her girls—she devastates that thing. And she does it with a wide grin, a loud laugh, and shouts of "look, Mama," excited by the time she gets to run and jump and flip, empowered by the strength and agility of her body.

As I watch her I realize that there, tangled in those beige bars, she is immensely free. She's not thinking about the mean thing her so-called friend said to her at recess, or how long it will take her to run through her violin practice that night, or how annoying it is that Mama is gonna wash her hair before bed. She's not just living in the moment, she is *reveling* in it, being her entire self.

There are so few moments that Black people get to experience that type of freedom. The type of freedom where you're not calculating (and laughing inside at) how "reverse racist" the other moms on the playground think you are when you tell them you're writing a book about dismantling White supremacy. The type of freedom where you're not forced to push back against the gaslighting that comes when you tell the administration that you're pulling your child out of their school because a group of White and White-aspiring kids touched her gorgeous fluffy hair and laughed at it. The type of freedom where you don't feel a twinge of trepidation the first time you

decide not to code-switch when it's your turn to speak at the parent association meeting.

In my freedom dream, I get to walk around this earth being my complete self at all times without having to worry about someone trying to kick
me out of a restaurant because I complained about poor service. I get to call
the police when someone majorly harms me without having to worry that the
officers will kill me within two seconds of arriving. I get to send my daughter
to school without having to worry that she will be suspended for the same
minor offense that her White peer was let off the hook for.

We're not there yet.

But I know a place where we can be our whole, free, Black-ass selves
right now: group text.

In my group texts with my closest friends, I don't have to censor myself. I can share my deepest concerns, celebrate my successes, talk shit about
people, and reveal how clueless I am about what's happening on the lust and
Soundcloud beats shows.

And I'm not the only one. Those blue bubbles pop up all day, as my girls
share funny tweets, impressive famous dick prints, and rants that we can't
share online 'cause jobs and oppression and trolls and respectability politics
and shit.

In the spirit of getting us *all* free, here are some actual messages that
appear in my group texts; names have been omitted to protect the shady.*

A: Question: Do you think one can truly fight for something they may not
have experienced? Is it off principle? Or do people truly only fight for things
they've experienced? Things meaning injustices, abuse, etc.
B: Yes. It sounds like an easy question, but maybe I'm not thinking of it
right.

---

* And I added punctuation, 'cause this is a book, not a text message, you heathen. Also, the letters just correspond to who spoke first, second, and so on. So don't try to figure out a pattern—
there isn't one, and you ain't slick anyway.

A: I mean, what does it mean to fight? Can you just say you agree with the cause, or do you have to be out front doing the fighting? Or is it enough to just put money out to help the cause? I don't know. Just some craziness I was thinking about when Jay-Z was talking about racism.

C: I say no. I guess it's the difference between sympathy and empathy.

A: He's experienced it. I've experienced it, but I don't know if *everybody* has truly experienced it. Like sometimes people give textbook answers of how they would handle it, but it's not always the way you can handle it.

B: Oh, so you are asking if people that haven't experienced racism and sexism can truly fight?

A: Yes.

B: I think they can, but it's important to note that fighting can look like different things.

A: That's true.

B: And I think it's important because Black people aren't gonna be the ones to fix racism. It's White folks. A racist dude ain't listening to my Black ass. They will listen to someone who looks like them.

C: Wait. Fight is an action. Yes, people can fight for or against things they haven't experienced. I think people can feel bad for people in a situation. But do they feel the pain? Not the same way.

B: Same with sexism, it's really gonna take men pulling each other up.

C: I'm not gay. I can march for gay rights, but I can't feel their struggle.

B: This is a broad generalization—I know the fight is more nuanced.

A: I mean, I guess what I'm asking is just because I show up, do I get credit for fighting for the cause? I'm a number, but what am I doing after that march?

C: Sometimes you just need numbers. *shrugging Black girl emoji*

A: Does fighting or standing up for something mean you do it every day or every chance you get or just that one time or whenever it happens to come across you?

B: I think so. 'Cause a lot of people won't even do that.

A: That's true. I mean I was just thinking, *Do I fight for anything?* Like, I try to stand up for people when I see them wronged, but do I really fight for stuff? Why don't I? Is it because I've been conditioned to fall in line and not ruffle the norm? I don't know. Is it because I was raised in the South?

B: Do what you can. You can't fight everything, so do what you can.

A: "She. Is. Playing. Taylor. Swift. In. My. Car. Can I toss her out?"

A: *Pastes in screenshot of an email sent to an annoying coworker.*

A: I sent this and now I feel like I was a little too angry Black woman in it.

B: It's clear. Was this a repeat issue? Clear meaning, the message was given clearly.

A: Fuck yes. I'm so frustrated with them. But I always try not to be a bitch via email.

B: Not angry Black woman, but annoyed about something you explained before. I don't think it was bitchy.

C: No. You were direct. Especially if you were clear in your previous email that no action was required.

A: I need new underwear. My booty eats all my draws.

A: I'm not sure why I'm feeling annoyed by the news talking about the girl Jholie Moussa, the teen who went missing and they found her body. They keep showing pics of her that are . . . provocative. Did she not have any pics where she's not licking her lips or looking back at it?

B: It's what they do.

C: *brown finger pointing upward emoji*

A: It's really blowing me. They showed a scholarly pic of Natalee Holloway. And let's be clear, she was being hot in the ass in Aruba. Didn't deserve any harm! But she wasn't a scholar on sabbatical. She was a teen.

C: Sadly, that's the norm in media. White supremacy touches everything. *sad downcast face emoji*

A: Maybe I'm cranky, but adult-ass women who wear chokers bother the hell outta me.

B: Lmao.

A: *Pastes in link to article: "Under Ben Carson, HUD Scales Back Fair Housing Enforcement"*

B: He is a disgrace. Damn sellout.

C: I've been watching eight minutes of *Jerry Springer*, watching these two women fight and cuss over a man. They brought this nigga out and I chuckled so hard. He looks like a baby roach! And yes, Ben Carson is a disgrace.

A: *Pastes in link to article: "WATCH: Big Daddy Kane Gets 'Raw' for Tiny Desk Concert"*

A: He. Can. Still. Get. It.

B: I love his old ass.

A: Love him!

A: Nigga.

A: Starbucks hired every high-powered Black attorney for help with the Blacks. They couldn't afford to lose us as patrons or workers. I appreciate the effort if nothing else.

B: They are doing this right. They are definitely trying hard.

A: *Pastes in surreptitiously snapped picture of adorable, clearly freezing newborn baby sitting in a car seat on the floor beside their mama*

A: White. People. This woman has on a winter coat. But she brings her newborn into the pediatrician office in a sleeper. No blanket. WTF??? This baby was *just* born. Like days old.

B: If you cold, that baby is cold. White. People.

A: Looking for gift ideas. Z's line is celebrating their anniversary, and I want to get them a gift from the wives. I was thinking this personalized flask and cigar case. But one of them is super religious. . . . Do you guys have another idea?

B: Tell that churchy muthafucka to chill and put pineapple juice in that flask.

C: It's so perfect! I want one.

A: Did y'all watch the *Black-ish* episode about Howard? Why did people like it? I hate it. It basically portrayed HBCUs poorly saying the kids that go there have a hard time adjusting to White folks in the workplace and are not exposed to White life.

B: I didn't like that either.

C: Same here. I wasn't a fan. I think *This Is Us* did it so damn perfectly anyone else would have fallen short.

A: Yup.

D: Yeah, I was upset the whole HU episode too. No one is out of the loop these days, and fuck knowing a White song.

A: Sista . . . you've been on my mind. Oh, sista . . . we're two of a kind. Sooooo, sista! *tilted crying laughing face emoji*

A: Am I missing something? This State of the Union is an entire speech of shout-outs. It's like one long-ass BET award acceptance speech. He's trash.

B: Ugh. Yeah, not watching that.

A: I know. I need to stop.

C: He's horrible at this!! He's sounding out each syllable. This is stupid!!!!

A: You know he searched high and low for Black people.

C: Locking the door on Dreamers to stop gang murder is like killing all White men to stop serial killing. This is insane.

A: I need to stay home today. My PTSD is flaring. My cousin got stopped twice this week coming home from work. Why is it okay for Black people to deal with this shit constantly????

A: "She clearly doesn't have any real friends. Why the hell did she tweet that instead of posting in her group text?"

~~~~~~~~

Akiba

I never learned how to jump double dutch. I have blamed this fact on my pigeon toes and bow legs. ("My feet point inward, my legs bend backwards. I can't *not* step on the rope.") I've gone as far as invoking an undiagnosed spatial problem. While I did manage to bust a blood vessel in my right eye opening a closet door as a kid, the truth is that my double dutch fail comes down to trust. I simply could not trust the inevitably screwface girls whipping that white, hard plastic–coated laundry line to a wicked rhythm. I sucked even when they were kind enough to designate me the "babydoll," the girl allowed to start in the center instead of jumping into already-turning ropes from the side. I hated that—I had my first-grade pride.

But seriously, name me one thing that is more beautiful than double dutch.

It is so very difficult for observer me to articulate what the end of White supremacy looks like. I can't tell you which set of policies, political victories, and global shifts will vanquish this crazy-making system. But what I *can* say is that the art and sport of double dutch offers some possibilities.

For one, double dutch requires a deep synergy with other people. If everyone is in sync, oh the tricks the jumper can do! But if you're turning double-handed or you're in the center jumping too slow, the whole enterprise falls apart.

The good thing about messing up in double dutch is that your mistakes disappear with every round. You can be trash at 1:20 p.m. and kill it at 1:32 p.m., after a few other folks get a turn. The reason why you get better doing the same thing isn't because you've had a twelve-minute emergency clinic. It's because you and the people turning the ropes shift how you work with one another. The democracy of rhythm takes hold.

Most double dutch takes place outside, in the sun, with Black girls in full control of their arms, legs, and minds. They are sweating and counting. No matter how absurd a sexual harasser is, he is not commanding girls to replace their skills-related grimace with a coerced smile.

You cannot leave your body when you're jumping or turning. The ropes know.

Also, I have seen with my own eyes how Black children who are not cis girls are welcome to learn and play double dutch. Outside of the game, these kids may very well be castigated and abused for being who they are. But within a double dutch context, they're flying—or failing—alongside the other people playing. It's all about jumping and turning, not being one way or another.

Try as you might, nobody can jump double dutch alone. And unless you are the rare professional, your team is place-based. The people you struggle with are in your neighborhood or schoolyard, or at your job where a group of sisters decided that double dutch is some of the most fun cardio on the earth.

Of course, like everything everywhere, all the time, double dutch can be problematic. Getting slapped in the face with a rope could happen. The person turning could get a surge of bitter energy and speed up the tempo so much that everyone is forced to quit. People can try to double the ropes to make up for weak spots in the first one, but thicker ropes lead to thicker welts. You can be a grown-ass woman like me who wishes that she'd mastered it as a kid and sees her lack of skill as a cultural forgetting.

But you can also be a grown-ass woman like me who is plotting on joining, creating, or renewing her membership to a league of other adults doing double dutch with varying degrees of skill, dreaming of a crew turning and jumping together in the sun.

ACKNOWLEDGMENTS

Akiba

Thanks to Kenrya Rankin, my amazing coauthor. Thanks to every single contributor. Thanks to my parents, Rochelle Nichols Solomon and James Solomon. To my sister, Asali Solomon, and her fam, Andrew Friedman and Adebayo and Mkale Solomon Friedman. Thanks to my cousin Rechelle McJett Beatty and her daughter, Damali Beatty. Thanks to chosen siblings Ayana Byrd, Norell Giancana, Karen R. Good, Marc Lamont Hill, Onitara Kimathi, Laini Madhubuti, Shakina McKibben, and Tracey Rose. And max gratitude to my ancestors who are always in the room: Carolyn Solomon, Mamie and Richard Nichols, and Yvette Kinyozi Smalls.

Kenrya

Thanks to Akiba Solomon for being a fab copilot on this journey. A huge shout-out to the amazing folks who contributed their freedom dreams to this project; I adore you all. Thanks to my parents, Henry Rankin and Kimberly Rankin, for equipping me with conviction. Thanks to my bestie Erica Easter for sending me tweets when I needed to look away from my laptop and for borrowing her goddaughter so I could work in silence and not share my candy. Speaking of which, thanks to Rips and Wild Cherry Pepsi for keeping me writing that one weekend after I was violently forced to give up my beloved Flamin' Hot Cheetos, RIP. One time for therapy for pushing me to write hella honest essays. So much love to Ayana Byrd for being an amazing friend and the best cheerleader a book could ever have, #GoBook! The hugest of hugs to Norell Giancana for her expert wrangling. Thanks to Shameeka Emanuel for showing me what happens when you live into what

God has for you. And my entire heart to my little, Saa Rankin Naasel, for being both an inspiration and a star.

Both of Us

Thanks to the *Colorlines* crew and publisher Race Forward, particularly Michell Speight and Jai Dulani. Love to our ace agent, Tanya McKinnon, who believed in this book from the start, landed us in the perfect place, and always made time. Thanks to her tireless associate Carol Taylor for getting us together. And major thanks to Nation Books editorial assistant Kleaver Cruz, and our peerless, never-scared editor, Katy O'Donnell. Katy, we are incredibly lucky to have you.

CONTRIBUTOR PHOTO CREDITS

Akiba Solomon	Courtesy of Kea Dupree Photography
Kenrya Rankin	Courtesy of Kea Dupree Photography
Hanif Abdurraqib	Courtesy of Andy Cenci
Mumia Abu-Jamal	Courtesy of Mumia Abu-Jamal
Tracy M. Adams	Courtesy of Sharief Cole
Tai Allen	Courtesy of Qaasim Barfield, Qlick Photos
Michael Arceneaux	Courtesy of Steven Duarte
Gina Belafonte	Courtesy of Gina Belafonte
Harry Belafonte	Courtesy of Pamela Belafonte
Haylin Belay	Courtesy of Setti Kidane
Mia Birdsong	Courtesy of Keith Mellnick
Dr. Yaba Blay	Courtesy of Chris Charles Photography
Elissa Blount Moorhead	Courtesy of Morgan Shea
Rev. Dr. Valerie Bridgeman	Courtesy of Tessa Berg
adrienne maree brown	Courtesy of Bree Grant
Stefanie Brown James	Courtesy of Hailey Photography
Mahogany L. Browne	Courtesy of Curtis Bryant
Tarana Burke	Courtesy of Kaia Burke, Strange Bird Productions
Ayana Byrd	Courtesy of Samantha Dion Baker
D. Bruce Campbell Jr.	Courtesy of Zamani Feelings
Ta-Nehisi Coates	Courtesy of Gabriella Demczuk
Shawn Dove	Courtesy of Tamara Fleming Photography
Tongo Eisen-Martin	Courtesy of Jeanesque Photography
Delphine Adama Fawundu	Courtesy of Delphine Adama Fawundu
Alicia Garza	Courtesy of kk ottesen

Quinn Gee	Courtesy of Quinn Gee
Xia Gordon	Courtesy of Laura Lannes
Aja Graydon and Fatin Dantzler	Courtesy of Madworks Studio
Christopher Rashad Green	Courtesy of Ava Reeves
Russ Green	Courtesy of Rebecca Dupas Photography
Dr. Joy Harden Bradford	Courtesy of Aspen Cierra Photography
Margari Aziza Hill	Courtesy of Margari Aziza Hill
Bishop Jacquelyn Holland	Courtesy of Kimberly Collins
Maori Karmael Holmes	Courtesy of Adachi Pimentel
Rickell Howard Smith	Courtesy of Donte Harris
Quentin James	Courtesy of Drew Xeron
John Jennings	Courtesy of Rob Mach
Olalekan Jeyifous	Courtesy of Olalekan Jeyifous
"MacKenzie Jones"	Not pictured
Robin D. G. Kelley	Courtesy of Lisa Gay Hamilton
Niya Kenny	Courtesy of Johnnie Gray
Sidney Keys III	Courtesy of Ashlee Nicole Artistry
Patrisse Khan-Cullors	Courtesy of Tristan Kallas
Bakari Kitwana	Courtesy of Renee C. Veniskey
Kiese Laymon	Courtesy of Kiese Laymon
Jamilah-Asali Lemieux	Courtesy of CASSIUS
Haki R. Madhubuti	Courtesy of Haki R. Madhubuti
Constance Malcolm	Courtesy of Tiye Rose
Wazi Maret	Courtesy of Texas Isaiah Horatio-Valenzuela
Kierna Mayo	Courtesy of Kierna Mayo
Pastor Michael McBride	Courtesy of Heather Wilson
Shane McCrae	Courtesy of Shane McCrae
Tiffany Mikell	Courtesy of Noah Gelfman
Denene Millner	Courtesy of Lila Chiles
Darnell L. Moore	Courtesy of Erik Carter
Ben Passmore	Courtesy of Tiff Cotard
Imani Perry	Courtesy of Sameer Khan

Marlon Peterson	Courtesy of Natasha Gaspard, Mane Moves Media
Tef Poe	Courtesy of Dazey Daze
Saa Rankin Naasel	Courtesy of Kenrya Rankin
Amanda Seales	Courtesy of Elton Anderson
Beverly "Bevy" Smith	Courtesy of Beverly Smith
Jay Smooth	Courtesy of Jay Smooth
Asali Solomon	Courtesy of Charlie Raboteau
Patricia Spears Jones	Courtesy of Mark Poucher
DeShuna Spencer	Courtesy of Lenzy Ruffin
Diamond Stingily	Courtesy of Sam Gamberg
Penny Wrenn	Courtesy of Penny Wrenn
Jasiri X	Courtesy of Leah Loves That
Bianca Xunise	Courtesy of David Garcia
Damon Young	Courtesy of Sarah Huny Young
Dr. Kortney Ryan Ziegler	Courtesy of Sarah Daragon

IMAGE CREDITS

Generations	Courtesy of Bianca Xunise	18
BLK PWR TWTR	Courtesy of John Jennings	45
Push	Courtesy of Ben Passmore	71
Cornrows, Afropuffs, and Joy	Courtesy of Delphine Adama Fawundu	92
Boo, Donald Trump	Courtesy of Kenrya Rankin	94
The Ease of Being	Courtesy of Xia Gordon	119
Kaas 4C	Courtesy of Diamond Stingily and Queer Thoughts, New York	153
Exhibit A	Courtesy of Kenrya Rankin	158
Variable Facility	Courtesy of Olalekan Jeyifous	243

Akiba Solomon is the senior editorial director of *Colorlines* and a National Association of Black Journalists Award–winning journalist and editor whose writing on culture, race, gender, and reproductive health has appeared in *Essence, Dissent, Glamour, Vibe,* and *Ebony,* among other outlets. She is the coeditor of *Naked: Black Women Bare All about Their Skin, Hair, Hips, Lips, and Other Parts.* Solomon has spoken about women's and social justice issues at the Schomburg Center, Stanford, Yale, and Harvard, among other institutions. A graduate of Howard University, she is based in New York.

~~~~~~~~~

Kenrya Rankin is an award-winning author, journalist, and consultant and the deputy editor at *Colorlines.* Her work has appeared in dozens of national publications, including the *New York Times, Glamour, Reader's Digest, Ebony,* and *Fast Company.* The Cleveland native is the author of several books, including *Bet on Black: African-American Women Celebrate Fatherhood in the Age of Barack Obama.* A graduate of Howard University and New York University, she is based in Washington, DC.